Y0-CCW-650

CHARLES C. PAINTER

# CHARLES C. PAINTER

The Life of an Indian Reform Advocate

VALERIE SHERER MATHES

PAPL
DISCARDED

UNIVERSITY OF OKLAHOMA PRESS : NORMAN

This book is published with the
generous assistance of the Kerr Foundation, Inc.


Portions of chapter 4 appeared, in a form since much revised for the present book, in "James Bradley Thayer: In Defense of Indian Legal Rights," *Massachusetts Historical Review* 21 (2020): 41–75.

Library of Congress Cataloging-in-Publication Data

Names: Mathes, Valerie Sherer, 1941– author.
Title: Charles C. Painter : the life of an Indian reform advocate / Valerie Sherer Mathes.
Other titles: Life of an Indian reform advocate
Description: Norman : University of Oklahoma Press, [2020] | Includes bibliographical
    references and index. | Summary: "A history of the Indian reform work of Charles
    Cornelius Coffin Painter as the Washington, D.C. agent for the Indian Rights Asso-
    ciation from his employment in 1884 to his death in 1895."—Provided by publisher.
Identifiers: LCCN 2020010070 | ISBN 978-0-8061-6632-2 (hardback)
Subjects: LCSH: Painter, C. C. (Charles Cornelius) | Indian Rights Association—History. |
    Indian Rights Association—Employees. | Indians of North America—History—
    19th century. | Indians of North America—Legal status, laws, etc. | Indians of
    North America—Government relations. | Indigenous peoples—Civil rights—United
    States—History—19th century. | Lobbyists—Washington (D.C.)—Biography. | Great
    Barrington (Mass.)—Biography.
Classification: LCC E91 .M38 2020 | DDC 970.004/97092 [B]—dc23
LC record available at https://lccn.loc.gov/2020010070

The paper in this book meets the guidelines for permanence and durability of the Committee on Production Guidelines for Book Longevity of the Council on Library Resources, Inc. ∞

Copyright © 2020 by the University of Oklahoma Press, Norman, Publishing Division of the University. Manufactured in the U.S.A.

All rights reserved. No part of this publication may be reproduced, stored in a retrieval system, or transmitted, in any form or by any means, electronic, mechanical, photocopying, recording, or otherwise—except as permitted under Section 107 or 108 of the United States Copyright Act—without the prior written permission of the University of Oklahoma Press. To request permission to reproduce selections from this book, write to Permissions, University of Oklahoma Press, 2800 Venture Drive, Norman OK 73069, or email rights.oupress@ou.edu.

To the memory of my dear friend and coauthor,
Phil Brigandi

▼ ▼ ▼

# CONTENTS

▼ ▼ ▼

# PREFACE

Charles Cornelius Coffin Painter, clergyman turned Indian reformer, has remained a continuous thread during my forty years of research and writing. I first encountered him in the late 1970s while researching Helen Hunt Jackson, author of *A Century of Dishonor* and *Ramona*, and I wrote an article[1] on his work on the California Mission Indian Commission, which was authorized to implement recommendations made in Jackson's government report. Research on the Women's National Indian Association (WNIA) to understand its part in implementing Jackson's legacy again led me to Painter and his role as the Washington, D.C., agent for the Indian Rights Association (IRA). To understand how the WNIA fit within the male-dominated Indian reform movement, I then turned to the annual forum on "the Indian question" held at Lake Mohonk, New York; there I learned that Painter not only had attended the first meeting but was an influential member. Between 1884 and his death in 1895, Painter had some role in most congressional legislation relative to Indians, either promoting it, opposing it, or drafting it.

By 1885 his interest was no longer limited to the Mission Indians; he was now responsible for representing all tribes. Unlike most reformers, who worked behind a desk, gave an occasional public address, or participated in a petition drive, Painter engaged in field work, visiting reservations far distant from his home in Great Barrington, Massachusetts. From his Washington, D.C., office, he wrote reports that were published and widely distributed, answered hundreds of letters from government officials and other reformers, lobbied Congress, and made public addresses. A major player in a crowded arena, he befriended presidents, Indian commissioners, interior secretaries, senators, congressmen, clerics, missionaries, government schoolteachers, and field matrons, and most of all, the Indians. Well known and influential during his day, Painter and the late-nineteenth-century Indian reform movement he represented have been largely overlooked by the scholarly community.

Writing in a narrative style and using his words when appropriate, I present his story, hopefully returning him to his rightful place. Limited by my sources, I did not set out to write a comprehensive biography of a life but a memoir of a career in Indian reform. The story here presented is based on Painter's letters to the IRA office, preserved by the Historical Society of Pennsylvania; a handful of letters in the American Missionary Association Archives at Tulane University and in the Samuel Chapman Armstrong Papers at Hampton University; and letters in the National Archives in Washington, D.C. Background material has been gleaned from his articles and his investigative reports, as well as IRA and Lake Mohonk annual reports and newspaper accounts.

The private side of Painter's life remains in the shadows. Although an avid letter writer by profession and absent from home for months at a time, his letters to friends, acquaintances, and especially to his wife, Martha, and son, Charles, have never been found. Nothing remains of his more personal reflections or most intimate thoughts. Also silent are the Indian voices. There are no letters, either of thanks or protest, about his effort on their behalf. No doubt if there were such letters, many would be critical of the agenda he and other reformers adhered to; like most of his fellow reformers, Painter was an unapologetic assimilationist. But he also was a man of his time, and his story needs to be told. Charles Cornelius Coffin Painter was a powerful presence in the Indian reform movement—a reformer who devoted his life's work to doing what he thought was best for America's Indian population and doing it with élan.

In forty years I have incurred debts to the staffs of numerous archives, historical societies, and libraries across the county, debts that can unfortunately never be properly acknowledged. I can, however, thank Phil Brigandi, my coauthor on two other books, and Patricia Heinicke, who read the manuscript and offered valuable suggestions. I especially want to thank my editor, Alessandra Jacobi Tamulevich, who continually supports my writing.

Sonoma, California, 2019

▼ ▼ ▼

# INTRODUCTION

In the Great Barrington, Massachusetts, Congregational Church on January 16, 1895, Rev. R. Dewitt Mallary presided over the funeral of Charles Cornelius Coffin Painter, who had died three days earlier in Washington, D.C., at age sixty-two. Mallary described his friend as a "Southern man with a Northern heart," born of "the stuff that reformers are made of without being narrow." Painter was a cultured man, "catholic in temper; swift to anger against wrong; [and] touched with the feeling of men's infirmities." Mallary recalled that Painter had moved from sunny Virginia to the "rigors and the beauties of Berkshire" to attend Williams College and later Hartford's Seminary of Theology. He had preached the gospel, putting his heart and soul into defending "the rights and conserving the interests" of the American Indians, making "earnest and eloquent appeals through the East" on their behalf. "What lynx-eyed vigilance has he put forth to see that Indian laws were not means of log rolling, thievery and oppression!" declared Mallary. It was "a grand work," hindered only by "apathy obstructed by base political chicanery mocked at by the thoughtless, checked by the ferocious savage's outbreak now and then, involving time and sacrifices and vast expense, but the prophet hero [had] struggled on, seeing his vision and wanting us to see it." Painter's name would "be sung in the future" and be "worthy to stand with those of other saviors of the Indians."[1]

Mallary's prophesy was true. Between 1884 and 1895 Painter had become an influential leader of the late-nineteenth-century Indian reform movement, known for extensive field investigations and well-written reports—work ended only by his untimely death. This book provides a portrait of Painter as one of the more powerful Indian reform advocates of that period.

Charles C. C. Painter, Washington, D.C., agent of the Indian Rights Association.
Cabinet card portrait by Boyce.
*Indian Rights Association Collection (1523), box 233, Historical Society
of Pennsylvania, Philadelphia.*

The "other saviors" Mallary referenced were the hundreds of middle-
and upper-class men and women—prominent religious, political, and cultural leaders—who came together amicably to focus on the so-called Indian
problem. They included clerics, former abolitionists, temperance workers,
educators, legislators, legal scholars, philanthropists, humanitarians, army
officers, and Indian Office personnel. They looked to Painter, who as a skilled

lobbyist and communicator was able not only to explain the complexities of any given issue to those most able to effect change, such as the president, the Indian commissioner, and the interior secretary, but also to achieve success more often than not.

Understanding Painter's fellow reformers and their organizations is crucial to understanding his work. Their membership generally viewed the solution to the Indian problem through the narrow lens of evangelical Protestantism, subscribing to the assimilationist beliefs of the day. Painter also believed that Indians needed to become part of mainstream society; however, his high-profile role and the responsibilities required of him as the Washington, D.C., agent for the prestigious Indian Rights Association (IRA) set him apart, primarily because of his intuitive grasp of the broader picture. His superiors described him as working in a "discreet, wholly honest, unselfish and devoted" manner. The Washington correspondent for the *New York Evening Post* portrayed him as "not only a reformer, but, what is rare indeed, a thoroughly practical one." An excellent judge of character, he worked successfully with Congress and its various Indian committees. However, "he was cordially hated by every trickster and jobber who had anything to make out of the Indian or out of the government over the Indians' shoulders."[2]

Operating within an era shaped by the Civil War, Painter's early reform work focused on African Americans, and his later work with American Indians was made possible by the abolition of slavery and the government's move to solve the next major social issue—the Indian problem. The solution devised by the administration of Ulysses S. Grant was the "peace policy," which incorporated the negotiation of treaties, the placement of western tribes on reservations, and the selection of Indian agents by Protestant missionary associations and religious societies, charged with their education and Christianization and with implementing other assimilationist policies to hasten the Indians' integration into mainstream culture.[3] This latter provision, designated as the "Quaker Policy," was strongly supported by Painter and praised in the *American Missionary*, the periodical of the American Missionary Association (AMA), which described these new agents as "far more trustworthy and efficient than their predecessors"—able to defend the Indians "from the frauds of ring speculators, and the temptations of the liquor dealers."[4]

To oversee these newly appointed Christian agents, representatives of the missionary societies that appointed them met annually with the federally funded Board of Indian Commissioners (BIC).[5] The *New York Tribune* described these annual conferences as beneficial to the administration of Indian affairs, saving "the peace policy from disaster."[6] Painter would play a vital role in these meetings, attending first as a representative of the IRA and later as a board member, presenting his views, recommending solutions, and undertaking investigations on their behalf.

Initially Painter was employed by the nonsectarian AMA. Founded in Albany, New York, in 1846 by white and black abolitionists, mostly evangelicals from more liberal Congregational and Presbyterian congregations, the association supported abolition, promoted racial equality and education for African Americans, and worked to spread Christian values—goals later promoted by Painter and the IRA. In addition to founding or assisting almost three hundred anti-slavery churches, the AMA also supported abolitionists as itinerant ministers and, with its strong New England heritage, established hundreds of freedmen schools, both elementary and normal, to train African American teachers.[7] By 1870 the association had founded seven institutions of higher learning, including Fisk University in Tennessee, with which Painter was affiliated for several years, and Hampton Agricultural and Industrial School (later Hampton Institute) in Hampton, Virginia. Hampton's founder, General Samuel C. Armstrong, had commanded African American troops during the Civil War and served as superintendent of Virginia's ninth district of the Freedmen's Bureau. Although Hampton initially educated young African Americans with a practical experience in industrial and craft skills, in 1878 the school received its first American Indian students. "The strong similarity that reformers saw between the needs of the ex-slaves and those of the Indians in preparing for full participation in American society made it reasonable to provide room for Indians as well as blacks at Hampton," writes historian Francis Paul Prucha.[8] Armstrong would play a pivotal role in Painter's reform work, befriending and advising him and recommending him as agent for the AMA and later for the IRA.

In 1848 the AMA began missionary work among the Chippewa (Ojibwa) Indians around Leech Lake, Cass Lake, and Red Lake in Minnesota, work initiated by the Western Evangelical Missionary Society of Ohio. With the

Samuel Chapman Armstrong, Civil War general and founder
of Hampton Institute.
*Indian Rights Association Collection (1523), box 234B, folder 5,
Historical Society of Pennsylvania, Philadelphia.*

implementation of Grant's peace policy in 1870, federal officials entrusted
the AMA with the appointment of agents to serve on four agencies: among the
Chippewas of the Mississippi, the Chippewas of the Lake Superior Agency,
the Menominees and Oneidas in Wisconsin, and the Skokomish of Washington Territory. In 1872–73, when these agencies were divided, the AMA

became responsible for eight agents. Its annual reports occasionally included agency reports,[9] as did its periodical, the *American Missionary*. Founded in 1846 and reaching a circulation of twenty thousand, the *American Missionary* covered religious and missionary subjects,[10] and for a short time, Painter would serve as its editor.

By its December 1879 issue, the periodical had added a short column by the AMA's Indian Committee, with an occasional longer article on the group's Indian work, some written by Painter. To guide this work, the AMA adopted three goals: to secure legal standing for the Indians in federal courts, to implement a procedure to grant land "in severalty" (that is, individually held as opposed to communally held), and to ensure full citizenship rights. AMA Indian Committee members resolved to press the Indian question until congressional legislation achieved these goals.[11] This Indian work became more important in 1882, when the American Board of Commissioners for Foreign Missions, founded in 1810 as the first American Christian foreign mission agency to direct missionary work of the Presbyterian and Congregational churches, transferred its Indian missions to the AMA.[12] Although Painter shifted his focus from African American education to Indian education as a result of this transfer, he never abandoned his interest in the former.

The AMA was joined in this Indian work by other associations, including the Women's National Indian Association, the Boston Indian Citizenship Committee, the IRA, and the Lake Mohonk Conference. Although each had its own catalyst, as we will see, the predominantly evangelical Protestant membership of all these groups had similar beliefs and goals, and they tended to work together congenially, especially with Painter.

### The Women's National Indian Association

The Women's National Indian Association (WNIA) grew out of a missionary circle, the Women's Home Missionary Society, which was organized on May 17, 1877, within Philadelphia's First Baptist Church. The founding of this missionary circle had been influenced by the establishment earlier that year of the Women's Baptist Home Mission Society of Chicago, whose goal was to engage in missionary work on behalf of Indian women and children.[13] In 1879, when the missionary circle's president, Mary Lucinda Bonney, learned that Missouri Senator George Graham Vest was pressuring Congress to open up for settlement lands in the Indian Territory (modern-day Oklahoma), she alerted her missionary circle members during their April 1879 monthly meeting and then turned to Rev. Heman L. Wayland, editor of the *National Baptist*, to draw up a protest petition to present before Congress. Bonney viewed this invasion as "a great injury to the moral sense" of the country and as "a vast hindrance to Indian missions" and their work of Christianizing and civilizing the Indians. Although petitions were prepared, the circle adjourned for the summer, forcing Bonney to turn to her friend Amelia Stone Quinton for assistance. The two "entered into a covenant," founding what would become the WNIA.[14]

Bonney provided the funding; and Quinton, the organizational skill.[15] Lacking the vote, they turned to petitioning as a tool of reform, and in their first petition Quinton deferred to male leadership in Congress and elsewhere, explaining that the signatories did "not suggest any political policy to be pursued, leaving such matters to wise statesmanship."[16] Thirteen thousand people from fifteen states signed their first petition, requesting officials to prevent the encroachment upon the Indian Territory and to guard the Indians in the enjoyments of their rights.[17] The second, signed by fifty thousand people from thirty-eight states, requested that the government deal honorably with all Indians, prevent white encroachment upon reservations, and recognize Indian treaties unless changed by the consent of both parties.[18] The third, signed by more than one hundred thousand people and calling for the granting of citizenship, common and industrial education, and land allotment in severalty, drew a heated response from Senators Preston B. Plumb of Kansas and Henry Teller of Colorado, who called the provisions too simple, inadequate, and sentimental.[19] Quinton described their stand as that of "senators, hotly expressing on the one hand Western impatience with Indians, and antagonism to Eastern sympathy, and on the other hand the moral sense of Christian men and women of many States."[20]

Securing a release from the First Baptist Church, the nonsectarian WNIA took up educational work and, under Quinton's guidance, organized outside Philadelphia while continuing to circulate its literature, send memorials to Congress, hold parlor and public meetings, and appeal to Christian clergymen, editors, and churches. The founding in late December 1882 of the male-dominated IRA enabled the WNIA to turn over much of its political efforts, petitioning excluded, and return to its original missionary roots, planted in the women's home mission movement.

### The Boston Indian Citizenship Committee

The Boston Indian Citizenship Committee was organized by nineteen prominent politicians, lawyers, businessmen, clergymen, and philanthropists[21] following the July 1879 fundraising tour of Omaha journalist Thomas Henry Tibbles, sponsored by the Omaha Ponca Relief Committee. Tibbles and the Omaha Committee were supporting a small band of Poncas led by Chief Standing Bear, intent on returning them to their former homeland and bringing a case before the Supreme Court to determine their legal status. The Indians had been arbitrarily removed from their Nebraska reservation in 1877 to inhospitable Indian Territory. Many died, including Standing Bear's son. Accompanied by his wife and a handful of followers, Standing Bear returned to bury the boy in his native land, only to be arrested by troops commanded by General George Crook and confined to Fort Omaha. Tibbles, convinced that the Fourteenth Amendment gave Indians certain rights, hired lawyers to file a writ of *habeas corpus* to determine the legality of their imprisonment. In *Standing Bear v. Crook*, federal district Judge Elmer Scipio Dundy ruled in the Indians' favor. Now freed, they were homeless, having renounced their tribal allegiance.[22]

Tibbles's speeches galvanized five prominent Bostonians to form a committee.[23] These were soon joined by others, and a new Ponca Indian Committee emerged,[24] sponsoring a public meeting to raise funds to pursue a case before the Supreme Court. Buoyed by his reception, Tibbles organized a speaking tour featuring Standing Bear and his interpreter, Susette La Flesche, the daughter of Omaha chief Joseph La Flesche. The tour began in Chicago and continued on to Boston and to New York City. In Boston the well-attended public meetings drew prominent literary figures, including poet and novelist Helen Hunt Jackson and poet Henry Wadsworth Longfellow, whose daughter, Alice Mary Longfellow, later became president of the WNIA-affiliated Massachusetts Indian Association. Jackson's attendance in November 1879 altered the direction of her life and her writing. Incensed by Standing Bear's story, she researched official government records on the Poncas and other tribes who had suffered land loss and abuse at the hands of government officials, incorporating her findings in *A Century of Dishonor* (1881), an indictment of government's dealings with the Indians.[25] Jackson's later writings on Southern California's Mission Indians would strongly influence Painter's California reform work.

A subcommittee of the Boston Indian Citizenship Committee investigated Ponca removal, recommending that the Indian be recognized not only "as a *person*, but as a *fellow-citizen*, entitled to the protection of law"; that treaty provisions be fulfilled; and that reservation land be "ceded to them by absolute title, inalienable for twenty-five years."[26] The last proposal, designed to break up communally held reservation lands and allot land in severalty, was later embodied in the infamous General Allotment Act, sponsored by Senator Henry Laurens Dawes—legislation that Painter would severely criticize.

### The Indian Rights Association

The IRA was founded in 1882 by Herbert Welsh, Henry S. Pancoast, and some forty distinguished Philadelphians in the home of Welsh's father, John Welsh, former ambassador to England and a leading businessman and philanthropist. The younger Welsh and Pancoast had been inspired to act following their tour of several agencies on the Great Sioux Reservation and by familiarity with the Indian problem gained from Welsh's uncle William, the first chairman of the BIC.[27] With the exception of George Dana Boardman, pastor of Philadelphia's First Baptist Church, where Bonney and Quinton were members, most who attended the founding meeting of the IRA were Episcopalians. The association, however, remained a "non-partisan, non-sectarian organization conducted by men whose services [were] wholly gratuitous." Through "intelligent, legitimate and persistent agitation among the people of the United States," it sought to secure for the Indians civil rights, impartial justice, education, and "a protected and individual title to land."[28]

Welsh had hoped to establish regional branches to diffuse knowledge of Indian reform through public meetings and publications. However, unlike WNIA branches, which governed their own activities, those few established by the IRA were used instead "to raise funds, distribute literature, and inspire letters and petitions in behalf of causes identified by the Philadelphia leadership."[29] The first branch, in Boston, drew in many members of the Boston Indian Citizenship Committee, while the Cambridge branch, organized by Welsh in March 1885 with Rev. Samuel Longfellow as president, openly welcomed women as members.[30]

Although initially the IRA's Executive Committee was the decision maker, Welsh, as corresponding secretary, took over that role as well. It was his willingness to run a central office staff that distinguished the IRA from the Boston Indian Citizenship Committee, which, without an office or a staff, functioned only when its busy members were able to find time. Like Quinton, Welsh addressed public meetings, organized, and made extensive investigations of western reservations, leaving Matthew K. Sniffen to handle affairs in the Philadelphia office.[31]

Painter's employment as the IRA's Washington, D.C., liaison between the IRA and Congress and the Indian Office marked a major shift in his reform work. One of the few paid IRA employees, he was politically astute and soon became indispensable. "Much of the effectiveness of the IRA was due to Painter's skills as a lobbyist," writes historian William T. Hagan.[32] To support Painter's work, the IRA established a law committee to draft bills for him to present before Congress. Painter also led efforts to oppose bills the association felt were ill advised, composed letters for various Indian commissioners to present to their interior secretaries, and defended Indian agents and tribes. His investigative reservation tours and lengthy reports, widely distributed by the association, alerted the public to major issues and supported IRA-sponsored legislation.

### The Lake Mohonk Conference of the Friends of the Indian

The Lake Mohonk Conference, founded by Albert K. Smiley near New Paltz, New York, was an annual three-day meeting held during the fall from 1883 to 1916.[33] A member of the BIC, Smiley was displeased with the limited time the board had to deal with issues brought before it by Indian associations and representatives of various missionary societies, so he began to host these gatherings at his family resort. Acknowledging the link between the conference and government policy, the BIC held one of its official sessions at Lake Mohonk, concurrent with the conference. A key component of the conference's success was the incorporation into its proceedings of Smiley's Quaker beliefs, especially the "tradition of seeking agreement through unity," although "unanimous votes were taken more to formalize the agreement than

Albert K. Smiley, founder of the Lake Mohonk Conference.
Portrait by George Steckel, Los Angeles.
*A. K. Smiley Public Library, Redlands, California.*

to secure it."[34] In addition, the adoption by the conference of the Quaker belief in female equality enabled members of the WNIA to attend this powerful forum on equal footing with male counterparts.

Attendance at the Mohonk Conference grew to include a wide range of individuals interested in Indian reform, with members discussing and ultimately setting government Indian policies. An "inner circle," eventually evolving into the Business Committee, determined the topics, selected speakers, and decided major points to be included in the conference's yearly platform. Painter, who attended the first conference in 1883 and most subsequent ones until his death, used the Mohonk Conference forum to deliver lengthy addresses on issues important to him and the IRA. According to historian Larry Burgess, the early conferences "established a tradition as working assemblies, clearly with the intent of doing a piece of altruistic and Christian work in behalf of the Indian wards of the United States." Painter and the others who met at the first conference in 1883 agreed in their initial platform of action that "civilization, Christianity and citizenship [were] necessary ends for any suggested reform goals in Indian policy." In subsequent gatherings other issues, such as land allotment, the application of Civil Service rules to the Indian service, and education, were added.[35]

▼ ▼ ▼

Painter's home base in Great Barrington, Massachusetts, allowed him to be closely affiliated with reformers in the Boston/Cambridge area, where the IRA had its Cambridge and Boston branches, the WNIA had its Cambridge Indian Association and Massachusetts Indian Association, and the Boston Indian Citizenship Committee convened when needed. One of his closest confidants was Joshua W. Davis, a founding member of the Boston Indian Citizenship Committee and a member of the Boston branch of the IRA.[36]

These major associations were well established by the time Painter joined the movement, enabling him to turn to these powerful religious, political, and cultural leaders for support. His strength, however, rested with the IRA, which had resolved though "the united, systematic, and persistent efforts of public-spirited men to bring about a rational and general understanding of the Indian problem." Its founding members vowed to provide Indians with a more general education, legal protection equal to that of the rest of the country, and ownership of land in severalty to be achieved through "the proper execution of the laws and regulations relating to Indian affairs."[37] Although at the time of its founding meeting Painter was an unknown, his employment and his widely publicized investigative reports written for public consumption would ensure that the original goals of the IRA were successfully met.

# CHAPTER 1

# FROM PREACHER TO INDIAN
# REFORMER, 1863–1883

"I came here from New York yesterday on the ill fated 'Granite State' [which] was burned on our way up the Conn. River yesterday morning," wrote Charles Painter to Hampton Institute's founder, General Samuel C. Armstrong, on May 19, 1883. "I made my escape by jumping from the upper to the lower deck and clambering down into a boat which came to my relief," he continued. "I hurt my back quite badly in my jump, but think I shall be all right again in a few days." The *Granite State*, traveling from New York to Glastonbury, Connecticut, had been anchored at Goodspeed Landing in East Haddam, Connecticut, when it caught on fire on May 18. Five people perished. Had Painter been one of them, the Indian reform movement would have lost one of its most prominent members.[1]

Charles Cornelius Coffin Painter was born on March 21, 1833, in Draper's Valley, Pulaski County, Virginia, to Jane Berry [Temple] and George Painter, a Presbyterian minister who founded the Draper's Valley Presbyterian Church. To augment his meager salary, the Reverend ran a girl's boarding school. The middle of ten children, Painter followed his father into the ministry, but as a Congregationalist. He attended Christiansburg Academy in Virginia and in 1854 matriculated to Williams College, founded in 1793 in Williamstown, Massachusetts, in the Berkshires in the northwestern part of the state, where he joined the Delta Upsilon fraternity and "won many friends by his warm heartedness and kindliness of nature," graduating with honors in 1858.[2]

Although other sources have him attending elsewhere, the Theological Institute of Connecticut, near Hartford, claimed Painter as a graduate of the class of 1862.[3] On September 23, 1863, Painter was ordained at New

Marlborough, Massachusetts, serving there as pastor until his dismissal on April 29, 1868. That same year, on June 2, he married Martha Gibson, daughter of Noah and Delia [Fairbank] Gibson of New Marlborough, and the couple moved to Grand Haven, Michigan, where in 1869 a son, Charles Fairbank Painter, was born. Painter served as an acting pastor in Michigan until accepting a position in 1869 in Naugatuck, Connecticut, where he remained until 1872. Beginning in June 1873, he became the pastor of the Congregational Church in Stafford Springs, Connecticut, serving until 1878.[4]

In December of that year, the *New York Times* announced his election as professor of theology at Fisk University in Nashville, Tennessee.[5] Founded by the AMA and named after Clinton B. Fisk of the Tennessee Freedmen's Bureau, Fisk had opened its doors on January 9, 1866.[6] Painter's employment was confirmed by the 1879 annual report of the AMA. The following year the title of "financial agent" was added to his name, a role described in the May 1880 issue of the *American Missionary* as "connected with [Fisk University's] financial management." Months earlier a *Berkshire Courier* reporter, covering Painter's public address in the Great Barrington Congregational Church, commented on the extensive funding necessary to send teachers to the South, remarking that Painter had successfully raised ninety thousand dollars for Fisk's Theological Department.[7]

Although AMA annual reports of 1881 and 1882 listed him as a Fisk professor as well as a financial agent, in May 1880 Painter had also taken over the editorship of the *American Missionary*. Three years later, along with Armstrong, he was listed as a member of the AMA's Committee on Indian Missions, with no explanation of duties.[8] Somewhere during this time period, at Armstrong's suggestion, Painter was also employed as a lobbyist for the AMA's missionary work among both African Americans and American Indians. His letters to the AMA corresponding secretary, Rev. Michael E. Strieby, confirm this.[9] This new responsibility required that he spend considerable time away from his wife, Martha, and their son, Charles, now eleven years old.[10]

That there are few extant letters and no contemporary biographical sketches make it difficult to chart Painter's movements at this time. However, according to the 1880 federal census, the family lived in the Berkshire County town of Great Barrington, described in a county *Gazetteer* as "a handsome post village" on the Housatonic River, with a population that year of 4,653.[11] The census listed Painter's occupation as "editor," a reference to his March 1880 appointment as editor and business manager of the *American Missionary*, to which he brought "a ripe scholarship, the pen of a ready writer, and a deep interest in the varied work in which the Association is engaged." Painter had assumed these duties with the May 1880 issue, and he would leave the position the following March.[12] During this time he commuted between his Great Barrington home and New York City, the headquarters of both the AMA and its periodical.

When his year-long editorial tenure ended, Painter began to write more. Two articles appeared in June and July, one on African American education and a second on graduation exercises at Fisk University, addressing an issue confronting many educators—should African Americans be given access to higher education, such as that offered at Fisk or Howard, or should they simply be taught the three Rs and manual labor tasks at Hampton Institute. The latter model allowed only "a very limited range of intellectual power, and require[d] the exercise of his muscles chiefly," Painter wrote. Taking the higher ground, he argued that until obstacles that prevented African Americans from excelling were removed, there was no way to know how much they could accomplish. "The time is coming when it will appear incredible that a man's place in the intellectual and social world shall be assigned to him because of the color of his skin, any more than because of the color of his eyes, or his clothes."[13]

Painter did not attend a graduation ceremony at Fisk until July 1881. Then, in an article for the *American Missionary*, he described the four-day ceremony, the presentation of diplomas by General Fisk, his "brief address full of pathos and good sense," exhibitions, tours, and the ceremonial laying of the cornerstone for the Livingstone Missionary Hall, a resident hall, named in honor of Scottish medical missionary and African explorer David Livingstone. Raised in the antebellum South, Painter was accustomed to seeing African Americans as inferior. He informed his readers that until recently he shared the belief that "nothing more should be attempted than a fair common school training." Now he wrote that the work of educating them was "no longer tentative"; they were "capable of taking on the same culture, and under it of reaching the same excellencies of thought and discipline, as the more favored whites attain under like training."[14] Painter would seamlessly transfer this new principle to Indian education.

## Indian Boarding Schools

Initially promoting African American education, the AMA had become involved in educating Indian youths after assuming its first missionary efforts in Minnesota, work that increased when in 1882 the American Board of Commissioners for Foreign Missions transferred their Congregational Indian missions to the AMA. Amory H. Bradford, chair of the AMA Indian Committee, reported on the successful practice of bringing young Indians to Hampton Normal and Agricultural Institute and Carlisle Indian Industrial School, the latter founded in 1879 by Captain Richard Henry Pratt. Located in the old army barracks at Carlisle, Pennsylvania, this school was the first federal off-reservation Indian boarding school.[15] Bradford cautioned that although the "possibility of civilizing the Indians [was] no longer an open question," the process must proceed slowly until "there is a radical change in the relation between the Indians and the United States Government." His committee reaffirmed that its aim was to secure for the Indians legal rights, land ownership in severalty, and American citizenship.[16]

In 1880 the government established a third off-reservation Indian school, in Forest Grove, Oregon, on the grounds of Pacific University.[17] Within two years the attendance at all three schools numbered almost 500, while some 3,937 attended reservation boarding schools and another 3,999 were educated at reservation day schools. In his October 1882 annual report, Indian Commissioner Hiram Price[18] described the industrial work at Forest Grove as meeting "with unusual success." Both the blacksmith and shoe shops had earned $772 for the school, while the apprentice carpenters had not only built school furniture but constructed two additions to the dormitories. Other students were learning practical agricultural techniques. Although Price did not provide annual costs for these boarding schools, he estimated the cost for an Indian student in a reservation boarding school at slightly more than $150 annually, and $30 for a day school student. He further noted it would cost over $2 million dollars to keep one-fourth of the school-age Indian population in school. Price lamented that congressional appropriations were never sufficient.[19]

A shortage of funding was an issue repeatedly echoed by Painter before BIC and Lake Mohonk meetings and in his published reports. In general, common school education was inadequately funded regardless of race, forcing Painter

Hiram Price, Commissioner of Indian Affairs, 1881–1885.
*Brady-Handy Photograph Collection, Library of Congress, Prints and Photographs*
*Division (LC-BH826-31181), Washington, D.C.*

to spend countless hours lobbying before Congress for monies to educate all
students—a task made more important with his appointment as corresponding secretary of the National Education Committee, formed in August 1882
with the sole object of seeking national aid for common schools. In an article
in the April 1882 issue of the *American Missionary*, Painter reported that
there were in the United States some 6.2 million or so individuals ten years

or older who could not even write their names. More than 75 percent lived in the "old slave States," and half of these were African Americans. It would cost the extraordinary amount of $18,719,958 just to educate these students for three months. Nevertheless, Painter believed that "every sentiment of justice to the negro himself as the subject of many wrongs and the possible avenger of them, and to the States themselves, requires that governmental aid shall be given to the common schools of the country."[20]

### Painter at the AMA, 1882

As Painter labored on behalf of the AMA and its goal of funding public education for all, he forged a close working relationship with Rev. Michael Strieby, who served as both corresponding secretary and recording secretary of the organization. Strieby was also a member of Hampton Institute's board of trustees.[21] Even after leaving the employ of the AMA, Painter remained professionally close to him, easily transferring to the IRA the experiences, ideas, strategies, and duties he had honed under Strieby's tutelage.

Painter's letters to Strieby reveal a constant and frenetic schedule, with hours spent writing news items for major national newspapers and hundreds of letters, memorials, and petitions. In between, Painter attended hearings before joint Indian committees, wrote legislation to present to Congress, conferred with congressmen and officials of the Indian Office, and attended conferences relative to educational and Indian-related issues, all while still engaged in fundraising for Fisk University. During his free time, he guided prominent officials and Indian reformers around Hampton Institute and Carlisle Indian School and gave public addresses, sometimes traveling long distances to do so.

A mid-January 1882 letter to Strieby is typical, describing a whirl of activity: Painter met with a prominent but unidentified Quaker reformer, conferred with several congressional members, and consulted with Indian Commissioner Hiram Price, who viewed the AMA's Indian work as "of the utmost importance," promising to help any way he could. Price, who had served in the House for a decade, understood the obstacle of congressional ignorance of the value of Indian education. Painter also met with Illinois Senator John A. Logan, who had proposed legislation turning over to education the entirety of the liquor tax receipts, some $70 million, with money appropriated to states

Michael E. Strieby, corresponding secretary of the American
Missionary Association. Still image.
*New York Public Library Digital Collections, Miriam and Ira D. Wallach Division of Art,
Prints and Photographs, Print Collection, New York City.*

based on population—legislation that was doomed to fail. Painter confided
to Strieby that the best way to ensure that the Indians would benefit from
congressional funding was to absorb them "as they ought to be, as citizens of
the states & territories and therefore partakers of the benefit, or be especially
provided for." Painter's position was supported by Commissioner Price and
General Eliphalet Whittlesey, secretary of the BIC,[22] both recommending
that the AMA "seek to extend the rights of Citizenship to them, and with
this the benefits of the fund." Painter also described his difficulty in finding

adequate housing in the capital; only "mean" rooms or those he could not afford were available.[23]

Financial insecurity would be a common thread in Painter's letters. To ensure that Martha was able to remain behind in Great Barrington among friends and family and that Charles graduated from his high school, Painter boarded away from home, doubling the family's household expenses. Nevertheless, according to Edgar J. Bliss, the editor and manager of the *Berkshire Courier*, he returned home often enough "to keep up his interest in the community and add the cheerfulness of his presence in many a home where he was ever welcomed."[24]

Painter's AMA duties were numerous. In addition to letter writing and meeting his other obligations, he was expected to attend the annual BIC conference with representatives of various Protestant missionary boards, who reported on their current Indian work. Therefore, on January 16, 1882, he joined Strieby and the other missionaries and educators for the twelfth annual meeting, called to order by Chairman Clinton B. Fisk on January 16, 1882, in Washington, D.C. Although Painter was new, halfway through the meeting Fisk called upon him, identifying him as "looking after the great national bill appropriating a large sum of money to the cause of education." Taking the podium, Painter described this bill, presented by Interior Secretary Henry Teller, as one of the best "that was ever introduced." Teller, explained Painter, had appeared three times the previous year before Congress, requesting an increase in education appropriations.[25] He described the secretary as sympathetic to their work; it was Congress that was "holding back, desiring to see the drift of the tide." This measure was part of a "new movement" whose "outlook is hopeful."[26] Unfortunately, Congress adjourned without passing the legislation.

In a late January 1882 letter, Painter described his various committee meetings as "all over crowded" and unable "to accomplish much." Two House bills relative to educational funding had been introduced. He foresaw "a great effort made to defeat the [Logan] liquor tax, and a fight made to retain it for educational purposes." Some proposed abolishing the tax altogether. "So far it is many men of many minds—but all these minds are gravitating to the point that something must be done." Painter also briefly discussed his interview with Pleasant Porter, a Creek (Muscogee) Indian statesman.[27] He described Porter as "a very intelligent Creek" who disagreed with Interior

Pleasant Porter, rancher, businessman, and the last elected principal chief
of the Creek Nation.
*Oklahoma Historical Society, Oklahoma City.*

Secretary Samuel J. Kirkwood's measure for allotting land in severalty and
instead believed "the tribes must develop *as tribes.*"[28] Thus Porter, like the
majority of Indians, strongly opposed the breakup of communally held Indian
lands and allotment in severalty to families and individuals. Unfortunately,
Indians were given no voice in the matter. And because the majority of Indian

reformers viewed severalty as the panacea for the so-called Indian problem, in early 1887 legislation to promote this principle became law, with Painter as one of its severest critics.

Painter's hectic Washington schedule continued into February and March. In early April he informed Strieby that he had sent out nearly eight thousand petitions, five hundred circular letters, and five hundred copies of one of his memorials. He had also taken the time to write both an article and a letter to the editor on education for the *Southern Workman*, a Hampton Institute publication. Then in mid-May he made a quick trip to Boston and Albany, explaining that the Massachusetts House of Representatives had unanimously passed a resolution requesting that Congress enact a bill for education and that the New York legislature "may yet pass such a resolution." In a June 19 letter he described his trip with Secretary Teller to Carlisle Indian School, where the secretary addressed the students, pledging "to do all he can for their education." Others supporting congressional educational appropriations included New Hampshire Senator Henry William Blair, who had, according to Painter, recently delivered a "capital speech" on the subject. Blair had assured Painter that even if the bill did not pass during the current session, he should not feel that his labor on its behalf was futile. The senator concluded that "an interest had been awakened all over the land which would not die but increase, and the members [would] return next fall impressed by the people that it was a measure demanded by them."[29]

Although much of Painter's time was spent securing educational funding, he also confronted a wide range of other issues, including securing appointments for competent Indian agents. On June 23, 1882, he informed Strieby that President Chester A. Arthur had appointed Edwin Eells as the agent at S'Kokomish Agency, in Washington Territory, an agency under AMA control.[30] Because the delegate from Washington Territory favored another candidate, Painter had been forced to make two visits to the Interior Department on Eells's behalf, conferring during his second visit with the territorial delegate. Ultimately Painter was successful, but it took months.[31] Later he would again defend Eells.

Although a quick learner, Painter often sought advice from General Armstrong. In late July he wrote Strieby that on his last visit to Hampton, the general "was very urgent that the effort" at Washington to increase educational appropriations be "pressed," strongly urging Painter to attend the educational assembly at Ocean Grove, New Jersey, "and do in papers or by letters what [he] could in this work." Armstrong had agreed to raise five hundred dollars for Painter's expenses, hoping that Strieby would do the same. Painter's plans, however, were almost side-tracked in mid-July, when Martha fell down the stairs at home. Fortunately, her fall appears not to have been serious, for Painter assured Strieby that he was looking forward to visiting with him; Martha was improving and would suffer no permanent injury, as first feared.[32]

### The National Education Assembly

Ocean Grove, New Jersey, was the site of the first gathering of the National Education Assembly, from August 8 to 9, 1882. It had been inspired in part by the failure of Congress to pass Teller's education bill, as well as the need to provide a platform for the country's Christian educators, party leaders, and churches to gather annually "to awaken and direct public sentiment in favor of enlarged National, State, and Church effort, for the education and elevation" of the "illiterate and degraded masses." Topics discussed that first year included general illiteracy in the country, the church and education, Indian education, and education in the post–Civil War South.[33]

Conducted by Rev. J. C. Hartzell, D.D., the assembly welcomed representatives of the leading Christian denominations engaged in educational work in the South. The AMA, a strong advocate of national aid for education, was represented by Dr. Strieby of New York City. John Eaton, U.S. commissioner of Education, gave the opening address, followed by Rev. Hartzell, who read a letter from Secretary Teller, informing the attendees that "the great mass of the people must depend on the public school system for the education of their children." Equal facilities free to all classes of children "cannot be too highly prized," Hartzell continued. If states were unable to carry out their educational obligation, then it was up to the general government "to make and wisely disburse proper appropriations, so as to encourage and stimulate the States that are the least able to carry on the work by themselves."[34] New Hampshire Senator Blair made the closing address on necessary measures to bring before Congress relevant to national aid to public schools. The *New England Journal of Education* described the meeting as "the beginning of a great national campaign, which will not cease till victory is inscribed on our banners."[35]

To inform government officials of the assembly's accomplishments, Senator Blair presented a brief description before the Senate, with his remarks printed in the *Congressional Record*, and Painter wrote an accompanying letter, enclosing a memorial petitioning Congress "to make speedy and adequate provision" to remove the current condition of illiteracy "by securing to all the children of the country the means for such education as is necessary to good and worthy citizenship." The gathering at Ocean Grove, he explained, represented "truly a national assembly" of the "earnest religious and educational forces of the country, its culture, philanthropy, and statesmanship." The practical outcome of the assembly was the appointment of a National Education Committee to continue efforts to secure national funding for common schools, with Strieby appointed as chairman, Armstrong as member, and Painter as corresponding secretary, accepting a requirement to live in Washington, D.C.[36]

In mid-August, after informing Strieby that he had written several newspaper articles, including a dispatch to the *Herald*, Painter addressed his concern about an upcoming meeting of the Executive Committee of the National Education Committee. He inquired how much money he would have to work with and the amount of his salary. "Of course it costs much more to live in Washington than it does at Fisk University," he reminded Strieby. He much preferred not to leave his family in Great Barrington alone "with all the risks of severe weather and heavy snow storms." Although he had recently turned down an offer of an unidentified job promising a good salary and "prospects of increase," he assured Strieby: "I did not succeed in persuading myself that I could afford simply to make money, yet I must use a proper prudence." Instead, he intended to "work right along now trusting that everything will be satisfactory in the final arrangement." Although the details are unknown, some sort of arrangement was made to enable Painter to continue his position, splitting his time between Washington and Great Barrington.[37]

Away from home now for several months, in December Painter informed Strieby: "If I saw my way clear to meet the expense [I] w[ould] have my wife come down after the holidays, for her life is lonely but I must know whether I shall get enough to pay postage & printing before I incur other expenses." Already he had sent out several hundred letters and thousands of circulars. His printing and postage expenses were so high there was nothing left to support his family. Not wanting to appear to be a "beggar," he ended his letter with a statement of commitment: "[M]y purpose is to see this through if possible."[38] It is unknown whether Martha spent the holidays with her husband.

In a late February 1883 letter to Armstrong, Painter complained that when the latest education bill he was supporting had come up in the House of Representatives, members adjourned before voting. The Democrats had filibustered all the previous day and "are still at it," he commented. Painter held out little hope the bill would get through.[39] The following month, he informed Armstrong that after speaking to the next chairman of the House Committee on education, he was assured the bill would be taken up "and pushed at the opening of the session."[40]

To advance his lobbying efforts on the value of Indian education, Painter often organized official visits to either Hampton or Carlisle. In early March he escorted fifty-four guests to Carlisle, including four congressmen, a number of clergymen, Interior Secretary Teller and his wife, and Indian Commissioner Price. In his February 27 letter he explained to Armstrong that in a couple of days he would be bringing a small party of prominent Indian reformers to Hampton by boat. The group would include anthropologist Alice Cunningham Fletcher, who had studied at the Peabody Museum of Harvard University, Francis LaFlesche, son of an Omaha chief,[41] and Kate Foote and her sister Harriet Ward Foote Hawley, members of the WNIA's Washington, D.C., branch. Born in Connecticut, the sisters lived in the capital, where Harriet's husband, General Joseph Roswell Hawley, served in the Senate.[42] Painter was rapidly gathering around him a group of Indian reformers who could help promote his current AMA agenda and later, his IRA work.

Painter returned home by the third week of March 1883, finding everyone in good health, although snow still covered the ground. "The sun is taking it off with great rapidity," he informed Armstrong. Home only a few days, he began to ask himself "What now? for I cannot be idle." He had already written a piece for the press on education.[43] His question was indicative of his tremendous drive for work, a drive that no doubt contributed to his early death, as his letters began to reflect more and more comments about health issues.

It is unclear when and why Painter left the employ of the AMA. However, sometime during the summer of 1883 he was hired by the IRA, which had been founded late the previous year. Armstrong, himself an IRA member, had suggested to founder Herbert Welsh that Painter might provide to the IRA the same services he was offering the AMA. Therefore in January 1883, Welsh contacted Painter, who then began work in the Boston branch of the IRA. The branch's failure to provide for a portion of his salary as pledged required the Philadelphia office to assume the obligation in April 1884.[44] Painter continued to write articles for the AMA magazine and retained his position as secretary of the National Education Committee, at least through 1884.[45]

Before he was hired by the IRA, Painter had been considered for the editorship of the *Council Fire*, which the IRA was in the process of acquiring. The periodical had been founded by Alfred B. Meacham, former Oregon superintendent of Indian affairs. When he died in 1882, Thomas A. Bland took over as editor. Bland, unlike most reformers, rejected the forced assimilation policy favored by the IRA and others, supporting instead communally held Indian lands. He and like-minded reformers founded the National Indian Defense Association in late 1885, referring to themselves as "friends of a sound and humane Indian policy."[46] Bland would at times prove to be a thorn in Painter's side. Unfortunately, the position of editor never materialized. In early May 1883 Welsh informed Armstrong that although he approved highly of Painter as editor, at the present time he could "promise nothing in the way of money." The acquisition fell through when the IRA's Executive Committee learned that they would have to assume all liabilities incurred by Meacham and Bland.[47]

## The Great Sioux Reservation

With no apparent responsibilities, in mid-May Painter informed Armstrong he planned to head west to visit various Indian tribes, although he was still undecided about whether to join up with the AMA delegation traveling to the Sioux country, or with the Senate Committee, or simply to travel "independently." He calculated he would need at least five hundred dollars for expenses. Funding was ultimately provided by both Armstrong and Joshua W. Davis, who had convinced Painter to join the AMA delegation and travel as far as the Crow Agency before setting out on his own. In a May 19 letter, Painter informed Armstrong that he wanted to see "as much of the country set apart for the Indians" as he could.[48]

Painter's trip almost failed to happen. The *Granite State*, upon which he was traveling, caught on fire on May 18 while at anchor in East Haddam, Connecticut, and while escaping Painter suffered a severe back injury and returned home to recuperate. Still in pain, he left Great Barrington on the afternoon of May 25 for Chicago, where four days later he wrote Armstrong that he had secured some passes and letters, enabling him to travel pretty much across the West. He planned to leave the following morning for Omaha and proceed up the Missouri River to Springfield, a small town outside the southern border of the Great Sioux Reservation (in today's South Dakota) to meet up with the AMA delegation. From there he hoped to secure a pass from the Union Pacific. His itinerary routed him through Salt Lake City, Albuquerque, Santa Fe, Pierre, Kansas City, and Minneapolis, requiring travel on the Union Pacific, Northern Pacific, Santa Fe, and Rock Island railroad lines. He intended to visit all of the Indian agencies up the Missouri River and various tribes in New Mexico and Arizona.[49]

Although Painter's few letters to Armstrong reveal an extensive itinerary, it is unknown how much of it he completed, for he left behind no formal report or additional letters on the subject. On June 1, at the Santee Agency on the Sioux Reservation, he met the delegation of the AMA Executive Committee, consisting of Rev. Strieby, the association's secretary; Rev. William Hayes Ward, superintending editor of the *New York Independent*; Charles L. Mead, commissioner of the American Missionary Society; and Rev. Addison P. Foster, a Congregational minister from Boston.[50] Intending to inspect missionary stations recently turned over to the AMA by the American Board of Commissioners for Foreign Missions, the group's final destination was the Santee Agency across the Missouri in Nebraska and the mission station at Oahe on the river's eastern side in modern-day South Dakota. Both the Santee Indian School and the Indian church with its Indian pastor were under the general supervision of Congregational missionary Rev. Alfred L. Riggs, while the mission station at Oahe, with its mission home, chapel, and two schools, was run by his brother, Rev. Thomas L. Riggs.[51] The delegation traveled almost four hundred miles into the heart of the Sioux Reservation, camping at night and passing "through a series of experiences not soon to be forgotten."[52] No further explanation of these experiences were recorded, and Painter's participation remains unknown.

On Saturday, June 2, twelve prominent reformers and clergymen met for three days in Rev. Alfred Riggs's parlor at Santee to consult on Indian issues. Two men, Albert Smiley and General Eliphalet Whittlesey, were members of the prestigious BIC, sent to Dakota Territory to investigate complaints of railroad fraud on Sioux lands and to learn the Indians' attitude toward the proposed reduction of their reservation. They were joined by Herbert Welsh, on an IRA fact-finding tour of the reservation, and by Painter and the AMA delegation. Also present were resident missionaries—the Right Rev. William H. Hare, Episcopal bishop of South Dakota and missionary to the Sioux; Rev. W. W. Fowler, a Protestant Episcopal Church missionary; and Rev. John P. Williamson, the first Presbyterian minister to work among the Sioux at the Yankton Agency.[53]

These men were most concerned with the Sioux Agreement of 1882, drawn up in August by a commission headed by Newton Edmunds, former governor of Dakota Territory, to replace the 1868 Fort Laramie Treaty, which had established the Great Sioux Reservation. The Edmunds agreement, prepared without Indian consultation, called for an 11 million-acre land cession, with the remainder divided into five small reservations. Ignoring the 1868 provision requiring the consent of three-quarters of the tribe's adult males to sell, the commission had forced a number of chiefs and headmen to sign. Those now gathered at Santee agreed that this 1882 legislation was unjust, that "undue pressure" had been used to acquire signatures, and that the offer was "not equitable." They were, however, in a delicate position. Although viewing the huge reserve as "a serious hindrance to the prosperity and welfare of the whites and a great impediment to the civilization of the Indians," they still had to appear to defend Indian rights while promoting a policy of civilization and assimilation.[54]

Bishop Hare, like the others, viewed the opening of the reservation to settlement as desirable, but it had to be done in a way that was consistent "with the principles of justice." His lucid arguments and objections to the current legislation convinced those gathered that he should present a public argument "stating courteously, in explicit terms, the nature of these objections."[55] Smiley later wrote that it was the "valuable conclusions" arrived at during the June meeting at Santee and the decision of those gathered to work together that had inspired his founding of the Lake Mohonk Conference.

Herbert Welsh, cofounder, member of the executive board, and corresponding secretary of the Indian Rights Association. Photograph by Haeseler. *Indian Rights Association (1523), box 342B, folder 4, Historical Society of Pennsylvania, Philadelphia.*

He would invite all who sat in Riggs's parlor that day to gather at the Smiley family resort at Lake Mohonk in the autumn to leisurely discuss not only the Sioux treaty but the entire Indian question.[56]

The insatiable demand for Sioux lands had followed the debacle at the Little Bighorn in 1876. That August the Indians had been forced to relinquish all lands in the unceded territory outside the 1868 reservation lines, as well as a large section of reservation land, including the Black Hills. Negotiators conveniently ignored the requirement of Indian consent. What's more, neither land-hungry whites nor railroad interests were satisfied with this immense cession. Because the remaining reservation land still barred easy access to the Black Hills, the Edmunds commission had been formed. The strong Indian protest that followed had galvanized the IRA to send Welsh to investigate.[57] A permanent solution, sponsored by Massachusetts Senator Dawes, would not be in place until 1888.

The unfairness of this Sioux Agreement continued to weigh on Welsh's mind, and during the August 1883 meeting of the second National Education Assembly in Ocean Grove, he addressed the issue in this more public forum. Describing his reservation tour, Welsh explained that although the cession would provide "a valuable tract of country for settlement by whites, permit free access of civilization from east to west of the reservation, and bring valuable advantages to the Indians by a closer contact with skilled farmers and mechanics," the friends of the Indian viewed the legislation as unwise and unjust and could not support it.[58]

This was only one of many issues discussed during the 1883 assembly, which had been enlarged by an additional day with more speakers and topics. Painter, as corresponding secretary of the National Education Committee, addressed the gathering on national funding for common schools. He reported sending out more than six thousand circular letters to educators and several thousand blank petitions addressed to Congress, later signed by between forty and fifty thousand citizens from twenty-three states and several territories. Eight states, either by petitions signed by state officials or by formal joint resolutions of their legislatures, had requested that Congress support the committee's work. Painter lamented that despite all his effort, the average congressman regarded these requests "as the opinion of sentimental educators and philanthropists, and not of the practical politician who constructs the platforms and runs the caucuses of his party." Because his past committee bills had failed to be placed on the congressional calendar, Painter had changed his strategy to interviewing congressmen to learn their attitude toward educational legislation and then trying to gain the cooperation of the more influential ones. On the positive side, leading newspapers had begun to "urge upon Congress the immediate and urgent necessity of national legislation in behalf of education," and major gatherings across the country had begun to emphasize the importance of this work. "Let it be the work of those represented here to-day," he concluded, "to convince our national legislature, that this is a work more vitally related to our national welfare than the opening of some stream for interstate commerce."[59]

Already acquainted with a number of influential Indian reformers through his AMA work, Painter's attendance at this second assembly enabled him to become reacquainted with some, such as Welsh, and to meet others for the first time, including Henry Pancoast and Amelia Stone Quinton, the feisty general secretary of the WNIA. Presumably he listened to Quinton's address on "Woman's Work in Solving the Indian Problem."[60] Painter would forge close working relations with both Pancoast and Quinton.

Painter's activities between the August assembly and his attendance on September 21 at the dedication of Great Barrington's new Congregational Church are unknown.[61] Then, on October 10, he attended the first Lake Mohonk Conference at Albert Smiley's elegant Victorian resort. One observer described "the fine estate [as] comprising thousands of acres, with number-less attractions of mountain views, ponderous rock-masses, its beauty-lined lake and distant fertile fields, . . . in gorgeous array of flaming foliage," and Smiley's hospitality as "royal."[62] Quinton, who attended for the first time in 1885, described "charming drives over the thirty miles of finely-graded roadway upon this magnificent mountain estate of 3,000 acres, so affluent in picturesqueness and variety of scenery."[63]

This first conference was small, with all participants receiving a personal invitation from Smiley. Painter and those present at Riggs's parlor the previous June were in attendance. They chose BIC chairman Fisk as conference chairman, Welsh as secretary, and Painter as a member of the program committee. Although Painter and his committee selected a broad range of topics to discuss, their primary concern was the 1882 Edmunds Agreement,

1893 brochure of Lake Mohonk resort.
*Mohonk Mountain House Archives, New Paltz, New York.*

a topic historian Francis Paul Prucha describes as "fitting in the light of the part the Santee Agency meeting had played in Smiley's determination to call the conference." Adopting the same sentiment as those who had met at Santee, the participants unanimously agreed that although a land cession was required, it was "expedient and necessary for each of the several tribes of Sioux to have its separate reserve." Whatever action was taken, it had to be "wisely and justly carried out." Conferees objected to the Edmunds Agreement not only because it had failed to protect individual Indian homes and farms and the property of the missionary groups in residence, but because it had been passed using "unjustifiable threats." Not all the Indians had been informed that a land cession was involved, and the consent requirement had been ignored.[64]

The conference then turned to the topics selected by Painter and his committee. Issues included citizenship for those "fitted for its responsibilities," allotment of land in severalty, additional boarding schools with industrial training, increased salaries for qualified agents, the licensing of Indians to engage in reservation trade, gradual withdrawal of rations, and expanded efforts by Christian churches to educate and civilize the Indians. Unlike future Lake Mohonk Conferences, the published proceedings included no notes on the discussions, leaving no record of Painter's role.

With his interest in education, his training as a Congregational minister, and his work for the AMA, Painter was a perfect fit at the first Mohonk Conference, where fully one-third of the attendees were ministers. As the conference grew in importance, it would come to include government officials, representatives from various religious societies, clergy from all denominations, members of congressional Indian committees, army officers, heads of Indian schools, presidents of universities and colleges, members of national Indian reform associations, and editors of secular and religious newspapers; sometimes hundreds attended. Lively discussion sessions along with opportunities to socialize over a meal or on a walk or a carriage ride over the beautiful property provided like-minded Indian reformers with opportunities to discuss all aspects of the Indian problem. The conference became a powerful forum for dictating government policy, and almost every time that Painter was in attendance, he presented the key address or directed the agenda.

With his role at Mohonk established, Painter's metamorphism from preacher to Indian reformer was complete. It had followed a natural progress, moving easily from his duties as a Congregational minister to the Theology Department at Fisk, where he learned the value of educating African Americans, and then to lobbying for the AMA. The association's assumed role in the appointment of a handful of Indian agents had brought Indian reform directly to Painter's door, making for a seamless shift to Indian work. His introduction to a myriad of prominent Indian reformers, his presence at Santee, and his attendance at the first Lake Mohonk Conference had assured him of a prominent position in the reform area.

# CHAPTER 2

# FIRST INVESTIGATIVE TOUR,
# 1884–1885

On the morning of January 22, 1884, almost thirty reformers, including women's rights advocate Susan B. Anthony, gathered at the historic Riggs House, built by prominent banker George W. Riggs on the corner of 15th and Pennsylvania Avenues in Washington, D.C. These reformers, including representatives of religious societies involved in Indian missionary work, were meeting to attend the thirteenth annual conference of the BIC. Although this was only Painter's second BIC meeting, he was no stranger to several of the attendees; Albert Smiley, General E. Whittlesey, and Rev. William Hayes Ward, who that year replaced Painter's friend Rev. Strieby as representative of the AMA, had been with Painter in Rev. Alfred Riggs's parlor at Santee Agency the previous year. Chairman Clinton Fisk called the meeting to order, inviting each attendee to describe their work. Representative of the recorded remarks are those of Rev. George L. Spining of Cleveland, Ohio, who complained that government policy and a lack of adequate appropriations often repressed the influence of his church's missionary efforts. As a case in point, he described as deplorable the physical condition of the Mandan, Hidatsa, and Arikara Indians at Fort Berthold (in modern-day western North Dakota). Their agent had drawn "a picture of the suffering of the Indians that ought to touch the heart of Congress," he noted. The Indians were starving because government appropriations had been drastically cut.[1] Within a few short months, Painter would experience that same scenario in Montana among the Piegans.

When it was Painter's turn to speak, he identified himself as the representative of the Boston branch of the IRA and the secretary of the National Education Committee, explaining that he had recently been asked by Rev.

Ward to serve as secretary of a committee created by the National Council of Congregational Churches. In addition, General Armstrong had charged him with writing legislation "creating a bureau of Indian education." To accomplish these ends, before the BIC meeting he had met with members of his newly formed committee to draw up resolutions, which he was now prepared to present. Because Painter and his committee had unanimously disagreed with Armstrong's request for an Indian education bureau, Painter instead had proposed the creation of a Division of Education within the Indian Office to be headed by "an eminent educator," reporting directly to the Indian commissioner and with authority "to put in operation a school system for all Indians excepting the civilized tribes," hiring the teachers, supervising the building of schools, and purchasing school supplies.[2]

Painter justified such a position as a means of removing the Indian agent from the hiring process; Indian education was often viewed as a vehicle for "compensation for the agent for his service," enabling poorly paid agents to hire members of their own family as teachers. Although he had found "most excellent schools" during his inspection the previous summer in the Dakotas, for the most part Painter believed good reservation schools were "the happy accident of having a good agent." Currently there was no system for good Indian education; thus he was proposing one to "cover the many individual cases of wrong and inefficiency." The existing superintendent of education had failed to accomplish the work Painter and his committee wanted done.[3]

The remainder of the morning session was devoted to the recommendation that an instructional farmer be hired for every fifty Indian families and to the question of land allotment, with opinions on that issue ranging from full acceptance to flat-out rejection.[4] The main opponent to allotment was Thomas Bland, editor of the *Council Fire*, who explained that by nature the Indian was a communist, viewing land "precisely as water that runs," with no desire to divide it. Painter disagreed, declaring that "no sentimentalism is strong enough to serve as a barrier which can hurl back these waves of immigration." According to Prucha, Indian reformers saw allotment as "an article of faith" and believed that Indian civilization "was impossible without the incentive to work that came only from individual ownership of a piece of property." There was "no panacea for the Indian problem [that] was more persistently proposed than the allotment of land to the Indians in severalty," he concluded.[5]

Before the conference reconvened at four o'clock, attendees had appointed a recommendation committee. As a member, Painter submitted the consensus report for debate, and under his expert guidance, the BIC voted in favor of eight resolutions. The first dealt with three fundamental issues viewed as the solution to the Indian problem: (1) "an indisputable but temporarily inalienable title to the land" upon which to build a home, (2) legal protection for that home, and (3) an education qualifying him to "assert and maintain his rights, and to discharge his duties as a citizen of the United States." The second resolution dealt with allotment. In May 1880, Texas senator Richard Coke, chair of the Committee on Indian Affairs, had introduced a bill calling for allotments in severalty ranging from 160 acres per family to lesser amounts to individuals, depending upon age. After some discussion, the conference came to "heartily approve the scope and chief features" of this bill.[6]

The third resolution called for the removal of the agent's power of hiring and firing teachers. Because of his intense interest in education, Painter had made a hasty trip to Commissioner Price's office to present this idea and get his approval before formally presenting it at the conference. The fourth called for the creation of a Division of Education within the Indian Office; the fifth, for the appointment of a committee to draft a bill creating this new division, with Painter as a member. The sixth called for an independent Indian Bureau with a single head, similar to that of the Agricultural Department.[7]

The seventh resolution supported the dissolution of the Great Sioux Reservation (Senator Dawes's Sioux Bill addressing this issue was still several months away). The conference resolved that this reservation west of the Missouri River (the western half of modern-day South Dakota) should be opened for settlement, with the several Sioux tribes or divisions selecting their homesteads and lands for grazing purposes. All proceeds from land sales were to be used for their benefit, both in furnishing agricultural support and in education. Painter informed his fellow reformers and missionaries that "whatever we may think about it . . . it is certain as fate that these reservations must go." He believed it was in the best interest of the Indians. However, he concluded, reformers must "get the best we can out of an inevitable wreck." Present treaties allowed the government to take every foot of the Sioux reservation by any method upon securing the signatures of three-quarters of the Sioux men and to "give or not give an old cow for it." The 1880 Coke Bill would provide greater protection than any treaty, for it called for personal titles, with all proceeds gained from the sale of surplus land to be held in trust. Congress, he explained, did not always regard treaty obligations, "but I believe never has perverted trust funds."[8] The eighth resolution called for copies of all the resolutions to be sent to the chairs of the Indian committees of both houses. Although Painter's resolutions were enthusiastically accepted by the BIC, Congress would be more hesitant, acting upon only two—the breakup of the Great Sioux Reservation and the implementation of allotment, neither original to Painter.

That spring Painter faced a health crisis, one of a number before his death a decade later of a heart attack. In April he informed Armstrong that he was finally feeling better. The doctor had informed him that his heart symptoms were all "functional" and would disappear as his "nerves recover tone," a diagnosis that was "itself tonic."[9] The anxiety of learning that same month that the IRA's Boston branch was unable to fund his salary could well have exacerbated the situation. The Philadelphia headquarters quickly assumed the responsibility, however, and soon he was engaged in lobbying work in the Washington, D.C., office, which had opened that year to serve as a liaison with the BIC and the Indian Office. From the beginning, Painter set his own course, describing himself to IRA executive secretary Herbert Welsh as a conservative when suggesting names for various positions, "holding that the government and not we must be held responsible for its appointees."[10] Welsh appeared to accept this declaration without question, reflecting the regard he held toward his new employee.

### Painter's Duties

Painter was the first Washington agent and the only paid employee of the IRA during the organization's early years.[11] His responsibilities included meeting with legislators and members of the various Indian committees, pushing before Congress measures the IRA believed beneficial and opposing those they disagreed with, making frequent investigative tours to Indian reservations, and remaining informed "as to the needs and progress of legislation on Indian matters." He was expected to communicate regularly with Welsh in Philadelphia and with the various branches, which by 1888 numbered twenty-eight.[12] Letters between Painter and Welsh were numerous and cordial, with

Painter addressing his much younger employer as "My dear Mr. Welsh" and Welsh responding with "My dear Prof. Painter." Welsh continually requested Painter's opinion, inquired about his health, asked pertinent questions, or forwarded letters for a response or to be included in Painter's reports. At times he requested Painter's presence at an Indian meeting or asked him to speak before a public gathering. Occasionally he praised him.[13] In addition to responding to Welsh, Painter corresponded with countless Indian agents, congressmen, Indian Office officials, and others, all demanding something of him.[14]

Painter performed his duties with "patience, courage, and success," prompting the IRA Executive Committee to declare that "perhaps the most important work undertaken by the Association, is that conducted by its representative at Washington." However, William Hagan in his institutional history of the IRA describes Painter as "not the smooth, ingratiating figure usually associated with the term 'lobbyist,'" for there was a "prickly" side to him.[15] He was foremost a skilled negotiator, who according to his contemporary Edward E. Hale, prominent Unitarian minister, journalist, lecturer, editor, and author, was "intimately acquainted with the course of Indian affairs in the national Capital," a knowledge that enabled him to alert IRA headquarters and various branches "at any moment when their action is required."[16]

Painter was also known for his scrupulously researched pamphlets and reports—written to sway Congress, to secure the public's support, or simply to be informative. In one report describing the duties of the IRA, he explained that it was neither an educational nor a missionary association, but one that sought to enforce treaties and other obligations. Therefore his "battle-field" was behind the scenes, working with various government committees and officials before the information reached the public. He called his work "the Court of final appeal," with an ultimate goal of ensuring "that the reservation system with all its pauperizing influences shall give place to homes built under the protection, not of Bureau Agents, but of civil law administered by Courts, in which shall be reared self-supporting, self-respecting citizens of our free republic."[17]

In a May 14 letter to Armstrong, Painter vividly detailed a Senate discussion, providing a rare insight into the complex environment in which he operated. His letter and a May 13, 1884, coverage by the *Chicago Tribune* described the arguments dividing the supporters and opponents of Indian education. Painter explained that the Indian appropriation bill had been moving along smoothly until an item appropriating $10,000 for industrial schools in Alaska was reached. Connecticut Senator Joseph Hawley, a Republican, stopped the proceedings to inform members that Interior Secretary Henry Teller had originally asked for $25,000—the House having reduced it to $15,000 and the Senate to $10,000. Hawley proposed returning it to the original $25,000. His motion was adopted, 31 to 11, but not, according to the *Tribune*, until after "a great deal of earnestness [erupted] in the Senate." The principal antagonist was John James Ingalls, a Republican Senator from Kansas, who not only disapproved of the present policy of Indian education but of the Indian service itself. Ingalls did not believe that education made "any appreciable change in the Indian character"; instead, it only "produced phenomena rather than results." According to Ingalls, any educated Indian who returned to his tribe found himself "an alien and outcast," with no allies. Massachusetts Senator George Frisbie Hoar, also a Republican, characterized the government's Indian policy as one of "broken faith and broken treaties," reminding the senators that President Lincoln had vowed that once the Civil War was over, he would address "himself to the remodeling of our Indian policy as one of the crying questions of the times." Although Hoar viewed the policy as broken, he nevertheless believed it was cheaper to educate Indians than engage them in war. Senator George Vest, a Missouri Republican, joined the fray, supporting the motion only if both sexes were educated.[18]

Painter then described Preston Plumb, a Kansas Republican, as making "a speech so brutal and shameful that he has not dared print it as yet." Other senators entered the fray, with Ingalls giving a more refined address but "equally false and devilish," and Vest speaking friendly and ably, exalting Jesuit schools but asserting that "*99 per cent of Carlisle and Hampton pupils collapse into barbarism*" upon returning home. As the debate raged, the Senate learned that the bill creating a government for Alaska had been approved by the House, with $25,000 earmarked for schools. That $25,000 and the $15,000 from the Senate bill provided $40,000 for Alaskan schools. Plumb immediately moved to strike the educational appropriation, but Painter informed Armstrong that this move was deemed out of order. Plumb then moved to set the total for Alaskan schools at $25,000; he was defeated 3 to 1. He then

Henry Moore Teller, U.S. Senator from Colorado, 1876–1882, and
Secretary of the Interior, 1882–1885.
*Library of Congress, Prints and Photographs Division (LC-USZ62–112543),*
*Washington, D.C.*

proposed that no monies be used for building schoolhouses. This time he
was "over whelmingly" defeated. It was clearly evident that the Senate "was
in no mood to listen to a policy" promoted by Plumb. "I think Plumb & Ingalls
are about as much sat-down-upon individuals as I have seen for some time,"
Painter concluded. In the end, Painter and his pro-education supporters got
far more than they had requested, prompting him to write: "Yesterday may be

put down as a red letter day, not alone for Alaska, but for Indian Education and Civilization."[19]

With the Indian appropriation bill still lingering in the Conference Committee, Painter organized a relaxing boat trip to Hampton for a number of congressmen. Then, with his affairs in good shape, in early July he made a quick trip home.[20] From September 23 to 26, he attended his second Mohonk Conference after again serving on the business committee to determine program topics, which included Indian citizenship, the Coke Bill, a new Sioux Bill proposed by Senator Dawes the previous March, and Indian education. Official conference proceedings, extant only in the news columns of the *Hartford Courant*, include scant discussion of debates, and thus little is known of Painter's participation. The *Courant* did report, however, that the seventh of the conference's resolutions praised him for "watching Indian legislation and furnishing information to Congress in the interest of Indian progress." His few letters to Armstrong provide no additional information about the meeting.[21]

Rev. Addison Foster, in his account of the meeting, described the sixty friends of the Indians as well familiar with reservation life. The conference "was notable for the breadth of its discussion and its substantial unanimity on all points at issue," he wrote, especially on the topics of Indian citizenship and criticism of the current system. He expressly singled out the Sioux bill, which had passed the Senate during the last session, as "largely influenced by the recommendations of the Mohonk Conference of last year." He concluded that beyond a doubt, the conference would have a large impact upon Indian affairs. During their free time, attendees were entertained royally by Smiley, who even furnished them with six four-horse teams every afternoon so they could drive around his property.[22]

### The Piegans

His obligations at Mohonk fulfilled, Painter set out in late October 1884 on his first IRA investigative tour to northeastern Montana to observe the condition of the Piegans, who along with the Blood and Northern Blackfoot made up the Blackfoot Confederacy. The IRA had been alerted to "extreme destitution and starvation" among these Indians as well as those at Fort

Peck and Fort Belknap agencies the previous October by Special Inspector Charles H. Howard, who had personally witnessed deaths by starvation.[23]

Officials should have anticipated this situation. Back in 1882, in his sixth annual report, John Young, the agent at the Blackfeet Agency, had informed Commissioner Price that for the first time in the history of his agency the tribes had spent the winter on their reservation. Over-hunting by white hide hunters, encouraged by both the military and government, had by the early 1880s depleted the once large buffalo herds, causing the Indians to become more dependent on government rations. Furthermore, the agency's annual appropriations were never sufficient, not even for half the year, forcing the Indians to supplement their food by hunting small game and harvesting the few crops they could raise in the Montana climate of severe winters and little summer rain. Then during the winter of 1882 an unidentified disease killed half of their horses.[24]

In his next report, Young repeated his dire observation: "[N]ow that all game is gone from their reservation, [and] no support can be derived from hunting," the Indians are forced to turn to tilling the soil and planting such crops that "the rigor of the climate allows." A wise guardianship required that the Indians be provided with "instructors and proper means as are necessary, with least delay, to bring them up to the point of self support," he concluded. "Until that is reached humanity requires that they and their children should not be allowed to suffer hunger."[25]

Decades later, from her station in Cut Bank, Montana, Helen B. West, regional historian for the Interior Department, reported that despite Young's frequent and urgent requests for aid, supplies remained insufficient, forcing him to watch his Indian charges grow weaker by the day. Blamed by the Indians for their hardships, Young then resigned after serving for seven years. Although maligned by the locals and the press (the *Benton Record* at one point described him as "that sniveling old fraud," according to West), Young's letters to Indian Office officials reveal his sincerity. West suggests that local newspapers, supported by stockmen and settlers eager to get rid of the Indians, did everything in their power to ensure that the Indian population was underestimated in an attempt to have their reservation reduced. Young, a dedicated Methodist, no doubted added to his reputation because of his running feud with the Jesuits, who operated the nearby Mission school, and his difficulties with the head chief of the Blackfoot, White Calf.[26]

Young's replacement, R. A. Allen, who took over on April 1, 1884, presented the same message, describing the Indians' condition as "deplorable," with many "gradually dying of starvation." The children, suffering the most, "were so emaciated that it did not seem possible for them to live long." In May he issued over two thousand pounds of condemned bacon, which he found "not to be in as bad condition as had been supposed." By June and early July the Indians' condition had become so desperate that they had stripped and eaten the inner bark of saplings growing along the creeks to "appease their gnawing hunger." Allen concluded that in order to civilize the Indians and make them "of any use to themselves or anybody else," they should be taught to farm, but to farm they must be fed to have the strength to do so.[27]

Painter, meanwhile, had secured an appropriation for the Indians the previous winter, although it ended up thirty-eight thousand dollars less than the IRA had requested. In July 1884, he wrote Armstrong that if he "could do anything for those starving Indians of Montana" he would return immediately from his home to Washington, concluding, "but do not think I could." He described the appropriation bill for their relief as "still hanging fire, and [it] will have to take its slow course." At this point only private charity would reach them in time. "I do not know what to do about it now," he confessed.[28] Welsh would take the decision out of his hands, ordering him to go to Montana, having raised three hundred dollars for his expenses.

The public learned of the situation in late June 1884, when the *New York Times* ran the headline "Indians Dying from Starvation." Five days later the *Times* reported that the agency carpenter had furnished thirty coffins in the past month. Then in early August it reported that the leading citizens of Helena had telegraphed Interior Secretary Teller, "urging immediate action for the relief of 3,000 Piegan Indians at the Blackfeet Agency who are actually starving." Their provisions were almost exhausted, and rations had been cut so severely that local ranchers reported that the starving Indians were killing off their cattle. Three weeks later the *Times* reported that Howard, the special agent sent by Governor John Schuyler Crosby, had described the Indians as "dying from the effects of gradual starvation at the rate of one a day." Because their situation was "an unnatural and inhuman state" of affairs,

Governor Crosby had called on Teller to issue full rations until Congress returned from recess.[29]

On August 31 the *Times* reported that the Indian Office was not to blame. The House had reduced Commissioner Price's $75,000 appropriation request to $40,000. Increased to $50,000 by the Senate, it was still insufficient. Quoting from Agent Allen's annual report, the *Times* concluded that at present the Indians were not suffering, but soon the berries would be gone, supplies would run low, "and the carpenter will again be kept busy making burial boxes unless something can be done in the way of getting them additional food."[30] The following day the *Times* reproduced Governor Crosby's lengthy telegram to Teller, protesting "against keeping the Nation's ward within the limits of this Territory in such a pitiable and starving condition." Crosby concluded that "humanity and justice demand their immediate relief." Two days later the paper reprinted Price's telegram to the governor, informing him that he had ordered additional supplies. Also included was Price's telegram to Agent Allen that supplies were on their way, with a report that instead of requesting money from Congress, the commissioner had used a provision authorizing him to apply any monies unexpended for the relief of another tribe.[31]

The *Christian Union* described this treatment as "an old story," often repeated in "the history of our intercourse with this people." Referencing Helen Hunt Jackson's novel *Ramona*, the *Union* called its closing chapters, tragic as they were, simply telling a "plain, unvarnished tale, which might be matched in the history of almost every other Indian tribe with which we have had dealings." Because the Piegans had been placed on a reservation without game and with soil that without irrigation was unproductive, "we have deliberately condemned an innocent people to the cruel torture and final death of starvation." The government had "no right to condemn a man to death except as the result of legal procedure." The *Union* concluded, "Such wrongs as these make one tremble for the future of the nation."[32]

In mid-October Jackson wrote Henry Chandler Bowen, a founder and later editor of the *New York Independent*, a weekly journal of Congregationalism and antislavery beliefs. She told Bowen that she had just read an article in a Chicago newspaper about an overabundance of wheat; in the same issue she had found an article on the starving Piegan Indians, "dying at the rate of one a day, literally of starvation." The reason was "that Congress reduced

Helen Hunt Jackson, author of *Ramona* and *A Century of Dishonor*.
*Courtesy of the Jones Library, Inc., Amherst, Massachusetts.*

the appropriation for the Indian Bureau,—and the Dept. was simply without money to buy necessary supplies." The "terrible antithesis of these two statements—these two conditions existing side by side with each other, in our land, has haunted me ever since," she confided. She had turned to poetry "to set it in a strong enough light to strike home to people's consciences." In "Too

Much Wheat," published on the front page of the *New York Independent* on November 6, 1884, she wrote: "Hundreds of men lie dying, dead, / Brothers of ours, though their skins are red; / Men we promised to teach and feed. / O, dastard Nation! dastard deed! / They starve like beasts in pens and fold, / While we hoard wheat to sell for gold."[33]

To Jackson, the Piegan situation was a continuation of the government's mistreatment of the Indians, one she had exposed in *A Century of Dishonor*; for Painter, as his first IRA investigation it presented a steep learning curve. Unlike subsequent tours, this one was hasty and insufficiently funded, hampering him from conducting as thorough an investigation as those he would later become known for. Furthermore, it took place months after the initial problem had been exposed. On October 11, the *Philadelphia Inquirer* reported his departure for Montana, adding that two bills with the "ultimate object" of ridding Montana of an Indian presence altogether were before Congress. The newspaper recommended these measures "be opposed and defeated," describing "in almost every instance the removal of Indians from their homes [as] unnecessary, cruel and unjust."[34] At one time Eastern populations had demanded the removal of their Indians; now, ironically, they were condemning westerners for engaging in the same practice.

Mistakenly identifying Painter's primary mission as looking "into the advisability of reducing the Northern Montana Indian Reservation," the Wednesday, October 29, issue of the *River Press* (Fort Benton) reported his arrival the previous Sunday on the evening train. The *River Press* identified the IRA as a philanthropic association organized to "settle the Indian question in a manner that will protect the red man's rights," favoring liberal appropriations "for assisting in the commendable undertaking of changing the wild warriors into peaceful plowmen." Only in the last sentence did the paper report that Painter was expected to leave the next day for the northern part of Montana territory and that while there he would "also examine into the condition of the starving Piegans."[35]

What he found was "sufficiently horrible to startle the conscience of the nation and to arouse our people to take such action as shall prevent their recurrence in future," wrote the IRA Executive Committee in its second annual report.[36] His observations galvanized the association to action. In his initial investigative report, Painter estimated that 400 out of slightly less than

2,000 tribal members had died of starvation during the previous winter and spring. However, a year later he revised the number to 482 deaths in a nine-month period. His displeasure with the incredible waste he had witnessed during his tour, including eighty heavy wagons full of useless candle molds and carpenter tools deteriorating on the prairie, was presented before the 1885 Lake Mohonk Conference. At the next year's conference, again using the Piegan situation as an example of the government's failure, he described the current Indian policy as a machine "too complicated, too widely scattered, too much turned in upon itself in its operation, presided over by too many independent dependents, who have diverse and antagonistic ends to subserve"—a policy that resulted in delayed appropriations and multiple deaths.[37]

From Fort Shaw, Montana, in late October 1884, Painter wrote IRA Vice President Dr. James E. Rhoads that he had arrived the night before after a visit to the Piegan [Blackfeet] Agency on Badger Creek.[38] The stagecoach had been so cramped that he had difficulty getting out and was taking a needed rest before setting out on yet another all-night and -day stage ride to Helena. From there he hoped to turn east and venture out to the Flat Head Agency. Because of threatening weather, he had decided against traveling the three hundred miles to Fort Belknap so late in the season, concluding that at this point he could "do nothing of practical value."[39]

At the Piegan agency, upon learning that the food on hand and those supplies on the way from a recent government contract and a special contract would be exhausted after March 31, Painter warned of a danger of starvation. He urged that supplies be started at once; otherwise, he re-emphasized, there would be a repeat of the previous year's situation, "an experience terrible to those who endured it; heartrending to those who witnessed, or even hear it, and disgraceful to those responsible for it."[40]

Although the roads were currently dry and hard, he described his own "light wagon cut[ting] in to the hubs in several places." He saw freight wagons loaded with flour stuck in alkaline flats and witnessed the struggle of twenty-six mules unable to haul out a single wagon, forcing the freighters to dig it out. Snow would soon make these roads impassable, preventing the supply wagons from reaching the agency. As an aside, he also noted that the twenty thousand pounds of corn that had been sent was "chaffy, light and musty." Even if cooked, it would be useless. The purchase of corn was a mistake because there was no mill to grind it. Painter suggested that it would have been better to have sent a few "large caldrons, or soup kettles," enabling the agent to "greatly increase the value of his meager supplies last year."[41]

The condition of the Indians at Fort Belknap Agency would have been as severe as those at Badger Creek had it not been for the large number of soldiers quartered at nearby Fort Assiniboine. Based on the sworn testimony of two citizens, one who had been Painter's driver for six days, he learned that these Indians had hired out their wives and daughters, even the very young, to the soldiers "for base purposes for money with which they bought food from the Post trader." More than fifty such cases had been witnessed by these two men, who heard the screams of these women and children "from the teepees and bushes under the brutal usage they were receiving."[42]

While Painter was touring the Blackfeet Agency, criticism continued to plague Commissioner Price. To head off blame, he admitted in his mid-October annual report that the newspapers had been "full of complaints for months past" that Indians in the extreme northern agencies were "suffering for food, and by inference the cause of this suffering was attributable to the neglect on the part of this office." Instead, he explained, the situation was "attributable *directly* and *entirely*" to the fact that congressional appropriations were made three months late and the amount given was less than what he had requested. Consequently, the Indians suffered during the winter and spring of 1883 and 1884. Forced to kill many of their horses and livestock, they had resorted to "eating bark, wild roots, &c., and there is little doubt that many deaths amongst them were the direct result of lack of food." However, during their most severe trials, few acts of lawlessness were reported. He did admit that the failure to make appropriations in a timely manner was "one great cause of embarrassment in the management" of his office.[43]

Based on Painter's preliminary report, a *New York Times* reporter described the Piegans' suffering as "a chapter too painful for publication."[44] Blaming the Subcommittee of the House on Indian Appropriations as responsible through their "insufficient and tardy action," IRA executive secretary Herbert Welsh and his brother-in-law, Robert Frazer, a member of the IRA Executive Committee, visited President Arthur on November 18, requesting that the president in his annual message call this matter to the attention of Congress. Because the supplies on hand at the Blackfeet Agency would last only until March 1885, Welsh stressed urgency. In addition, personal letters were sent to E. John Ellis of Louisiana, chairman of the Subcommittee of the House on Indian Appropriations, requesting that action be taken immediately to secure additional funding.[45]

The *Philadelphia Inquirer* reported in early December that Painter, who had recently sent in his report to the IRA, had received sworn evidence revealing that at Fort Assiniboine the previous winter and spring "the distress involved facts too frightful for publication."[46] Although it is unclear when Painter returned home, it is known that on December 12 he accompanied Welsh, Robert Frazer, General Armstrong, and Clement M. Biddle, a Quaker merchant and IRA Executive Committee member, to visit Ellis and Thomas Ryan, a member of the House Committee on Indian Appropriations. Their object, according to Welsh, was to "present some practical suggestions as to Indian appropriations for the coming year, so as to influence in the right direction the work of this committee, and thereby increase the efficiency of the whole Indian service."[47] They proposed an immediate appropriation of fifty thousand dollars for relief, adequate monetary support for all Indian schools, an increase in agent salaries to ensure the employment of more competent men, an increase in pay for Indian police and for judges of Indian courts, and more stringent measures to suppress the whiskey traffic.[48]

In a December 13 letter, Welsh wrote that although initially Ellis and Ryan "seemed hardly disposed to give us a hearing," they later "manifested such interest" that the meeting lasted more than an hour. Ellis even appeared sympathetic, calling the previous year's starvation "an 'infamy.'" Welsh described the attitude of both men as "all that we could desire," and the formal IRA annual report noted that they "conveyed the impression that it was their intention to use their influence to carry them into effect." However, in the end, Ellis refused to bring the matter before his committee.[49]

On December 18, a very vexed Painter informed Welsh that Ellis and Ryan had agreed that as soon as they received the deficiency estimate for the Montana Indians from the Interior Department, they would introduce a joint resolution and see to its passage in two days. Painter "exerted himself strenuously," running between various governmental departments and finally getting all the paperwork to the Speaker of the House late on December 17. After the Speaker reported the resolution to the House, it was referred to

Ellis's committee and then ordered to be printed. On the morning of the following day, Painter also met with Senator Dawes, who promised to put the legislation through the Senate after it passed the House. "I saw a fair ending to all my hard labors for these poor people," Painter informed Welsh, "but hear the conclusion." Meeting with Ellis following the committee meeting, Painter asked if he had brought the matter up. Bluntly Ellis said "that he had not and would not." Expressing his frustration, Painter informed Welsh that Ellis "wanted to know whom I represented, and thought the Indians had rather too many friends about here." It was now too late to get the legislation passed in time to avert the "danger that stares this poor people in the face. May God pity them! An appeal must now be made to the country."[50]

Painter's appeal took the form of a December 24 open letter to Ellis, published and circulated by the IRA to various newspaper editors. Painter complained that Ellis's committee had appropriated only $176,000 of the $260,000 requested by the Interior Department. This action, along with the failure of Ellis's committee to heed the warning of the special inspector who had appeared before them, was threatening these Indians "with absolute starvation." Painter held Ellis personally responsible. "As all known methods for securing relief for these Indians from your Committee have been exhausted," he wrote, "I am forced to appeal to our citizens at large." He was confident that the public did not want to see these Indians starve to death or turn to prostitution to save themselves. Three days later the Executive Committee of the IRA sent a petition to Samuel J. Randall, chairman of the Committee of the House on Appropriations, requesting fifty thousand dollars "to relieve the threatened starvation among the Indians of Montana." Explaining that Ellis and Ryan had initially promised "immediate favorable action" but had since reneged, the petitioners asked for Randall's assistance in securing the funds necessary "to avert the recurrence of starvation among the Indians of Montana."[51]

Painter and the IRA were joined in their public efforts by WNIA President Mary Bonney, who during her November 19, 1884, annual conference address, informed members and visitors that while they were gathered at St. George's Hall in Philadelphia, in far-off Montana the Piegan Indians were starving to death. "Should news come across the ocean of a similar state of things in Ireland, Congress and the people would be alive to the exigency" and ships laden "with provisions [would be] ploughing the Atlantic eastward." And yet, "the wards of the nation send forth their cries with little response." She asked members to express "the depth of [their] convictions that these dying Indians should be speedily relieved." The conference unanimously adopted a resolution to petition Congress and the president to immediately send food and supplies so that "the spectacle of such scenes of want and distress permitted in a Christian nation may not be again possible among us."[52] IRA and WNIA petitions, graphic newspaper accounts, public pressure, and Painter's persistence paid off. On January 6, 1885, the IRA Executive Committee received a telegram signed by Pennsylvania Congressman Charles O'Neill that fifty thousand dollars had just been appropriated by the House for immediate use for the support of the Indians at Crow, Fort Belknap, Fort Peck, and Blackfeet agencies.[53]

Ellis was furious with Painter's open letter, denouncing the lobbyist on the floor of the House for "the grossest misrepresentations and statements . . . utterly and infamously false." He characterized Painter as "one of those self-constituted friends of the Indian."[54] On January 23 the *Springfield Republican* reported that Massachusetts Congressman Francis W. Rockwell defended Painter, using Interior Department statistics Painter had provided to show "conclusively that the Montana Indians have been for two years shamefully neglected by Congress." According to the *Republican*, Ellis "squirmed in his seat" when faced with these figures, proving that Painter's accusations were true. At the end of the session, "Ellis contented himself with saying that he reiterated all his previous utterances, but the general impression is that Painter and Rockwell have a decided advantage in the matter."[55]

In late January 1885, Painter thanked Rockwell for his "prompt vindication," describing "this seemingly personal controversy" with Ellis as "disagreeable." The IRA, Painter explained, had no other choice when facing the "fearful scenes of starvation and suffering," and he refuted in detail each of Ellis's accusations, concluding that "the reckless character of Mr. Ellis' charges may be judged from the statement that for five years I have been annoying [his] Committee." Openly critical of the Indian system as it currently existed, Painter informed Rockwell that "so long as we furnish the means and almost necessitate the conditions of a shiftless life [for the Indians], it will be continued." He believed that if Indian policy "would but furnish the conditions and lay upon these people the necessity of a better life, and teach them how to attain it, we would at least test the question whether or not they are capable of it."[56]

During the January 8, 1885, BIC meeting, Ellis's criticism of Painter was also balanced by praise from Rev. Henry Kendall, secretary of the Presbyterian Board of Home Missions. "Nobody says in Congress any more that the dead Indian is the best Indian," declared Kendall. "Look at the way in which Professor Painter reached Congress in the appropriation for the Piegans," he noted. "There was no trouble about it after the Tribune containing his publication [the open letter] reached the Senate. The bill went through in fifteen minutes." He concluded that three or four years earlier, that could never have happened.[57]

Months later Agent R. A. Allen of Blackfeet Agency reported that since congressional appropriations had not been sufficient, he, along with the territorial governor and the Helena board of trade, had called the Indians' situation to the attention of the Interior Department. Additional supplies were purchased, and during the last congressional session another appropriation was made. "These extra allowances enabled me to issue such quantities of food as prevented any suffering from lack of food," he wrote, and "the death rate was much less than in the preceding year." Inflating his own role, Allen made no mention of Painter's actions or the support of the IRA.[58]

Painter's first investigative tour had been a success. He had ably represented the Piegans' condition, served effectively as a member of the IRA Executive Committee, worked closely with Commissioner Price, appealed to the public in his letter to Ellis, and pushed through legislation to alleviate the Indians' suffering. The only thing lacking was his formal report of the investigation; such reports would later become his signature. According to Hagan, these reports "featured colorful and sometimes caustic descriptions of government personnel which made his pamphlets widely read on the reservations." The IRA did, however, publish two pamphlets devoted to the Piegan Indians, quoting from some of Painter's letters. Years later Welsh remarked to Armstrong that "half, or more than half, the value of our organization would be gone if Professor Painter left it."[59]

On January 8, 1885, Painter participated in the annual BIC conference. The number of attendees had grown annually, and although members representing the Washington auxiliary of the WNIA had attended the previous year, this year the national association's general secretary, Amelia Stone Quinton, was seated for the first time. She reported on the work of her association, which had grown to include thirty-eight branches in ten different states, after which Welsh complimented their activities, remarking that certain things "in the present age can be pushed better by men, but the two societies stand side by side, the slight divergence being that men have more to do with political matters."[60] Such collegial acceptance of the WNIA's Indian work had made it possible for the organization to support Painter and the IRA on the Piegan situation.

Painter ably presented his work at the BIC proceedings, emphasizing what he had learned in Montana. At the Blackfeet Agency he had found between five hundred and six hundred children and only two teachers, both "inexperienced young girls put in to help out the agent's salary." He again complained about the agent's power to hire teachers, emphasizing that Indian education continued to be sacrificed to support the agent. He also recognized Blackfeet land as useful only for grazing, describing the error of the government in allowing such land to be homesteaded. If these Indians were to be forced to depend upon agriculture, it would "simply be going against nature." One steer required fifty acres of land.[61]

## Crow Creek

A month after the appropriation to save the Montana Indians was authorized, Painter was confronted with a scheme to confiscate thousands of acres of reservation land. Involved from the beginning, he quickly and efficiently solved the problem. In late February 1885, during the last week of Chester A. Arthur's administration, at the direction of Interior Secretary Teller, the president hastily issued a proclamation opening up to white settlement half a million acres of the 635,000-acre Crow Creek Reservation (in what is today central South Dakota). Teller later defended his actions, claiming the matter had been before the department for a year; whatever the case, the appropriate congressional committees and outgoing Indian Commissioner Price had not been consulted. Upon learning of this proclamation, Painter immediately telegraphed Welsh. On March 1, even before the proclamation became official, two thousand settlers had rushed onto the reservation—home for the last two decades to one thousand Yanktonai Sioux. On March 2, Painter visited the Interior Department and late that evening paid a formal visit to Secretary Teller, urging him to instruct "the local land Agent not to issue certificates to whites until the Indians had first selected." Painter returned on successive days to the department, also visiting the land office to learn what sections were exempted from the order. Meanwhile, Welsh met with the IRA Executive Committee, which directed the association's Law Committee, chaired by Henry Pancoast, to draft a legal brief protesting the action. Aided by the press, the IRA blanketed the country with pertinent facts. Faced with IRA lobbying, incoming Interior Secretary Lucius Q. C. Lamar suspended implementation of the proclamation until he could examine it. In mid-April, incoming President Grover Cleveland revoked the opening of the reservation to settlement.[62] A month later Painter wrote Welsh that he had no doubt "that these settlers went in *good faith* onto this land; strong in the confidence that no land once wrested from the Indian would ever be restored to him."[63]

Cleveland would prove to be a valuable ally to both Painter and the IRA. Largely uninformed on Indian affairs, he treated Painter and the association with respect, following their direction and consulting regularly with him. Painter had a similar arrangement with Indian Commissioner John D. C. Atkins and Interior Secretary Lamar, whom Painter later described as beginning to "understand better than he did the nature of our work, and, to some extent the necessity of our methods." Painter assured Welsh that if in the future the IRA explained its views fully, he was confident that Lamar would give them all his aid.[64]

While Painter was gaining experience and confidence, the IRA was growing, with a membership of two hundred and fifty by the spring of 1885 in twenty-three branches. By 1889 membership would rise to nearly twelve hundred. Despite the association's emerging importance, Painter, Welsh, and co-workers were dealing with a complex Indian bureaucracy. A simple reservation visit required not only authorization from Washington officials but the agent's cooperation. In addition, by the late 1880s, the Senate, responsible for ratifying treaties, was controlled by the Republicans, while the House, which held the purse strings, was Democrat-controlled. It was not uncommon for IRA-sponsored legislation to pass one house and die in the other. Painter would wrestle with this complex bureaucracy during the rest of his tenure.

He could, however, take great pride in his first year. He had played a major role during his second BIC conference, exhibiting organizational skill and an astute vision of the direction Indian reform should take. In late fall, he had played a key role in easing the suffering of the starving Piegans, manipulating the resources he had available and obtaining congressional funding. Finally, he and the IRA had quickly come to the defense of the Yanktonai Sioux, who had been in danger of losing a vast amount of their land through a hastily issued presidential proclamation. His next task, defending the land rights of California's Mission Indians, would become his most enduring legacy.

▼ ▼ ▼

# CHAPTER 3

# FIRST VISIT TO MISSION INDIAN VILLAGES, 1885–1886

Seeing the "Last Poems of Helen Jackson" in the December 1885 issue of the *Century*, Painter was convinced that the July 1 poem entitled "Acquainted with Grief" had been the very one he had seen "lying unfinished, by her side, during one of the interviews" he had with Jackson in late June as she lay gravely ill. Her face during that visit was, he later wrote, "the face of an angel with the glow of earth's sunset, and the ruddy flush of heaven's sunrise," bearing "testimony to the completeness of her victory over her enemy Grief." It was not claiming too much, he wrote, that "among the comforts of her closing days, not the least to her, was the fact that the Indian Rights Association had sent its Agent out to investigate the condition of those people whose sad story she has told in *Ramona* with such moving pathos, and whose wretched and hopeless condition weighed so heavily upon her heart." Jackson, already familiar with the IRA's work on behalf of the Piegans and at Crow Creek, had joyously welcomed Painter, exclaiming: "Oh, is this you! There is no one in the United States whom I so much wanted to see." At her "earnest request," he had returned to the Mission villages for a second look. His interest piqued, he would return to their remote villages numerous times.[1]

The Mission Indians' situation was unique in the United States, for their ancestral lands were not settled by Protestant northern and western Europeans but by Catholic Spain, which from 1769 to 1823 established twenty-one Franciscan missions along the Pacific coast from San Diego to Sonoma, the last during the Mexican period.[2] In the 1820s Mexico declared independence, taking California and the southwestern borderlands along. Less than three decades later, at the successful conclusion of the Mexican-American War and the signing of the Treaty of Guadalupe Hidalgo, California and neighboring areas became part of the United States, bringing their indigenous occupants under American rule.

Indian lands in the rest of the country were generally acquired through the treaty process, with the Indians receiving smaller reservations carved out of their cessions. However, Congress failed to ratify the eighteen treaties negotiated with California Indians between 1851 and 1852, forcing them to live on unprotected lands with unresolved titles.[3] Over the next half century, minimal protection was afforded through a patchwork of military and executive order reservations, and California's indigenous population suffered extensive loss of land and population.

### Helen Hunt Jackson

The Mission Indians found a champion in Helen Hunt Jackson, who poignantly portrayed their struggle in her novel *Ramona*. Her activism had begun in Boston in the fall of 1879 after attending a lecture by Ponca Chief Standing Bear, describing his tribe's removal and loss of their homeland. Her research had led to the publication of *A Century of Dishonor*, a condemnation of the government's Indian policy. Then during the winter of 1881–82, on assignment for *Century Magazine*, she toured Mission Indian reservations and villages, witnessing their poverty firsthand. Interior Secretary Teller, convinced that Jackson was capable of making an investigative tour and writing a government report on the Indians' conditions, appointed her as an official agent for his department. In 1883, accompanied by co-commissioner Abbot Kinney of Los Angeles, whose knowledge of California land laws and ability to speak Spanish proved useful, she returned to California, charged with visiting the villages and making recommendations for reservations. Jackson and Kinney's official report was submitted to the government in July 1883, and on January 10, 1884, the draft of a bill for the relief of the Mission Indians accompanied by a printed copy of the Jackson/Kinney report was submitted by Commissioner Price to Secretary Teller, who presented it to President Arthur, who sent it to Congress. The bill, with Jackson's recommendations, passed the Senate but failed in the House. Submitted annually thereafter by the Indian Office and strongly supported by Painter and the IRA, it finally became law in 1891.[4]

Disappointed with public reaction to her exposé, Jackson wrote *Ramona*, basing it on her newfound knowledge of the Mission Indians. In April 1884, a month after the novel was completed, she wrote Amelia Stone Quinton: "I do not dare to think I have written a second Uncle Tom's Cabin—but I do think I have written a story which will be a good stroke for the Indian cause."[5] Quinton recommended it to the WNIA membership, and a pamphlet alerted the IRA's members, describing it as written "not so much with the intention of pleasing the public by a fascinating story as of touching the conscience of the American people, and stimulating them to redress wrongs of which they had been guilty."[6] After reading *Ramona* and Jackson's *New York Independent* articles,[7] many reformers, including Painter and Quinton, were drawn to the plight of the Mission Indians.

Leaving Great Barrington on May 25, 1885, Painter met with Jackson during his three-month summer investigative tour of western reservations. His interest in education had prompted him to first go to Indian Territory to attend the closing exercises at the Indian University at Muscogee in its newly dedicated building. He was pleasantly surprised with that section of the territory, describing it as "one of the loveliest regions of the Southwest"; the people, as "one of the richest"; and their lifestyle, one to which "other Indians ought to conform."[8] From there, he made a quick detour to Arizona at the same time that Geronimo and a few of his followers had fled the San Carlos Reservation there. Blaming "a double-headed and not harmonious management" for this outbreak, Painter described the Chiricahua Apaches at the reservation as "corralled in a sort of Andersonville, on short rations, and almost absolutely naked." Fearing an even larger outbreak, he informed the secretaries of the interior and of war that instructions should be given for their relief. From San Carlos he traveled to Tucson to visit the Papago and Pima on their reservation, discovering there twelve thousand residents plagued by whisky sellers.[9]

## Mission Villages

Painter visited a number of Mission Indian villages before heading north to San Francisco in late June to meet with Jackson. He was convinced that she was comforted about his IRA investigation, writing that it "helped to sweeten the bitterness of death to that sainted woman, when she could commit, as she did, her unfinished work to our hands," fully aware that the IRA would take up the case of these Indians and "urge it persistently."[10]

Following Painter's visit, Jackson wrote Antonio F. and Mariana Coronel of Los Angeles: "I have been much cheered by an interview with Prof. Painter." If he really "undertakes to get something done for those Indians, he will be worth more than all the Senators and Congressmen put together." She had met the Coronels during the research trip for her *Century Magazine* articles. Antonio Coronel had influenced her views of Mexican California, drawing up an itinerary of old ranches and missions to visit for local color.[11]

Painter also wrote Coronel about his visit with Jackson. He had revisited the Mission Indians, he wrote, and would be coming to Los Angeles to consult with him, accompanied by Joshua W. Davis and his wife, Elizabeth.[12] Painter explained to Coronel that the IRA intended to pursue a court case to establish that under the Treaty of Guadalupe Hidalgo the Mission Indians had become U.S. citizens. Therefore he hoped to confer with other reformers at the Coronels' home to "settle on a practical line of conduct" and requested that they organize such a gathering to include Abbot Kinney, who had served with Jackson as a special agent for the Interior Department; Horatio Nelson Rust, a friend of Kinney who later served as the Mission Indian agent; and Henry H. Markham, a member of the House of Representatives from California. Painter also wanted to meet as many of the village leaders as possible. "I know that I am asking much," he wrote, "but no more than I am confident your great interest in these poor people will lead you willingly to undertake."[13]

Painter and Davis had specifically requested that the village leader, or captain, at Santa Ysabel assemble as many Indians as possible on July 15. In response, twenty-eight village captains representing as many villages gathered, along with almost four hundred Indian men, some of whom had traveled a great distance. Painter and his party, however, failed to show up. Three days later the Santa Ysabel village captain received a letter from Painter and Davis, explaining that the hot weather had made it difficult for the ladies to travel. (Along with Davis's wife, Elizabeth, Rust's daughter had also been there). The "Indians were sadly disappointed," noted Father Antonio Dominic Ubach, who had received ten dollars from the two men to defray travel expenses for the village captains. Ubach, who had escorted Jackson through various villages during her visit in the spring of 1882, was particularly critical of Painter. In his letter to General William Starke Rosecrans, Democratic congressman from California, Ubach described Painter and Davis as members of a special committee "sent out from Washington to investigate matters about the various Indian Pueblos." Mistakenly assuming they were official government agents, he wrote Rosecrans: "I cannot see for the life of me what *report* can these two gentlemen make to the Government after acting in such a manner." After all, he explained, Jackson and Kinney had not mistreated the Indians but had "done their duty nobly and faithfully by going from one Indian Pueblo to another seeing for themselves the real condition of the poor Indians, and their report to Congress will be an eternal monument of the truth, justice and fair play which has received the applause and admiration of everyone that has read it."[14]

Despite Ubach's displeasure, Painter's published report was widely distributed throughout the country, and it presented the condition of the Mission Indians in sympathetic terms, generating good will and generous support. This report included a brief quotation from a *Los Angeles Herald* article describing their current problems and the text of a February 7, 1878, petition to the interior secretary from the San Luis Rey Indians, requesting protection for their land. Painter also presented a history of Mission villages in danger of being dispossessed—villages whose stories he would elaborate on in future IRA pamphlets. Painter's tour had left him impressed, and his report described these Indians as "Christian, civilized, [and] self-supporting" but crowded off of lands from which "they have always lived"—lands to which lawyers believed they had "a valid legal, as well as a just and equitable title." He accused Congress of knowing these facts but being content with spending money for "special commissions and committees, and elaborate reports, giving comfortable jobs to white men." It had allowed "the cry of these poor people to die out amid the din of white interests, and the reported facts to lie buried out of sight."[15]

### Lake Mohonk Conference and Other Meetings

From Southern California, Painter and the Davises continued on to Nevada and Oregon, ending up at the Fort Hall Reservation in Idaho Territory, where Painter found encouraging progress among the Bannocks and Shoshonis. They were cultivating more crops that year and were selling their hay to the local cattlemen. From there, Painter traveled home in time to take Martha to the annual Mohonk Conference the first week of October 1885. On the opening day of the conference, with knowledge gleaned from his recent tour, Painter discussed the condition of the Mission Indians and his interview with Jackson, noting how the Indians "lay upon her heart, and how her interest and prayers were all in this work." The Indians' condition, which he described as "very sad," would appeal to even "the hardest-hearted person you could find, unless it be a California land-grabber."[16]

Painter expanded his remarks to include the condition of all Indians, blaming government policy, which treated them as foreigners, leaving them without legal protection, subject to easily broken treaties. The solution was congressional legislation, which until recently had been controlled "by the greed of the Western land-grabber." If a bill "does not conflict with any white man's interest," it might have a chance of passing, he explained. The Indian, however, "has no voice, and few friends—nobody to push it against the interests of the white man." Worse yet, the responsibility for Indian matters "rests nowhere." It was divided between the Treasury Department, the Indian Office, the Department of Justice, various congressional committees, and finally Congress—another reference to the Indian policy as a large disorganized machine. "The time has come," Painter explained, to "sweep this whole system away and put the Indian on the basis of a white man, and give him a man's chance in this country under the law." Quinton, who was attending for the first time, described his address as "stirring."[17]

Painter dominated the discussion during the morning session on the second day, describing the reservation system as not only isolating the Indian but keeping him "aloof from our civilization," denying him "the opportunities of a citizen and a man"—an "incubus upon every effort" for his advancement. As to the issue of citizenship, Painter declared that since the country had taken into its body politic and extended citizenship opportunities to others, he had "no particular objection to extend[ing] the ballot to such Indians as you can chase down, lasso, and bring to the polls." Fifty thousand Indians "scattered over the country, armed with the ballot would [not] create any great damage to our institutions," he concluded. He reported that he had also conferred with some Sioux Indians about the Edmunds modification of the 1868 Sioux Treaty. Inquiring whether they had indeed given their consent, he learned not only that they had not but that they had been threatened with cuts to their

Amelia Stone Quinton in 1898, cofounder, first general secretary, and longtime president of the Women's National Indian Association.
*William H. Weinland Photograph Collection (photCL 39 [202]), Huntington Library, San Marino, California.*

annuities, removal to the Indian Territory, and during a terrible cold spell, prevented from visiting their agency for two weeks until they signed. Painter concluded that this was one of several illustrations of the "*sacred* charter of our so-called treaties with the Indians" being subverted.[18]

On the third day, conferees paid tribute to Jackson, who had died of cancer on August 12, 1885. They resolved "that the brilliant and useful life of this truly grand woman still appeals to the people of the United States, to Congress, and to the Executive to continue and complete the work inspired by her pen, and labored for to the end of her life." Painter spoke about his visit with Jackson. He explained that after learning from her nurse that she was too feeble to receive visits, he had been about to leave when Jackson herself welcomed him. Propping herself up in bed, she inscribed the last copy of her government report to President Grover Cleveland, exclaiming: "Give him my thanks for the Crow Creek matter," a reference to his revocation of the order to open that reservation. Painter described her as apprehensive, fearful that "the artistic part" of *Ramona* would be overshadowed by its "philanthropic purpose." As a last request, she asked that he and other reformers give the Mission Indians their "constant attention."[19]

During the closing session, Painter described his visit with the Missions Indians, explaining that with California statehood had come the creation of a land commission before which all claimants had to appear to make good their title. The Indians had not been invited; therefore, no matter where they lived, they held an uncertain land title and were threatened with displacement. It was a shame "that in this Christian country, and with our boasted institutions, this people should be treated worse than under the old Mexican government." The only recourse was for the federal government to "send some reliable man from the East to defend the title of the Indians to these lands."[20] Ultimately, he would be that "reliable man."

To emphasize the seriousness of the situation, Painter described two endangered villages. One, located in the Temecula Valley, where descendants of the San Luis Rey Mission Indians lived, had been used by Jackson as the home of Ramona's fictional husband, Alessandro. Although the Indians' claims to their village had been based on a protective clause in an old Mexican land grant, the current ranch owners had brought a removal suit before the San Francisco District Court. Unsuccessful in their arguments, the Indians had been evicted in 1875, some moving to the small, arid Pechanga Canyon.[21]

The second, the Serrano village of Soboba, was located on an 1844 Mexican land grant, Rancho San Jacinto Viejo. The ranch had been purchased in 1882 by San Bernardino businessman Matthew R. Byrne, who had been granted an eviction order by the San Diego Superior Court. In early April of the same year, Jackson first visited the village and conferred with Byrne; she returned the following year as an agent of the Interior Department.

Aware of the eviction, Jackson then contacted the Los Angeles law firm of Brunson & Wells, appending to her official government report their opinion: based on Mexican law and the respect the United States gave to property rights legally recognized by prior sovereigns, the Indians had a legal right to their land.[22] In late June 1883, at Jackson's urging, Anson Brunson and G. Wiley Wells were appointed special assistants to the U.S. Attorney to represent the Indians. Their compensation, left to the discretion of the Department of Justice, had been determined by Attorney General Benjamin Harris Brewster at a miserly rate of no less than two hundred dollars annually.[23]

In late 1883, Byrne brought action in the Superior Court of San Diego County in *M. Byrne v. Antonio Alas, et al.* against Antonio Alas and eighty other defendants, all Soboba residents. The following May, Brunson & Wells filed a petition to have the case removed to the federal court as a test case; however, Brunson's election that fall to a superior court judgeship resulted in the dissolution of the firm, endangering the lawsuit. Now Painter informed the Mohonk Conference that he had visited Wells in June 1885, only to learn that the judgment had gone against the Indians for failure to appear. At that time he also learned that Brunson had left the partnership, forming a new firm.[24]

At the conclusion of Painter's address, the conference unanimously resolved to send a petition to Congress, calling for immediate and effective steps to protect the Mission Indians in "whatever rights they may have to the lands they now occupy."[25] Individually and collectively, reformers would carry on Jackson's work. While the IRA and the Lake Mohonk Conference provided financial and legal support, the WNIA supported missionary work, including the funding of a medical and educational program in one isolated village.[26]

A month later, on November 19, 1885, Painter attended the opening session of the IRA convention in New Haven, Connecticut. Here he addressed an informal afternoon session on the "status of the Indian question at the national capital." He deplored "the indifference" on the part of Indian officials in implementing the "good work begun by President Cleveland in restoring the Crow Creek lands in Dakota and compelling the whites to leave the domain."[27] The following day he addressed the condition of the Mission Indians. However, the principal speaker that evening was Massachusetts Senator Henry Laurens Dawes, who spoke on the issue of land allotment in severalty. On this occasion Dawes cautioned that severalty "might" be good on some reservations but impractical on others.[28] (Once the Dawes-sponsored legislation was passed in 1887, however, he did little to make sure that reservations were carefully selected. It was Painter who would spend countless hours discussing, implementing, explaining, and criticizing the legislation.)

Painter, who was becoming sought after as an expert speaker on the Indian problem, joined IRA members in mid-December for their annual meeting in Association Hall in Philadelphia. First on the agenda was a concert of music performed by some thirty young Indian students from the Lincoln Institute and Educational Home. That evening Painter was the main speaker, describing scenes he had witnessed during his most recent tour.[29] Four days later, in an interview printed in the *Philadelphia Times*, he returned to sentiments expressed during the recent Mohonk Conference, placing the blame for the Indian problem on a government policy that "has been to float [the Indian] along on the advance wave of our Western immigration, outside our social institutions, out from under the protection of our laws and with no opportunity to work out anything for himself by his own genius or industry." He described "an elaborate and complicated system of book-keeping" that was so intricate that even the Indian commissioner had to guard against "being overwhelmed." He concluded that "the more the governmental Indian machinery is studied the more wonderful does it appear and the more is one's admiration excited that any man or set of men can run it and not be caught in it."[30]

Painter finished the year with the publication of an upbeat article on the AMA's Indian Committee. Never before in the committee's recollection had Congress "been so sensitive to the criticism of the public press," and never before had the criticism of the press "been so justly, so intelligently, and so freely made." Congressional appropriations for educational purposes had been increased from $600,000 to $1.1 million, indicating that legislators were finally beginning to see the value in Indian education. However, obstacles still existed, including a governmental system that made the Indian "the abject and helpless victim of an absolute despotism." He concluded that immediate steps needed to be taken to "do away with the tribal relations."[31]

Painter's growing familiarity with the inner workings of the federal government's Indian policy was promoted by the IRA in its fourth annual report, which included a lengthy discussion of his reform work for 1886 and a list of his ten public addresses. Although the speaking engagements were mostly in New England, he also spoke in Philadelphia and Chicago. Throughout the remainder of his career, Painter was a frequent guest speaker, spreading the good work of the IRA and soliciting financial support before such disparate groups as the Great Barrington auxiliary of the WNIA and Sunday School assemblies. However, his most thought-provoking addresses were before the Mohonk Conferences. The IRA soon recognized his efficiency, crediting him with speedily acquiring "more complete knowledge of the facts involved than any one else can bring to bear." As such, he frequently exerted "a perceptible and most wholesome influence upon the course of legislation and administration affecting Indian interests."[32]

In 1886, as in other years, these interests were widely spread across the country. Learning from Congress that 166 land allotment patents for the Puyallup Indians on Puget Sound had been suspended, Painter moved quickly to get them issued. When the House Committee on Indian Affairs voted nearly unanimously in favor of Indian schools being located near reservations, he demonstrated the value of Eastern boarding schools, a subject he was familiar with as a constant visitor to Carlisle and Hampton. Informed that the Indian agent on the Cheyenne River Reservation had ordered that the Indians living near La Beau could not trade with the merchants there, forcing them to travel 150 miles to trade at the agency, he immediately informed the Indian commissioner, and the order was revoked.[33]

### Shirley Ward and the Mission Indians

Although Painter addressed these and many other problems in 1886, much of his attention remained focused on the Mission Indians. Returning home from his 1885 visit, he had advised Welsh and other IRA officials of their perilous situation. The association was determined to defend their rights and to support the legal efforts of Shirley C. Ward. The son of Mission Agent John S. Ward, the younger Ward was formally appointed special assistant

U.S. attorney for the Mission Indians of California by Attorney General Augustus H. Garland in mid-January 1886. Not until February of the following year was Painter able to get an appropriation bill passed authorizing the payment of one thousand dollars to Ward, who even prior to his official appointment had been working on the Soboba case, as well as preparing an argument to be filed on behalf of Indians on another reservation in several land disputes currently before the General Land Office.[34] Explaining that the Indians were crowding upon him "thick and fast with their troubles," Ward informed Welsh in late March that he "never dreamed that their interest would require the attention" that he was now giving them.[35]

The Mission Indians were on Painter's mind on January 9, 1886, when, accompanied by Welsh and IRA president Dr. James Rhoads, he paid a visit to Indian Commissioner John Atkins. Atkins was pleased with the work that Ward had already accomplished, an assessment confirmed by the IRA Law Committee, which had examined the young lawyer's legal brief. Painter, Welsh, and Rhoads then conferred with President Cleveland, who showed "a marked interest" in the Mission Indians and asked Painter to call upon Attorney General Garland to request that he "have the validity" of the Indians' land title "tested in the courts." In a February 25 letter to Welsh, Painter explained that before the attorney general could prepare such a test case, he had to have a formal request from the Interior Department. After a consultation with Garland and Atkins, all agreed to await the decision of *M. Byrne v. Antonio Alas, et al.*[36]

Painter was favorably impressed with Ward, describing him as "earnest and vigilant in the discharge of his duties," honestly making "the best fight he can for his clients."[37] However, he was displeased with Ward's salary, which remained the same as that paid to Brunson & Wells. Because the original law firm had "a philanthropic interest in the Indians," they had been willing "as an act of charity to undertake their defence [sic]" with little compensation, only two hundred dollars for expenses, payable with proper vouchers. Painter had learned from Garland that on orders of Interior Secretary Lamar, Ward had been given the same financial arrangement. Unable to make Garland budge, Painter informed Ward that because the IRA "did not want the case to suffer because of red tape," the association would "within reasonable limits" pay his expenses.[38]

### New BIC Responsibilities and Ongoing Political Intrigue

Like Painter's interest in the Mission Indians, his obligations to the BIC had grown. On January 8, 1886, he informed Welsh that he had been appointed by the Mohonk Conference as chairman of a committee "to draw up resolutions & present business" for the BIC meeting later in January. He described the committee meeting, held at the Riggs House, as "the largest and most interesting ever held," spending eight out of the nine pages of his letter detailing all the machinations that transpired. He noted that those in attendance had been very "anxious to know the chances that the President would sign the Dawes bill." Painter was also aware that Thomas Bland's National Indian Defense Association was actively engaged in preventing the bill's passage. Painter had learned that three of the six committee members appointed by Bland had defected, concluding that the bill was "excellent" and suggesting only one clause that would not change the bill's provisions. Initially none of the six men had even read the bill. After being presented with a copy, three had immediately approved. Bland was furious. "It was in the air that there must be collision and that the time had come to prick Bland's bubble," declared Painter. His dislike for the man was palpable, ultimately resulting in a heated argument between them and ending in Bland's withdrawal from the committee. "The provoking cause of this outburst on my part," wrote Painter, "was the man himself . . . his simple presence."[39]

Senator Dawes had also been present in the crowded parlor of the Riggs House and when asked to speak, "spent nearly half an hour lamenting that the feature of his bill which he regarded as its most important had been left out." He continued on for another three quarters of an hour on the dangers reformers would face when his bill became law, "dangers which seemed to him so overwhelming that he was now forced to feel at times disposed to drop the whole measure," Painter explained. "Bland and his clackers" had applauded from the back of the Riggs parlor. Painter described Dawes's tirade as both "amazing and humiliating," for the senator had not "studied the bill he had so long championed and was now criticizing." The section of the bill that Dawes complained had been removed "was put in as clearly as language could express it," explained Painter, who would have liked to have read the first section of the bill out loud "had it not been for overwhelming the old

Henry Laurens Dawes, senator from Massachusetts and sponsor
of the Dawes Severalty Act.
*Library of Congress, Prints and Photographs Division (LC-DIG-ppmsca-07783),
Washington, D.C.*

man with shame." He continued, "you can well imagine that we all felt pretty cheap." Painter, who had no doubt that the Dawes legislation would pass, lamented, "but I do wish that some asses could be suppressed."[40]

The animosity between the IRA and Bland's National Indian Defense Association would only increase as the Dawes severalty legislation moved through Congress. In early 1887 President Cleveland inquired of Painter if an understanding could be made between the two associations, prompting Painter to respond: "[O]ur views of the policy to be pursued are diametrically opposite." He continued: "[I]t seems to me as if they are defending the Indians' right to be an Indian, and would perpetuate the conditions which force him to remain Indian." Cleveland then questioned why the representatives of the Five Civilized Tribes, the most advanced of all Indians, were so hostile to the Dawes legislation. Painter's response was "Mr. President when you hear of a league entered into by the barbers of the country the object of which is to dissuade people from shaving, you may expect to hear that indian chiefs and leading men who handle tribal funds are in favor of such a measure." Painter informed Welsh that the president laughed, saying that "he apprehended that this was about the level of it," prompting Painter to assure Welsh that the president would ultimately sign the final bill. However, one day after Cleveland signed, Painter would warn Welsh that the IRA should call its various branches together and organize to "aid the President, if he will allow us, and watch everything that is done with the closest scrutiny whether he will or no."[41]

The annual BIC meeting with representatives of various missionary boards and reformers was held on January 21, 1886, two weeks after Painter's contentious Lake Mohonk committee meeting. During his presentation, Painter commented on his recent visit to the Modoc Indians, originally from northern California and southern Oregon and now living in Indian Territory. Settler pressure on their homeland had resulted in warfare, culminating in their forced removal. "I saw nothing so encouraging in the Indian Territory as the progress among these people," Painter informed the conference. "It was natural development and growth, the power of their manhood asserting itself," he concluded. Later in the proceedings, he addressed Indian education, especially the difficulties of maintaining reservation day schools. As reformers they must insist that Indians had rights, including the right to send their children to public schools.[42]

## Mission Indians Again

His obligations to the BIC successfully concluded, Painter turned his attention again to the Mission Indians. During 1886 the IRA produced two publications to generate public attention and solicit support for the Indians' defense: On March 1, *The Case of the Mission Indians in Southern California* was published out of "a sense of responsibility" for the execution of the trust that Jackson had placed upon Painter and the association during the deathbed meeting. This pamphlet included excerpts from Indian Office officials and the 1883 Jackson/Kinney report, as well as the history of the Soboba village, the role of Brunson & Wells, and the reinstitution of the case by Ward. Weeks later, the IRA published Painter's lengthy formal report of his visit to the Mission Indians and other western tribes. Broader exposure was gained with a lengthy review in *Lend a Hand, a Journal of Organized Philanthropy.*[43]

May was busier than usual for Painter. Engaged in copying material for Ward to use in his legal work, on May 10 Painter apologized to Welsh for not sending in his monthly report and missing an IRA meeting. The research had "required a good deal of reading, and taken much time," he wrote. Three days later he mailed sixteen pages of notes and references that he thought would be of value to Ward, who a week later responded: "Your research [has] involved such labor that I regret very much to have given you so much trouble." He informed Painter that he had no doubt he would "be successful in the long run" on behalf of the Mission Indians, although the case might have to go to the U.S. Supreme Court.[44] Then two days later, Antonio Coronel wrote Painter that because Dawes's "bill for the relief of the Mission Indians" was currently before the House Committee on Indian Affairs, he suggested that the House subpoena both Agent John Ward and himself to appear and testify on behalf of the Mission Indians. "I am and have been for thirty years intimately and minutely acquainted with their condition, rights, troubles, and needs," he informed Painter, "and Mr. Ward by his careful attention and solicitude for their rights and interest, has become thoroughly conversant with their needs, and would be prepared to lay their entire case before the committee." If Painter thought the idea a good one, Coronel asked him to "lay the matter before the committee without delay." It is unknown whether Painter took the suggestion. The Dawes legislation that Coronel referenced was the annual submission by the Indian Office to Congress of a Mission Indian bill based on the Jackson/Kinney report.[45]

Although still attentive to the needs of the Mission Indians, Painter returned home to Great Barrington to attend the funeral of his pastor, and in mid-May he joined prominent congressmen, educators, ministers, and Indian reformers at Carlisle School's seventh annual open house. Guests toured the campus, visited workshops, listened to student recitations, and enjoyed a parade. Painter was also collaborating with the Indian Office in an effort to send fifteen students from the band of Chiricahua Apaches living captive in Florida to be educated at Hampton Institute. "I think there is no doubt but it will be done," he informed Welsh. However, a week later he wrote that the students instead would be attending Carlisle.[46]

Also in May, Painter's article on Indian citizenship and the Supreme Court was published in *Lend a Hand*. Reformers viewed citizenship as essential to the process of bringing the Indians into the body politic. For a time the Senate Judicial Committee had recognized that Indians who severed connections with their tribe and took up white ways should qualify for citizenship and be allowed to vote, but the negative decision in *Elk v. Wilkins* (1884) ended that premise. In his article, Painter described this decision as being "of great interest and importance," explaining that John Elk, an Indian who lived in Omaha, Nebraska, had tried to register to vote; when denied, he sued. For clarity, Painter included the full text of this now two-year-old decision that even though an Indian had "voluntarily separated himself from his tribe," he was not recognized as a citizen under the Fourteenth Amendment. Quoting Judge Thomas M. Cooley, Painter agreed that when an Indian dissolved his tribal relations and adopted "the habits and customs of civilized life," it would "seem that his right to protection" must be that of "any other native-born inhabitant."[47]

In mid-July Painter visited his family in Great Barrington, keeping Welsh up to date on his efforts on behalf of the IRA. He joined General Armstrong for meetings with fellow reformers in Lennox, Stockbridge, and William-stown, Massachusetts, to raise money to pay some of the expenses for his next visit to the Mission Indians. In late August he informed Welsh that checks were beginning to come in.[48] The following month he had speaking engagements in Glastonbury and Hartford, Connecticut, with good attendance.

He planned to leave for California either the Monday or the Tuesday after the Mohonk Conference and already had his railroad passes from Chicago to Mohave, California, and back again. Just days before leaving for the conference, he made another hasty trip to Washington, reporting to Welsh on the more than a dozen tasks he had recently completed.[49]

## Lake Mohonk

On October 13, 1886, Albert Smiley called the fourth annual Lake Mohonk Conference to order. Painter and his wife, Martha, were among the over sixty attendees. The Mission Indians were the first topic during the morning session of the opening day, with Joshua Davis, who had accompanied Painter on the previous year's investigative tour, addressing the conference first. Since each member had been given a copy of Painter's report *A Visit to the Mission Indians of Southern California and Other Western Tribes*, Davis kept his remarks brief. When Painter spoke, he concentrated on his meeting with President Cleveland, the attorney general, and the interior secretary and their decision to allow the case of *M. Byrne v. Antonio Alas, et al.* to move forward. He explained that the case had been decided against the Indians on July 3, 1886, but that Attorney Ward had gotten it restored to the court's calendar[50] and Welsh had sent his personal check of $3,300 as an indemnity bond for Byrne, who pending the appeal would be deprived of his property.[51]

Months earlier Painter had expressed concern about the bond, hoping to avoid it. To do just that, Attorney General Garland had telegraphed Ward, suggesting he associate his father's name as defendant with the Indians. As the elder Ward was a government Indian agent, it would make the U.S. a party to the case and remove the need for a bond. To expedite matters, Painter made a hurried trip from Great Barrington to confer with Garland. Upon his return he wrote Welsh that he was glad he had gone, and that in the future the IRA would be on much better terms with the Justice Department. Later he informed Welsh that the judge in the case would not accept this idea "as sufficient guaranty that damages would be paid." At one point Welsh had opined that he could be risking his money, to which Painter responded: "[T]he risk is just as great as that the case may go against the Indians." Describing their current case as "just and good," Painter expressed hope that the bond would be given "and the rights of these Indians may be definitely settled."[52]

During the morning session of the third day at Lake Mohonk, Mrs. Osia Jane Joslyn Hiles, a well-to-do Milwaukee widow and member of the Wisconsin Indian Association, a WNIA affiliate,[53] continued the discussion on the Mission Indians. During her allotted ten minutes, she described her recent visit to some of their villages. Her address, which Painter later described as deeply moving, generated a conference resolution that the issue of legal protection for the Mission Indians be referred to a committee. When Hiles agreed to contribute five thousand dollars, thirteen others joined her, and the Committee for the Legal Defense of the Mission Indians was born. Conference members also declared that IRA work on behalf of these Indians "must be enlarged and broadened," delegating Painter to investigate and determine which cases should be pursued and to locate a competent attorney to take on the cases the committee decided to prosecute.[54] He chose Frank D. Lewis, of Pomona.[55]

To protect the rights of the Mission Indians and other tribes and repair the government's broken Indian policy, Painter harnessed the power of the emerging reform movement that had recently moved onto the national stage with the emergence of IRA and WNIA branch associations. Collectively, they could now package a message for wider distribution through pamphlets, newsletters, and newspaper articles. Painter was perfectly positioned to be a major leader in this effort, especially given his congenial relationship with Quinton of the WNIA and Davis of the Boston Indian Citizenship Committee, and his position within the IRA. He also had the perfect vehicle to promote his ideas—the Lake Mohonk Conference, with its audience of prominent religious leaders, newspaper editors, government officials, and reformers. On the second day of the 1886 conference, he read his paper "Our Indian Policy as Related to the Civilization of the Indian," comparing the government's antiquated Indian policy to that of a machine. He criticized each part of the machine and presented his solutions.[56] Painter had alerted Welsh about this address in late August, calling the topic "the unrelatedness of the Indian Bureau to the Indian problem." Believing the subject "demanded immediate attention," he had turned to General Armstrong for advice. A month later he informed Welsh: "I shall be surprised if we do not stir up things."[57]

Painter described the relationship between the government's Indian policy and the end reformers sought—the civilization of the Indians. "So long as we travel without having a point at which we are purposing to arrive," he informed them, "we are in danger of mistaking simple movement for progress." For the past 260 years the government's Indian policy, like Topsy, had grown with no purpose, "nailed and glued together, piece by piece, by divers workmen, acting without concert or plan." This antiquated policy was a machine that did not recognize "the fact that the material on which it grinds is more than dead matter"—it was human beings. This machine was comprised of treaties, the reservation system, the agency system, and all branches of the government. And "nowhere, from first to last, does the idea of the manhood of the Indian find place, and by none of these agencies of department is the end we seek for the Indian definitely recognized."[58]

The first part of the machine Painter addressed was the treaty process, designed to serve a present purpose or to settle a present difficulty. Rather than being agreements between equals, treaties were "simple arrangements between superior intelligence on the one hand and superior brute force on the other," broken as soon as their purpose was achieved and replaced by a more profitable agreement. "Nowhere can we find intentions wise or generous with reference to the welfare of the Indian." He then turned to reservations—a "wall which fence[d] out law, civil institutions, and social order, and admit[ed] only despotism, greed, and lawlessness." On an earlier occasion he had described the reservation system as one of "isolation and non-absorption," holding Indians "aloof from civilization," denying them "the opportunities of a citizen and a man."[59]

Under the current system, the Indians would never become "industrious, self-reliant, self-supporting," and law-abiding citizens, Painter declared. They were ruled by an agent who was often "an irresponsible despot," a "disburser of provisions and annuities" turning the Indians into "helpless and pauperized dependent[s]." Instead of being selected by a "commission of angels specially charged by the Almighty with the duty of extreme vigilance and care," the agent's position was often a reward "for the most disreputable and impecunious of partisan political workers." The continual change of political parties in Washington meant that between 80 and 90 percent of the agents were changed at election time. If a "good, wise, and strong man" was appointed by "happy accident," the machine displaced him as soon as he was useful.[60]

Painter was equally critical of the Indian Office, which was under the control of the interior secretary, who had a corps of special inspectors reporting directly to him, all independent of the Indian commissioner. Painter recalled the case of the Crow Creek Reservation, where the commissioner learned from either the newspaper or the IRA that the reservation had been opened for settlement at the same time as he was making plans to settle the Indians upon it. After listing all the employees of the Indian Office, Painter compared this bureaucracy's relation to the government "as the book-keeper is related to a business house." This bookkeeper was, however, "elaborate and expensive, and so confusing that the condition of things cannot be easily discovered." Estimating that six hundred thousand dollars was paid in salaries to white employees alone, Painter described the office's main job as satisfying the needs of those who wanted a job, while failing as an agency for Indian civilization. Policies were implemented by political hacks—"drunken livery-stable men sent to teach Indians to plant potatoes—a hatful to the hill—and so-called doctors who prescribe a spoonful of iodine to be taken internally for a sore throat."[61]

Congress did not escape his criticism, describing some members as ignorant and indifferent to the needs of reservation Indians, cutting appropriations and throwing them "back into hopeless and listless apathy," while others, members of various congressional Indian committees, spared no expense on their junkets and vacation jaunts to learn about Indian conditions and then more often than not misreported or misunderstood what they had witnessed. "No legislation can be secured for the Indian beyond the necessary appropriation bill," he noted. Even when correct information was incorporated into legislation, it was not passed. More than one hundred and fifty Indian-related bills were introduced in the Senate during last winter and more than two hundred in the House, but only three bills pushed by friends of the Indians actually passed the Senate before failing in the House. Even the BIC suffered. Initially well funded with the aim of reforming abuses and purifying the Indian service, of late those contractors who "could no longer enrich themselves at the expense of the Indian and of the Government" made their opposition felt in Congress, and for the past few years the board had only enough funding to pay for an office and a secretary.[62]

Painter did not spare the president, interior secretary, or Indian commissioner, although he provided only a few examples of their transgressions. He did point out that an unidentified president, through misinformation, had come to see the BIC as "simply ornamental and of no utility," appointing members from only one party. Painter described the entire machinery as complicated, with too many individuals running the show and with "diverse and antagonistic ends to subserve." Before outlining his solutions, he described egregious cases he had personally witnessed. At one agency he had discovered a first-class sawmill where there were no logs, while at this same agency, Indians hauled their wheat fifteen miles to the railroad, where it was shipped elsewhere to be ground. At another, a freight contractor had dragged an engine and boiler over two hundred miles of alkaline plains to an agency that had no possible use for it. Painter concluded that "anything is possible in connection with this service, excepting the one end we desire."[63]

He recommended breaking down reservation walls in order to let civilization in, and securing "inalienable possession of sufficient land, by personal title, for the use of each one." To protect these lands, he suggested placing them "under the administration of a wise commission" such as those charged with the "Peabody and like funds." Next he proposed to subject the Indians to the laws of the land, giving them legal protection, and finally, he urged immediate citizenship, with all its duties and privileges. When funds from the sale of excess reservation lands were exhausted, there should be nothing remaining "to separate the Indian from other citizens, except the bronze of his skin, and the memory of his great wrongs softened and made tender by the grace and sufficiency of our tardy atonement."[64] *Lend a Hand* described this address as "striking, original, and [a] valuable paper, presenting and describing the present Indian policy as it really is, a mass of inconsistencies, contradictions, and injustices."[65]

## Mission Villages

Returning home, Painter finished preparations for his next tour. Writing Welsh on October 20, 1886, he outlined the itinerary for his upcoming Southern California visit and thanked his employer for sending a check for five hundred dollars. Davis had already secured railroad passes for the California part of the journey; for the eastern part Painter had a pass on the Atlantic and

Pacific Railroad. Two days later he set out on his third investigative tour of Mission Indian villages, now burdened by additional responsibilities placed upon him by Mohonk's new legal defense committee. After spending three weeks in San Francisco, where he consulted with "reliable men nearer the seat of our war," he headed for Los Angeles and then on to San Diego, where he toured the unfinished buildings of Father Ubach's Saint Anthony's Indian Industrial School, where currently forty boys and girls were crowded into a single classroom. Even under the watchful eyes of the sisters of Saint Joseph of Carondelet, such conditions made it difficult to practice individual exercises.[66]

Required by Mohonk's new committee to identify cases for legal recourse, Painter had chosen the heart-wrenching story of Rogerio F. Rocha,[67] an elderly Indian who along with members of his household had been tossed off their San Fernando Valley land by sheriff's deputies during a pouring rain on November 12, 1885. According to his affidavit, Rocha (or Roch), a native of the mission of San Fernando, was seventy-six years old and a blacksmith by trade. His title to the land dated from an 1843 grant to the Indians by Mexican Governor Manuel Micheltorena. Unfortunately, this grant had not been patented under the U.S. federal government. Instead, three years later the land had been purchased by E. DeCeles, supposedly with the condition that the Indians not be disturbed. Upon his death, in the summer of 1874 his son, E. F. DeCeles, with permission from the Los Angeles County Probate Court, sold the land initially to George K. Porter and Charles Maclay, who assured DeCeles that the Indians would not be disturbed. DeCeles's attorney concurred. Then in 1885 R. M. Widney, Maclay's attorney, bought in. In the meantime, Rocha had been paying taxes on his clearly marked ten-acre plot, with a fine spring, two adobe houses, two wood sheds, chickens, a blacksmith forge, and assorted utensils.[68]

According to Rocha's affidavit, Maclay, accompanied by an interpreter, had informed him he had to leave, and on November 1 two deputies arrived with removal orders. Shortly thereafter, they returned with a cart and began loading all the Indians' belongings, dumping them on the roadside some two miles distant. Rocha described the sight of his wife and three elderly women walking behind the cart as "the saddest event of [his] life." They endured eight days without shelter, with rain spoiling their meager food and thieves stealing their few belongings. Then, while Rocha was in Los Angeles getting

Rogerio Rocha of San Fernando Mission. Photograph by Charles C. Pierce.
*C. C. Pierce Collection of Photographs (photCL Pierce 01716),*
*Huntington Library, San Marino, California.*

permission from the local priest to occupy an old shed connected with the mission church, his wife died of pneumonia. Painter had pointed out that Rocha was simply one of four to five hundred "self-supporting, civilized, Christian Indians" with titles to their homes as good as his—all in danger of being evicted. Their cases "must be remedied in the courts," he declared.[69]

Painter defined three levels of evil facing Mission Indians—those remedied only by a legal suit; those requiring congressional action, necessitating the arousal of public opinion; and those needing only an executive order to create a reservation. Since December 27, 1875, nineteen reservations had been set aside by executive order, some of them currently in danger. At the San Gorgonio Reservation, which adjoined the town of Banning on the Southern Pacific Railroad, forty white squatters had pre-empted all the water and the best land on the reservation. At Capitán Grande, some thirty miles from San Diego, white intruders had "made filings on the lands which had been occupied by the Indians, who were forced back to the mountains." In response to the federal government's order for settler removal, San Diego's leading men maintained that the settlers were respectable and law abiding. "It is always much easier and less troublesome every way to do an Indian substantial and irreparable wrong, than to inflict a seeming hardship upon a white man," Painter wrote in frustration. "No chapter in the sad and shameful history of our dealings with the Indians," he concluded, "is more disgraceful than that which tells the story of these Mission Indians."[70]

Several months after the Mohonk Conference, Painter informed Welsh that trespassers had been ordered from the Capitán Grande Reservation and that he was looking into the progress of two Indians from the San Jacinto Reserve (Soboba) who had asked to have certain sections restored to the public domain so they could file on them. Unfortunately, the Indian Office had restored different lands, and Painter learned that the Indians' request for the correct lands had been pigeonholed three weeks earlier. The clerk had promised Painter that he would "take steps at once in the matter." Now it was two weeks later, and Painter informed Welsh that following a visit to Atkins, the commissioner had agreed to personally tend to the matter.[71]

Writing from Los Angeles on November 11, 1886, Painter informed Welsh that the night before he had met with Horatio Rust and a man named Barrows[72] to organize an IRA branch, with Antonio Colonel as vice president and Rust as secretary. They were planning a public meeting the following week, and Painter would give the public address. "I have thought it of the utmost importance that the Agent who is making a good fight here for the Indians, and our attorney, Ward, [should] have the moral support of such an organization," he wrote. They should be aware that the IRA "has its eye upon them." He had gathered together a number of "strong and influential men," and "if it starts off as it now promises it is almost worth the trip." He praised Agent John Ward and his son, Attorney Shirley Ward, for scoring several victories and some partial ones. He reported that he was leaving for San Diego the next day and had arranged to meet the leaders of most of the Mission Indian villages for a conference.[73]

Two weeks later Painter was home, the plight of the Mission Indians seldom far from his thoughts. In late November, he informed Welsh that he had just written Davis, who was treasurer of Mohonk's Committee for the Legal Defense of the Mission Indians. Painter firmly believed that it was important that this committee pressure the House in favor of the annual Mission Indian bill. "I have a much clearer idea of the Mission Indian Question than before," he informed Welsh, adding that he felt "justified in giving this visit to them." A week later he wrote Welsh that he had sent Shirley Ward's brief and the transcript of *M. Byrne v. Antonio Alas, et al.* to Austin Abbott of New York, a member of the Mohonk legal defense committee and a prominent legal scholar, so "he might have data for an opinion as to the strength of our case." He urged Welsh to make sure that the association pushed the current Mission Indian bill, which still faced congressional opposition. On December 13 Painter appeared before the full House Committee on Indian Affairs to urge the bill's passage.[74]

During the second week of December, Painter traveled to Cambridge to attend an IRA branch meeting and to listen to Welsh's address there. Branch president Rev. Samuel Longfellow invited Painter, whom he described as "the picket guard of the Association," to give a short talk. The *Cambridge Chronicle* reported that his address "bristled all over with the most delicate needle points of sarcasm." Painter, stressing a "love for the Indian, and a withering contempt for the policy of the Government towards him," described several absurd attempts of the government to civilize the Indian, including the dumping of a portable sawmill hundreds of miles from "a stick of timber."[75]

A yearly pattern was emerging in Painter's Indian work: In January he attended the BIC meeting; and in October, the Lake Mohonk Conference. The latter became the sounding board not only for his personal philosophy of Indian reform but for his solutions. The publication of the Mohonk proceedings ensured that his ideas were widely spread. Although by now secure in his position, 1887 would prove to be a difficult year as he struggled with solving the problems of the seriously flawed General Allotment Act, otherwise known as the Dawes Act.

# CHAPTER 4

# THE DAWES ACT
# AND A RETURN TO THE
# INDIAN TERRITORY
# AND CALIFORNIA, 1887

The year began on a positive note for Painter. He telegraphed Welsh the first week of January that the "Indian appropriation bill passed, no attack on schools this time."[1] On the eighth of February, however, President Grover Cleveland's signature on the General Allotment Act set the stage for difficult times. Painter would struggle to fix the legislation and walk a tight line in support of James Bradley Thayer's bill, intended to provide the Indians with legal protection the Dawes legislation had failed to deliver. His summer investigative tour to California brought a bit of a respite and no small excitement: he discovered and reported an illegal flume crossing the Capítan Grande reservation and found five saloons in full blast, he then spent most of one day with General Nelson Miles, preparing to raid the saloon keepers "after my statement of the case to him." This raid, he concluded later, was "a most important move and will go a great way toward clearing the reservation of intruders."[2]

Painter began his official duty of the year by attending the sixteenth annual conference of the BIC. On January 6, 1887, Board President Clinton Fisk opened the meeting in an ebullient mood. "We have never convened when we have had such cause for gratitude as just now, when we could set our work upon such ground of joy and satisfaction as at the present condition of progress in the Indian matters," Fisk declared. His mood was due in part to the passage of the General Allotment Act by the House of Representatives—news that the conference initially hailed "with great pleasure.[3] This legislation, more commonly referred to as the Dawes Act, would become law the following month and prove to be one of the most destructive pieces of Indian legislation in the nation's history.[4]

### The General Allotment Act

The idea of dismantling communally held reservation lands and allotting them in severalty was not "a latter-day solution thought up to meet the crisis in Indian affairs in the 1880s," writes Francis Paul Prucha. It had deep roots. As early as 1633 the General Court of Massachusetts decreed that certain Indians should be given allotments. By the early 1800s treaties began to incorporate the concept, and as of March 3, 1875, nontribal Indians were given the opportunity to homestead public lands. Few applied, because to do so required that they relinquish their tribal affiliation. The emergence of the WNIA and the Boston Indian Citizenship Committee in 1879 provided a new impetus. That year Indian Commissioner Ezra A. Hayt drafted legislation for an allotment bill, which he had announced at the January BIC meeting. Its failure prompted similar bills, including one from Texas Senator Richard Coke, chair of the Senate Committee on Indian Affairs, introduced in May 1880, requiring the consent of two-thirds of all adult males. The Dawes version excluded this provision.[5]

Many reformers viewed private property ownership as essential to the civilizing process. The Dawes legislation authorized the survey of reservation land and its allotment by appointed allotting agents into parcels of land in quantities of 160 acres to heads of households, 80 acres to single individuals over eighteen, and 40 acres to orphans under eighteen, inalienable for twenty-five years. Citizenship was to be conferred upon allotment. Surplus lands would be opened to white settlement, divesting the Indians of millions of acres of land. Reformers who opposed tribalism cheered the legislation, which promised economic advancement via assimilation into mainstream rural American life. Merrill E. Gates, former president of Rutgers and Amherst colleges and president of the BIC, described it as "a mighty pulverizing engine for breaking up the tribal mass," while the IRA viewed it as a "vital and important step" and as a "definite and comprehensive" Indian policy. Quinton in her 1887 WNIA presidential address called it the "Indian Emancipation Act."[6]

One of the legislation's more outspoken critics was Colorado Senator Henry Teller, later secretary of the interior, who had described the act's predecessor, the Coke Bill, as "[a] bill to despoil the Indians of their land and to make them vagabonds on the face of the earth." Although Teller recognized that the legislation's supporters acted in good faith, he was aware of "the inherent objection in the Indian mind against land in severalty." During Senate debates in January 1881, he had explained that so long as the Indian "remains anything like an Indian in sentiment and feeling," he could not be made to take individual lands. It was part of the Indian's religion "not to divide his land." Teller also recognized that the Coke Bill would benefit land speculators, not Indians. He believed that decades later, when "Indians shall have parted with their title, they will curse the hand that was raised professedly in their defense to secure this kind of legislation." Instead of improving the situation, he viewed this legislation as turning "things right around." Indians had to be civilized, educated, and Christianized first to make them understand the value of private land ownership. And issuing land in severalty would not civilize them.[7]

The Dawes Act required corrective legislation from the beginning. The leasing of allotments to the young and the elderly was not included. Married women, easily turned out of their homes through divorce, were not protected. A more equitable method would have granted 160 acres to every Indian, man, woman, and child, but that would have meant less land opened to the non-Indian public. Since much of the land was better suited to grazing, livestock raising should have been encouraged instead of farming. And finally, it was naïve to think that Indians, especially those who did not come from an agricultural background, could succeed during the late 1880s and 1890s, when many of their white counterparts were failing—forced into foreclosures and tenant farming, turning to state Granges and the Populist Party for support.

Painter, who agreed with breaking up tribal lands, had originally lobbied on behalf of the legislation, calling attention to certain amendments the IRA "deemed inexpedient," advocating for others as he met with influential members of Congress and the president to secure its passage.[8] To explain this legislation to reformers and the public, in March the IRA published his pamphlet *The Dawes Land in Severalty Bill and Indian Emancipation*, in which he described the government as finally recognizing "the manhood of the Indian and [throwing] wide open a door closed against him, through which he is invited, and even urged, to enter whatever places he may choose to occupy as a citizens of this free Republic." Painter concluded that under the legislation eventually all reservations would be broken up and every Indian would become a citizen, resulting in the "utter overthrow" of the "whole miserable policy and cumbersome machinery under and by which we have hitherto pauperized and crushed these people." However, he also recognized the strong opposition to the bill among Indians, especially from the Five Civilized Tribes (Cherokee, Creek, Seminole, Chickasaw, and Choctaw), who viewed the bill as being in direct conflict with federal treaty obligations. Their position was supported by Thomas Bland and his National Indian Defense Association, which simply rejected any forced assimilation.[9]

On the positive side, Painter wrote about the one group who would benefit—those Indians living on executive order reservations (non-treaty reservations, numbering some 90 of a total of 159 reservations), who had no "valid title [other] than that of occupancy by sufferance of the President," who could merely "take all their vast territory from them by a stroke of his pen." Under severalty, these tribes would be given a permanent home secured by "a personal patent" and money to be "used as the tribe may determine" after the sale of excess land. Thus in this case, Painter argued, instead of viewing the legislation "as a bill to rob the Indians of their land," as some said, it should be seen as the "only practical measure" to save their lands. By its passage reformers had succeeded in securing "the conditions under which it is possible to develop the manhood they believe there is dormant in these people," concluded Painter.[10]

Painter also addressed the negative side, alerting fellow reformers to the dangers as well as the opportunities. They should not make the same mistake as had the leaders of the temperance movement, who after getting a law forbidding the sale of liquor passed in the 1850s, ceased further effort. Reformers now had "what they never had before, opportunity for hopeful work" on behalf of the Indians. They must not fail to meet their responsibilities. For one, it was essential that the president appoint honest and informed men to carry out this legislation and not mere politicians, interested in dispensing patronage for the "flocks of hungry vultures" circling "over this fat carcass, determined that its dry bones alone shall be thrown to the Indian."[11]

Senator Dawes, the bill's sponsor, shared some of the same concerns as Painter, and he had expressed them during the January 1886 BIC meeting. "I begin to fall back and ask myself seriously, whether, after all, too much risk is not being taken." If the bill were to become law "and is administered in bad faith, and by bad men, it first wipes out all of the heritage of the Indian," he explained, "and then it scatters him among our people without preparation for citizenship, and without the capability of maintaining himself, really in a worse condition than he can be in now." Using the analogy of seaworthiness, Dawes declared: "If every sailor on deck is not true, how can he keep his rudder true?"[12]

These concerns were valid. Honest men were not always appointed as allotting agents, and Painter soon became one of the legislation's severest critics. The IRA had early misgivings. Its fifth annual report described the legislation's passage as the "beginning of a transitional period" of indefinite duration, "certain to bring with it fresh problems and unforeseen complications, and demanding our increased study and effort." Education at this crucial time was even more important. It was also essential for every civilizing agency to be "brought to bear upon [the Indian] with increased earnestness and energy." Because the Dawes Act dealt primarily with land disposal, the IRA determined it was desirable to supplement its provisions with additional legislation "for the ultimate extension of law over the Indians." Therefore, they supported legislature proposed by Harvard law professor James Bradley Thayer, a prominent figure in the evolution of American constitutional jurisprudence. Unlike Teller, who opposed the Dawes Act outright, Thayer believed that it had not gone far enough to protect Indian rights.[13]

### The Thayer Bill

On February 13, 1887, five days after President Cleveland signed the Dawes Act, Professor Thayer addressed a meeting at the First Unitarian Church in Worcester, Massachusetts, sponsored by the Boston Indian Citizenship Committee and the Worcester Indian Association, a WNIA affiliate.[14] In his address, Thayer focused on reservation Indians, at the time numbering

James Bradley Thayer, Harvard law professor and Indian reformer, 1852.
Photograph by Pach Brothers photography studio, New York.
*Harvard University Archives, Harvard Library (W710969), Cambridge, Massachusetts.*

around 250,000. He condemned the government's policy toward these Indians and the "gigantic, complicated, costly, and in a great degree, needless body of laws and administration" that had grown up around them. He proposed a new bill to augment the Dawes Act by replacing the faulty system of Indian administration—"and with it the whole class of political Indian officials, commissioners, agents, traders, and the like"—with a system that would guarantee legal rights to the Indians through the establishment of courts.

Thayer's proposal would work in tandem with the Dawes Act: "The Indians should be made citizens just as soon as it can be done . . . as fast as their land is allotted to them in their own application."[15]

In a letter to Painter, Welsh described Thayer's proposal as "a new & radical plan for the solution of the Indian question," while the *Boston Daily Advertiser* described it as "the initial step" in "an agitation" originated by the Boston Committee with details perfected by Thayer. The intent was to "present a radical reform bill" to Congress the following winter and in the meantime to create "a public sentiment in its favor." The *New York Times* reported the proposed legislation as including the abolition of the Indian Office (an idea soon dropped) and the granting to Indians of "all civil rights, except the right to vote and the right to sell his land, the latter point being acceptably covered by the Dawes bill." The *Times* quoted Thayer as claiming that "his scheme will cost not more than one-fourth of what it now takes to run the expensive and cumbersome machinery of the Indian bureau."[16]

Welsh was skeptical. Enclosing a news account in his letter to Painter, he described Thayer's proposal as a "substitution of new machinery for old, with a multiplication of points of responsibility" and asked Painter's opinion. The following day Painter responded that he did not have enough information to address the question intelligently, reminding Welsh that during the 1886 Lake Mohonk Conference he had laid out his own solution, consisting of a commission to take charge of "all property rights of the Indians," similar to the one in charge of the Peabody Fund. The Indians would then become citizens under the jurisdiction of civil courts, "not under any special machinery set up for them," as Thayer proposed. "I prefer my own plan in so far as I understand this proposed at Worcester differs from it," he wrote, concluding that the Boston Indian Citizenship Committee had simply taken his plan and given it "a somewhat different shape."[17]

Although initially neither Painter nor Welsh were supportive of the Thayer/Boston Committee proposal, they realized that the Dawes legislation did not adequately protect Indian legal rights and that additional legislation was necessary. Therefore, the Thayer proposal was reworked, with Welsh and Thayer corresponding and consulting,[18] while Painter and the IRA Law Committee smoothed over other features. Additional consultation with Boston Committee members took place during the fall Lake Mohonk Conference.

In the end, the Executive Committee of the IRA reported that if the Thayer bill could successfully be introduced in Congress, it would "without question" become the "most important piece of legislation respecting the Indians before the country."[19]

Despite the changes, the intent of the original proposal was preserved. The Thayer bill provided for equal protection of the law for all Indians, on or off a reservation; a modification of the Dawes Act to allow leasing; extension of state or territorial laws over reservations; appointment of court commissioners or judicial officers with the authority to hear and decide civil and criminal cases; annual sessions of U.S. district courts to hear appeals; and a plan for education commissioners who would establish and maintain free common schools with compulsory attendance for all Indians not yet citizens. In addition, it provided for the appointment of clerks for the commissioners and magistrates for each reservation, at least one being an Indian. Indian agents were granted the powers and duties of a sheriff, and a new position was created, that of a U.S. circuit court–appointed officer, versed in the law, to serve, among other duties, as a district attorney in each agency. Like the Dawes Act, Thayer's bill excluded those tribes in the Indian Territory, any Seneca reservation in New York, and the eastern band of the Cherokee in North Carolina.[20]

It was agreed that Senator Dawes would present the bill before the Senate, which he did on March 29, 1888. Thayer later remarked that "it was always understood by us that Mr. Dawes did this by request, and that he did not then intend to express his own approval of the measure." Dawes, Thayer explained, had "much doubt as to the expediency, and even the constitutionality, of the bill," believing there was "no need of any legislation of this sort." In mid-April, Thayer confided to Welsh that all concerned with writing this new legislation had done their "best to make the scheme simple & inexpensive."[21] The bill was referred to a subcommittee of the Senate Committee on Indian Affairs. On April 24, Painter wrote Welsh that the committee would "hear the friends of the Thayer bill" on May 1. On that day he presented it for consideration.[22] Two hearings were held, during which Thayer, Painter, and other supporters defended the legislation. According to Thayer, Dawes, "whose name is never to be mentioned in any company of friends of the Indians without honor and respect, even when we must differ from him" was present, taking an active part in the discussion. The Harvard professor remarked that privately the Senate subcommittee admitted they did not share Dawes's negative opinion and "freely expressed the opinion that something must be done in the direction we wished."[23]

Dawes's opposition dealt the bill a fatal blow. He confided to his wife, Electra Allen Sanderson Dawes, his distaste of the reformers' "impractical schemes," especially that of "Thayer's aerial project."[24] In summarizing the fate of this bill, Painter succinctly stated that it had been "pronounced by the Senate Committee [as] too elaborate and costly." A substitute proposal by Alabama Senator John Tyler Morgan, although simple and inexpensive, was no improvement. Painter described Morgan's bill as "most disastrous as well as absurd," enlarging and legalizing "the despotic powers of the Indian Agent."[25] Fortunately, this bill never became law.

Complexity and cost may not have been the real reasons for the IRA's tepid support. In 1884 the IRA Law Committee had drafted a bill with the main object of extending the criminal law of either the state or territory over Indian reservations, thus providing the Indians with the right to sue, among other powers. Although Thayer's bill was more comprehensive, with educational provisions and modifications of the Dawes Act, it shared some similarities with this IRA bill. When their own legislation failed, Painter and Welsh may well have been reluctant to give extensive support to Thayer, a relative newcomer to the Indian reform movement.[26]

Dealing with the Dawes Act was trying for Painter. On February 15, 1887, he wrote Welsh of an unsettling episode in the Indian Commissioner's office. He had walked in as Lone Wolf, a Kiowa chief, was informing Commissioner Atkins that he "feared he could not restrain his young men from going to war if he undertook to carry out the provisions of the Severalty bill [Dawes Act]."[27] Lone Wolf was not alone that day. There were other Kiowas, including Joshua Given (later a WNIA missionary),[28] who was serving as interpreter, and several Comanches, Seminoles, and Creeks. These Indians had been stirred up by Thomas Bland and some Creeks and Cherokees who strongly opposed the allotment legislation. According to historian Joseph Genetin-Pilawa, Bland, who rejected assimilation, was focused "upon using the federal government to provide resources and opportunities for Indigenous nations while simultaneously protecting the integrity of communally held land."[29]

Although Painter definitely agreed with Bland about using resources and opportunities for the Indians, he totally disagreed with him on the value of communally held property. In his letters, Painter's distain for Bland was evident.

To diffuse the situation, Painter handed Given his card, inviting him to escort the Indians to a meeting that evening. There he explained to his visitors that "no more could be done under this bill than could be done before under the treaty of 1868." Painter tried to convince them that this new severalty legislation "had not been urged & passed by those who were robbing of Indians, but by their best friends" and assured them that the president "did not intend to use the power this bill gave except as he saw it would help them and not hurt them." Given found it difficult to "believe that any white men would act simply for their good." During the interview Painter learned that Bland had indeed met with the Indians, promising that the National Indian Defense Association would have this new law set aside. They had already retained as counsel Judge A. J. Willard, former chief justice of the South Carolina Supreme Court. Painter explained to the Indians that since the Dawes legislation had been passed by Congress, Bland and his association could not change it.[30]

A month later Painter informed Welsh that he had learned a bit more about "the secret history of the Thayer affair which is confidential for the present and not fully unfolded to me." His confidant was Joshua Davis. Apparently in one of the Boston Indian Citizenship Committee meetings there had been talk of a "measure *supplementary* to the Dawes bill," but the matter had been postponed. "They were startled and greatly shocked to hear the report of the meeting at Worcester in sensational head lines." Davis had concluded that this address was the result of "some one more jealous than wise, in representative of the other, and in default of their knowledge." Painter did not believe anything serious would come of this. "The gravest thing was the seeming want of good faith on the part of the Boston men," he concluded. To clear matters up, Senator Dawes planned to meet with them.[31]

Late in February a perplexed Painter wrote Welsh, who had requested a comprehensive report of his accomplishments to date. From memory, Painter listed activities but provided no dates, so it is impossible to know if the list reflected a week's work or a month's. What it does clearly reveal is the crucial role Painter was playing. He had appeared before the House Committee on Indian Affairs and urged the passage of various bills, including the Dawes legislation and the Mission Indian bill. The latter, he noted, had "been blocked by objection." He then appeared before Commissioner Atkins, Interior Secretary Lucius Lamar, and President Cleveland on behalf of Mission Indian complaints of squatters on their reservations. Those cases that had "gone through the land office," he noted, "were ordered off." The action on others was delayed until the fate of the Mission Indian bill was known. If the legislation failed, "these reservations shall be cleared off at once." After numerous visits to clerks and Indian Office officials, Painter had succeeded in securing land for two Indians on the Soboba Reservation and successfully added pasture lands to the Cahuilla Reservation. Using the power of the press, he had been able to force the Interior Department to give the Hoopa Valley Indian agent the monthly use of a clerk; had interceded on behalf of the absentee Shawnees;[32] and had interviewed the president numerous times on such issues, including Civil Service rules. He had counteracted the effects of Bland and his association. He had prepared a circular and revised another report for the Mohonk Conference. He concluded that his diary showed almost daily notes, such as "Called to Sec. [secretary], Con. [Congress], or Committee, or some one about some matter which it would seem foolish gravely to report, but the doing of which makes up largely the routine of my daily life here."[33]

In mid-April Painter attended a public meeting of the Jamaica Plain branch of the Massachusetts Indian Association, a WNIA affiliate. Although not the keynote speaker, he was called upon to give a short address on granting Indians all rights guaranteed to American citizens. In discussing the decision against Indian citizenship in *Elk v. Wilkins*, Painter concluded that the case was decided against Elk solely because he was an Indian. He then reviewed provisions of the Dawes Act, explaining that although the act was "a positive necessity," land divisions must be "fair and impartial." He concluded that the "friends of this persecuted race must stand firm for the next two or three years; they must be ready to put their hands in their pockets and help support those who would see that the Indian was respected and that the government did its duty."[34]

When Congress adjourned for the summer, Painter prepared for his tour to the Indian Territory and Southern California, jointly requested by the IRA

Executive Committee and the Mohonk Conference's Legal Defense Committee, chaired by Davis. Although the trip was mostly funded by the IRA, some support for the California leg was provided by the Mohonk Conference and the Boston Indian Citizenship Committee, of which Davis was a member. Therefore Painter addressed most of his lengthy letter-reports to Davis, who copied and forwarded them to Welsh.[35]

## The Indian Territory

Painter left Great Barrington on May 2, 1887, with letters of introduction to military posts and Indian agents en route from the acting secretary of war and Secretary Lamar. He traveled first to Washington and met with President Cleveland, who specifically called his attention to the "tremendous pressure to have a territory created out of 'No Man's Land' the 'outlet' and the territory embraced in Oklahoma." He then visited Lamar, who, although sick in bed at home, invited him to his room, where the two men conferred for two hours. Painter was convinced that Lamar understood his position on Indian reform, explaining to Welsh that the secretary had "fully read and inwardly digested" his earlier Mohonk Conference paper equating the government's Indian policy to a machine, accepting the analogy with "much intensity of feeling."[36]

Both Cleveland and Lamar had ordered Painter to investigate the advisability of moving certain tribes living on executive order reservations in the western part of the Indian Territory, such as the Wichitas, Cheyennes, Arapahos, Comanches, and Kiowas, to the eastern section, opening up their lands to white settlement—a scheme urged by congressmen from Iowa and Illinois. The Wichita treaty had never been ratified, and the rest of the reservations had not been set aside through the treaty process, so little stood in the way of their removal. Painter strongly disapproved, describing it in his IRA annual report and a separate pamphlet, *The Proposed Removal of Indians to Oklahoma*, as "an outrage" that would be "a disastrous step backward."[37]

Following orders, Painter spent two days traveling across the eastern Oklahoma countryside designated as a potential new home for the Wichitas and other tribes, finding it no better than much of their current home. "They [should] not be forced or persuaded, nor enticed to move," he reiterated. Traversing the Wichita, Caddo, and Delaware lands on his return from Anadarko to Darlington, Painter again had an opportunity to scan the landscape. He wrote Welsh that removing the Indians would be to commit "as great an outrage as if they [should] remove the farmers from my town from their homes by violence. A greater more infernal outrage could scarcely be committed." It would be better for President Cleveland "to violate treaty obligations touching *empty territory*," concluded Painter "than to violate all principles of right and justice as touching living men in order that he may silence a clamor for land."[38]

In addition to investigating the potential removal of these tribes, Cleveland and Lamar had requested a report on government schools. The best in the Indian Territory were the Cheyenne school at Caddo Springs, the Mennonite Mission School at Darlington, and the school among the Otoes, where Painter described the teacher, a Miss Emma De Night, as putting "her whole soul into her work." The rest were pretty much "worthless." The condition of school buildings varied from "close, nasty, and unbearable" dormitories that smelled of urine to buildings that were merely "a miserable thin brick shell, which threatens perpetual collapse." He found a similarly unfortunate range among the employees, from a superintendent who was "utterly incompetent" to a teacher who "looked as if he had gotten out of his grave to find a 'chaw of terbacher' and had lost his way & could not find his resting place." Painter fled from one school as soon as he recovered use of his legs, describing the experience as "a hideous night-mare." On the positive side, he thoroughly enjoyed participating in the site selection for a new Comanche School at Fort Sill. He found better facilities in Southern California, visiting a school that Agent Ward had recently built at the small reservation of Mesa Grande, where a young schoolteacher from Mississippi, Miss Carrie E. Hord, was not only doing a good job but also spending time teaching the Indians how to care for their sick. The best schoolhouse in all of the Mission Indian villages was at the small village of Soboba, with its mixed Serrano, Cahuilla, and Luiseño residents.[39]

In a May 23 letter, Painter wrote he had reached Arkansas City, Kansas, in time to sit in on a Senate committee meeting investigating fraudulent activities relevant to reservation trading posts. In his longer published report, he criticized the entire system of trade, "which is of itself an abuse," doubting "that anything would come of this investigation." From there he visited the

Cemetery of a Soboba Indian Village.
*Courtesy of the A. K. Smiley Public Library, Redlands, California.*

nearby Chilocco Indian School,[40] beautifully located on elevated land not far from Arkansas City. He described the school superintendent, a relative of Interior Secretary Lamar's first wife, as an infidel from Tennessee with no business abilities. He found "everything nasty and unsatisfactory." From Chilocco, Painter headed to the Ponca, Pawnee, Otoe and Oakland (old Nez Perce Reservation) Agency, under the care of Major E. C. Osborne of Tennessee, who had just killed a farmer at his Otoe subagency. Apparently the farmer, a Mr. Smith, had been armed and was threatening the agency clerk, the blacksmith, and Osborne. "It was doubtless a case of self defence [*sic*]," Painter exclaimed, "but [it is] a bad state of things when Agent, Clerk, farmer, &c are carrying deadly weapons and are ready to use them at the slightest offense." In a June 7 letter, Painter remarked that after Osborne dropped the farmer's body off at the undertaker to have it shipped to Tennessee, "he went in for a high old time." Because Arkansas City was a temperance town, Painter had no idea where people got their whiskey. All participants in the Osborne situation belonged to a "class which ought to have no representatives in the work of Indian civilization," he concluded, cautioning Welsh not to make public any of his remarks. In general he found agency employees from Tennessee and Mississippi a "poor lot, and if you do not think them a nasty lot why then just come down and try it for a week or so."[41]

Painter held a conference with Indians at the Ponca Agency, listening to a "long list of grievances" before riding all over the cultivated areas of the reservation, finding it "to be a magnificent body of land." He learned from the more progressive tribal members that government employees took no interest in their welfare. Months later, in an October 31 letter to Welsh, who had specifically inquired about the "character of the appointments in the Indian service," Painter described the superintendent at the Ponca school as "an infidel of the blatant kind." Neither he nor his wife, a teacher, were qualified. The school itself was "very poor indeed." From the Ponca Agency he headed to the Pawnee Agency, where he also found a bad state of affairs. The clerk was doing little work, the farmer was ignorant about farming, the school superintendent was "wholly unfit for his position," and "everything about the school premises . . . [was] in a fearful condition." Impassable streams made a visit to the Sac and Fox, Shawnees, and Pottawatomies impossible; instead he boarded a train for Fort Reno to visit the Cheyenne and Arapaho Reservation near Darlington and the Kiowa, Comanche, and Wichita Agency at Anadarko. He wrote Welsh of a disturbing situation among the Kiowas, placing partial blame on Bland and his association. During his conference in Washington, D.C., with Bland, Kiowa Chief Lone Wolf had become emboldened, believing he was more important than the Kiowa Indian Agent, Capt. Jesse Lee Hall. Furthermore, after returning from the conference, Lone Wolf now claimed he had a letter from Commissioner Atkins, requiring the agent to do all of the Kiowa business through him. Then, several weeks previously, a Kiowa medicine man became involved, calling for the killing of all white men, the breaking up of schools, and the restoration of the old ways, and inviting the neighboring Cheyennes and Arapahos to join them in their uprising. When the Indians converged around the schoolhouse, located a mile west of the agency, threatening to burn it to the ground, the superintendent and his wife fled. Painter explained that the enraged Indians left only after Agent Hall ordered soldiers to protect the schoolhouse.[42]

Painter was impressed with Fort Sill, located some forty miles from the Anadarko Agency, describing it as beautifully built, mostly of blue limestone. While there on a Sunday morning, he officiated at a marriage ceremony, visited the Sunday School at the Wichita School, attended a Sunday School for white children at the agency in the afternoon, baptized a small child, and delivered a sermon at the close of the school day. That evening he preached before some thirty-five or forty whites, learning firsthand the needs of a missionary among both the white and Indian residents. Putting aside his clerical duties, Painter continued on to the Wichita Indians. While describing their fences as the best he had seen and their corn as "splendid," in his October 31 letter he portrayed their school superintendent as "a miserable, brutal, drunken, profane witch." Painter described Captain Hall, the Kiowa, Comanche, and Wichita agent and a former Texas Ranger, as "a swearing, drinking man," but he had been impressed with him. However, because the man was independent and displeased with the lazy, ineffectual employees sent him by the Interior Department, Painter was convinced that Hall would not last long; the "system of terrorism operated by the Department," which sought to "enforce absolute approval of all its men and methods as to the price to be paid for continuance in office," would soon cause either his dismissal or his voluntary departure. Dissent was "treated as proof of insubordination and unfitness for the service." Finding incompetency almost everywhere, Painter believed that the quality of agency personnel had deteriorated and work had regressed.[43]

The one exception was John H. Seger, whom Painter described as the most successful man he had ever met in the Indian Service. In the early 1870s, Seger had moved onto the Cheyenne and Arapaho Reservation to build houses and agency school buildings for the government, but he was soon put in charge of the Arapaho Mission School. With allotment about to commence, Seger and his family were ordered to vacate the reservation in the fall of 1885. The agent, however, relented, asking Seger instead to establish Indian families in an agricultural colony on the Washita River. In the colony's first year, 1886, some sixty Indians moved there, each to their own farm. Guided by an interpreter and traveling "in four-mule grandeur" courtesy of the commandant at Fort Reno, Painter described his first visit to the Seger Colony as "the most interesting and instructive part" of his whole journey, finding some three hundred in residence, all actively farming and raising cattle.[44]

### Mission Villages

Arriving in California on June 10, Painter's first task was to learn to what extent President Cleveland's orders to remove intruders from several Mission

Indian reservations had been enforced—orders issued after Painter's visit to the president following his previous California trip. Painter was also to inspect existing reservations to determine their capacity to support resident Indians, explain the provisions of the recently enacted Dawes legislation, locate unoccupied public lands for potential Indian homesteads, determine the legal worthiness of defending Indian title to old land grants from which they had recently been ejected, and learn in general what "intelligent" actions could be taken by local reformers to defend Indian rights.[45]

Accompanied by Agent John Ward, Painter set out for the Morongo reservation east of Banning, finding some dozen families in residence as well as thirty to forty white trespassers.[46] Ward pointed out that shortly after the Indians had plowed the fields for their crops, white interlopers had run "their furrows clear around and enclosed the patches the Indians were breaking up, and then drove the Indians off and would not suffer them to plant." Ward's solution "as a cure-all for the difficulties of the situation" was to gather all the Mission Indians onto two reservations, force them to farm, and send their children to school. Painter, on the other hand, believed that with the removal of these trespassers, this reservation could easily accommodate an additional eighty families. Ward had planned to accompany Painter on his entire tour, but he resigned, effective immediately, before Painter could take another step.[47]

In his report, Painter expanded on the agent's resignation. Intending "to go out in a blaze of glory, in the estimation of the people of California among whom he lives," Ward had sent to the *Los Angeles Herald* a copy of his final report, in which he had belittled the Indians, "showing how easily the whole problem would be solved if his practical common sense could only be utilized." Especially decrying the Dawes legislation, Ward had described it as the promised keynote "in the grand chorus of emancipation from the thralldom of the white man."[48] Painter obviously was not impressed with the agent.

Although initially traveling solo, at one point Painter was accompanied by John T. Wallace, a special justice department inspector charged with investigating reports of illegal liquor sales. As a result, Painter not only "materially lessened" his expenses but took the opportunity to explain the IRA's work to his traveling companion. Painter informed Welsh that Wallace became so interested that he "strongly urged its supreme importance upon the Bureau through his reports to the Department of Justice, asserting that our methods are the only common-sense methods which have been applied to the Indian problem, & recommending that the work of allotting and settlement be turned over to us."[49]

Together they visited Cahuilla in southern Riverside County, finding the 340 residents growing crops of barley and corn and raising cattle. Painter determined their 17,420-acre reservation to be large enough to grant in severalty nearly 51 acres to each man, woman, and child, or 250 acres to a family of five. Unfortunately, the land was better suited to grazing. Always interested in educational facilities, Painter visited the Cahuilla school, where he met with Mrs. N. J. Ticknor, who had been there since the school started. She and her young daughter lived at the rear end of the schoolhouse, which he described at length, relating her reminiscences of one winter when the snow sifted in, covering the tops of the desks.[50]

Twenty-four of Ticknor's forty students were attending school the day of Painter's visit. He noted that several were adult men. Painter also visited a Cahuilla woman he identified as the *Ramona* of Jackson's novel. She was in fact Ramona Lubo, widow of Juan Diego, whose murder Jackson had skillfully woven into her novel to explain the death of the fictional Ramona's husband, Alessandro.[51] Writing to Davis, Painter related some details of the actual murder, complaining that "Ramona impresses you more favorably as to beauty and intelligence as described in the book, than as seen by her hut. She is full-blooded and homely." Jackson's portrayal of Ramona had been so vivid that many, including Painter and Quinton, believed that she really existed.[52]

From Cahuilla, Painter and Wallace headed for Warner Ranch, owned by former governor John Gately Downey, who had not yet ordered the eviction of its Indian residents. At the Cupeño village of Agua Caliente (Warner Hot Springs), one of five on the ranch, Painter and Wallace found some 175 Indians residents and a hot springs that provided almost boiling hot water, "afford[ing] relief to all but the most stubborn cases of Rheumatism." Dusty from the long ride, Painter took advantage of a dip before meeting with the men of the village to explain the provisions of the Dawes legislation, inform them that the IRA was defending Soboba's land claim, and warn them that their Warner Ranch lands were also in jeopardy. Learning that at best they had only occupancy and use rights, the Indians declared that "this had always

Ramona Lubo, widow of Juan Diego, ca. 1906, viewed by many
as the Ramona of Helen Hunt Jackson's novel.
*Ramona Bowl, Hemet, California.*

been their home, and they wanted to stay there." Next, Wallace lectured them
on the liquor traffic, encouraging them to provide proof against liquor sellers.
It being too late in the day to travel on, the two men and their driver spent
an uncomfortable night in the schoolhouse. Arriving at Santa Ysabel the
following day, they found the school closed because the teacher had measles.
They continued on the six miles up to Mesa Grande—a small reservation of
some 120 acres of mostly good and well-watered land. A broken horseshoe
prevented their journey to San Felipe, with its sixty residents. This village was
on a confirmed grant that had been issued a patent by the U.S. government,
although the grant had recently been sold "with the understanding that the
title is to be cleared of the Indians' right of occupancy," Painter later wrote.
Unable to visit San Felipe, they set out for La Jolla, Rincon, Pauma, and Pala.

These villages were threatened by the Oceanside Land & Water Company, which was buying up land and claiming water rights.[53]

On June 28 at Pala, some one hundred Indians from principal villages in San Bernardino and San Diego Counties (Riverside County had not yet been formed) gathered at the request of Antonio Coronel to listen to Painter discuss the Dawes Act. Reporters and photographers from Los Angeles and San Francisco also attended, reporting and taking candid photographs. According to the *Los Angeles Times*, one pose in front of the Old Pala campanile "particularly pleased the Indians." With Coronel interpreting, Painter discussed the Dawes provisions, explaining what the IRA and other reformers were doing on their behalf, making no promises and holding "out no misleading hopes," he wrote Davis. Wallace then addressed the group, requesting help to remove whiskey sellers. Coronel, described by Painter as a staunch friend of the Indians, then addressed them in a "most fatherly way." Although the day was "very laborious," Painter nevertheless found it "valuable in every way."[54]

Painter and Wallace continued on to Rincon by way of La Peche on the La Jolla Reservation, where they toured a school. In a letter to Davis, Painter described the teacher at La Peche, a woman from Georgia, as not very good. Her schoolhouse fared even worse. Although newly reconstructed by Agent Ward, "It would be as easy almost to warm the country about it as the inside of it." Their detour to visit Le Peche brought them into Rincon late in the afternoon, and school was out. Although unable to observe the teacher, Hattie E. Alexander, in action, Painter described her as "a pleasant, sensible sort of woman." To his dismay, Painter learned from Agent Ward that the federal government was closing all Mission Indians schools with an enrollment under twenty, with the exception of Father Antonio Ubach's boarding school in San Diego. This left only the schools at Soboba, Cahuilla, Rincon, and La Peche (La Jolla). Painter later wrote that "it would be an outrage to enforce the order, and doom to perpetual ignorance the children of those who have suffered so many wrongs at our hands." He described this order to Davis as "simply infernal and worthy of the contemptible scrubs who are running the Bureau." He learned that the low enrollment at these schools had been the result of an unexpected measles outbreak.[55]

Now alone, Painter toured Capitán Grande Reservation, which President Cleveland had ordered cleared of white intruders. Although Agent Ward had

Indian Council at Mission San Antonio Pala, 1887. Antonio Coronel, in the front row
just to the right of center, has a white beard and holds his hat in his left hand.
To Coronel's left is Horatio N. Rust, bearded and turned to the side, holding a hat
in his right hand. Between them is Painter, who appears to be holding a cane;
he had several serious bouts of illness around this time.
*Horatio N. Rust Photograph Collection (photCL 11 [48]), Huntington Library,*
*San Marino, California.*

claimed he had complied, Painter discovered five fully operating saloons. In a
late July letter, he informed Davis that the previous spring Ward had actually
ridden by two of them, and although he had taken down all the necessary
information from the saloon keepers, he had left them undisturbed, informing no one of their presence. By mere chance, Painter encountered Wallace,
informed him of his findings, enabling Wallace to organize and lead a raid.
On July 12, Painter wrote that he had spent most of that day conferring with
General Nelson Miles, whose troops were stationed nearby in San Diego
and would participate in the raid. In his July 17 letter, Painter wrote that
Agent Ward and the U.S. Marshall had already set out for Capitán Grande,
the raid to be carried out early the following morning. According to the *Los
Angeles Herald*, Wallace claimed to have "found some of the vilest dens in

Close-up of participants at the Pala Council, with Painter on the left holding
a straw hat and Horatio N. Rust on the right.
*Horatio N. Rust Photograph Collection (photPF 20851), Huntington Library,*
*San Marino, California.*

full blast, liquor being sold openly in tents and shanties." Seven men were
arrested, their wares destroyed, and they were imprisoned in Los Angeles.
Painter complained that naturally the departments of the interior, justice,
and war would receive praise for this raid. "Well, we must let them have
it, and not offend them by saying anything publicly to the contrary," he
concluded. However, "it was a commentary on the way officials discharge
their duties that this raid had to be instigated by the agent of the I.R.A.,"
he concluded.[56]

Painter had also discovered a San Diego water company building a flume
across the Capitán Grande Reservation, another intrusion Ward had failed to
report.[57] When he returned home, Painter alerted the Interior Department to
this situation. He later learned that the new Mission Indian agent, Joseph W.
Preston, not only made an agreement on January 16, 1888, with the San Diego
Flume Company to furnish water to the Indians but succeeded in getting

a payment of one hundred dollars per mile for the right of way across the reservation—a monetary arrangement that Painter described as "more than justice to the Indians."[58]

Painter's final stop was Soboba in the San Jacinto Valley. He informed Davis that the Indians there were living on fine lands with a good schoolhouse built by Capt. William P. Fowler and his wife Mary Sheriff Fowler. Mrs. Fowler had been the school teacher until she married, whereupon Ward removed her, supposedly because of a policy that only single women could be employed. Painter, however, had seen a letter from Commission Atkins to Ward, a copy of which was sent to Mary Fowler, denying such a policy existed. In fact, Atkins believed it was "very desirable that women in such isolated places shall have husbands." Although he did not meet the former teacher, Painter learned that she "had the confidence of the Indians to an unusual, I may say unlimited extent."[59]

Months later, as Painter was finalizing his report, he learned that the village of Soboba had been saved. On January 31, 1888, the California Supreme Court in *M. Byrne v. Antonio Alas, et al.* had ruled in favor of the Indians, arguing that Mexican land grants included the Indians' right of occupancy. A congratulatory article in the *Springfield (Massachusetts) Republican* described the outcome as "a measure of justice done," praising the IRA, Painter, and Helen Hunt Jackson for befriending the Mission Indians. The IRA had two thousand copies of the article reprinted and published as an undated document, entitled "The Saboba Case," which praised Painter's persistence in achieving the victory, entitling him "to feel that he has in part at least redeemed his promise to Mrs. Jackson made but a few days before her death."[60]

Painter's Southern California tour had not been limited to visiting Mission villages. He had also conferred with local non-Indian officials, including a land office registrar and the new superintendent of Christian Mission schools in San Diego. He described the superintendent, a Professor James, "as a nice old gentleman who has vague ideas of his mission, and large expectations as to what he can do." When time permitted, Painter also delivered four public addresses—one on the evening of Sunday, July 17, before a large audience in the Congregational Church in Los Angeles, where according to the *Los Angeles Times*, he gave "illustrations" of the Indians' treatment and solicited on their behalf "the sympathy due to [these] outraged people." He also spoke in Riverside, Santa Barbara, and Pasadena, describing the latter as "one of the best Indian meetings" he had ever attended.[61]

On July 19 Painter informed Welsh that he was tired of the heat, ready to "turn feet and face toward the east." His plans to leave that next morning for Santa Barbara and then on to San Francisco and home were interrupted by a telegram from Davis. In an appeal for public funds to aid the Mission Indians, Davis had sent out circulars, the text of which had angered Judge R. M. Widney and Charles Maclay, purchasers of the San Fernando grant from E. F. DeCeles. Describing these circulars as "grossly and maliciously false," the two men claimed they misrepresented their actions. Because Painter had written the original text, Davis was now requesting that he "investigate the facts anew." Painter immediately responded that he had no idea what had stirred Widney up. The circulars may have struck the match, but Painter himself had added fuel by discussing the San Fernando case during his public addresses. Although Painter made no mention of their names, both men lived in Los Angeles and the audiences remembered the event, describing the men as "notorious."[62]

To strengthen the IRA's position on the San Fernando case, Painter had requested four affidavits from Antonio Coronel to include in his report. The most damning was Rogerio Rocha's affidavit, which thoroughly contradicted Widney and Maclay. Rocha clearly stated that at the suggestion of the original owner, in 1871 he had his property surveyed and paid all taxes due, only to be told in 1885 by Maclay that the land was no longer his. At that point his belongings and those of the women had been thrown out on the public road.[63] These affidavits, Painter explained, had put the two men "in a very bad plight for men whose good names are dear to them."[64]

Home by August, Painter began work on his hundred-page report and a separate five-page pamphlet on the proposed relocation of the Wichitas, Cheyennes, Arapahos, Comanches, and Kiowas. Although believing that all reservations should be done away with and white settlers allowed to homestead remaining lands, he found this third attempt by Commissioner Atkins to resettle certain tribes to be "the most objectionable, as it involve[d] a removal of Indians who had taken root in their present homes." Painter had twice travelled through the entire length and breadth of the Oklahoma District and found this land no better than their current home. Although he never supported moving Indians merely to satisfy white desire for land, in this case

because of the absence of formal treaties, a removal was possible. The Cheyenne and Arapaho Reservation had been established by an executive order,
while that of the Wichita had been set aside by an unratified treaty, although
the Indians claimed they had always owned the land, building their homes
and opening up their farms there. Painter warned that numerous Indian
wars had grown out of such misguided removal attempts, and that in the
absence of reservations, the Indian must have secured to "him enough land
to furnish him a foundation for and the means of achieving his civilization."[65]

### Lake Mohonk

By late September, Painter and Martha were among the almost one hundred
participants of the fifth annual Mohonk Conference, opening on September 28, 1887. Attendees represented various educational institutions, missionary societies, and Bible societies, as well as the American Missionary
Association and the three major Indian reform associations: the IRA, the
WNIA, and the Boston Indian Citizenship Committee. Fully one-third
of the male participants had brought their wives. The beautiful location
and numerous activities Smiley provided made this three-day conference a
mini-vacation. On October 2 Painter wrote Welsh, who was unable to attend
because his wife, Fanny Frazer Welsh, was ill, that this meeting was *the* most
important and interesting conference of the whole series." He was pleased
that his paper, the first one of the conference, had been published in the *Hartford Courant*, with an editorial notice. He hoped that Welsh approved of the
resolutions adopted. The Mohonk proceedings would be published as soon
as he and General Eliphalet Whittlesey had finished the editing process.[66]

Painter's assessment was accurate. This conference would be different, for
the previous February the Dawes Severalty Act had become law. Clinton Fisk,
unanimously chosen as conference chair, opened the morning session of the
first day by describing the passage of this legislation as the "beginning of a new
epoch in Indian Affairs." There was still much that remained to be done, and
therefore the executive committee had proposed a series of questions for free
discussion, beginning with "What changes in Indian governmental administration are required by the abolition of the Indian reservation system."[67]

In his address on the proposed question, Painter explained that the passage
of the Dawes legislation was "not the end" that reformers had been seeking,

only "a needed means to its attainment." There was much work to be done. "We can not hold ourselves innocent of disasters which may come to these people through these enlarged opportunities," he declared, "unless we do all we can to improve them." The Indian was "about to be thrown into the seething activities of our complex civilization and take his chances in free competition with other races." He was stepping "out of his undifferentiated, impersonal tribal relation into one of individualized, responsible citizenship," requiring the immediate adoption of a change of policy. To Painter, the key was education. New schools must be built and others enlarged to educate the two-thirds of the Indian population who were not in school. And more governmental control was essential.[68]

President Cleveland had proposed an advisory commission of army officers and citizens to oversee Indian education. Painter suggested that if created, such a commission should have absolute control over all Indian school matters, as well as the responsibility of implementing the Dawes legislation, ushering the Indians through this "transition period, as they pass out from the bondage of the bureau into the liberty of men and citizens." Dawes strongly disagreed, arguing that the president currently had the same powers that Painter wanted to transfer to this proposed commission. Painter responded that the old machinery of the Indian Office was incapable of handling the allotment process because of the considerable amount of property involved. "I think it is a much simpler thing to blow up the old machinery," he argued, "than try to readjust it." Let the commission have the "discretion to use this property for the Indian and apply it to his benefit," he concluded. Although no action was taken on Painter's suggestion during the conference, a lively discussion followed on all aspects of Indian education. The *New York Times* described Painter's paper as "one of the most important" of the conference. The reporter noted that although former Commissioner Hiram Price and Dr. Lyman Abbott, a Congregational theologian and member of the Lake Mohonk Conference, had approved of the commission idea, he doubted that Congress would agree. The *Times* complained that "not one in four understands the Indian question or cares for it. There is less business sense in the management of the Indian bureau than in the management of any other department in the world."[69]

The evening session on the second day was devoted to a discussion of the Dawes Act. Prucha describes Dawes's remarks as revealing a "defensive attitude toward the law that bore his name, but also a realistic appreciation that the legislation by itself did not solve all the problems."[70] Initially Dawes was reluctant to speak. "I hardly see the need of my occupying any portion of the time of this conference upon the matter under discussion to-night," he explained. The provisions had been "so fully comprehended and expounded" that he had no expectation of making them clearer. Aware that Thayer and members of the Boston Indian Citizenship Committee and the Boston branch of the IRA wanted to discard the "cumbersome and effete Bureau of Indian Affairs," the senator remarked that this would not happen "until the Indian as an Indian passes away." He explained that although his law had "only enacted an opportunity and nothing more," it had markedly changed the condition of the Indians and presented reformers with new obligations. "If you fold your hands and say, I did my duty when I set him on this course, you fail, you do not comprehend your duty," he explained, encouraging his fellow reformers to assume their responsibility for implementing his legislation.[71]

Early complaints that the process would move too slowly proved incorrect. Dawes assured attendees that President Cleveland had initially intended to apply the legislation one reservation at a time. However, already half a dozen had come under its provisions, prompting Dawes to recognize that the "greed of the land-grabber" would press the "application of this bill to the utmost."[72] He was pleasantly surprised to learn of the success of the Crow Indians. During his last visit four years earlier, he had found them "wretched, degraded, uninviting, and unattractive—very bad indeed"—not one of them seemed "capable of being made a man." They had since been moved to a better location and a school had been constructed. One Indian even owned a small cattle ranch. "If the Crow Indians, in four years' time, can be made fit to be homesteaders and citizens," there were indeed grounds for encouragement.[73] He stressed the important role that reformers would play in the process, especially by the elevating influence of their Christian religion, which would inspire the Indian to "obey the laws of the land, and the laws that govern him in his relation to his fellow-man and his Creator."[74]

When Thayer took the podium, he both praised Dawes for his legislation and noted its flaws. It failed to allot land at once to any entire tribe, to make citizens of those whose land was not yet allotted, or to make an Indian a full citizen immediately. He stressed that the Indians still lacked laws and political institutions. Thayer then presented a summary of nine proposals offered by the Boston Indian Citizenship Committee, somewhat modified from the original, to ensure the protection of Indian rights. These were the extension of state or territorial laws over all reservations; protection of rights under the Constitution for all tribal Indians, on or off a reservation; reservation courts analogous to territorial courts; a county or town organization for reservations; modification of the Dawes bill to allow leasing and partition of the allotments; equitable ownership of Indian monies held by the government; assumption by the government of all taxes and fees during the term of inalienability; use of proceeds of Indian-held funds for educational use; and citizenship to those Indians who had taken their allotments and had proven to the reservation judge that they could manage their own affairs. Absent was Thayer's earlier proposal of abolishing the existing Indian administration. He then opened up the floor for questions.[75]

The discussion deeply troubled Boston Committee member Frank Wood, a printer and current treasurer of the Mohonk Conference. An admirer of Dawes and an original supporter of his legislation, Wood, like Thayer, believed "something in the nature of laws and courts and training for these poor people" was essential. The Constitution had been amended after the Civil War to guarantee the Freedmen their rights; if necessary, the same should be done for the Indians. Wood concluded that "if the government was to give no more aid to these Indians, [he] was sorry that [he] ever commenced to turn the Boston crank." He then moved that a committee be formed to look into the matter and report on additional legislation necessary to achieve the goal.[76] Thayer was appointed to chair this new Law Committee, along with Austin Abbott, a prominent New York legal scholar and dean of the New York Law School, and Philip C. Garrett, a Philadelphia lawyer and executive board member of the IRA.[77]

The Lake Mohonk Business Committee concluded that the Dawes Act had not solved the Indian problem; it only presented an opportunity for its solution, requiring missionary and educational bodies to organize and combine "their various energies to one great end, the Americanizing, civilizing, and Christianizing of the aborigines of the soil." Viewing education as the most pressing issue, the conference called upon the government to provide increased appropriations because "the most vigorous and united efforts are required to prepare the Indian for citizenship as rapidly as the Dawes bill will confer it upon him." Even Dawes had noted that Indian families would need direction until they "could get their little habitations erected, or a little seed into the ground and secure agricultural implements and learn how to do things."[78]

On the morning of the third day, Painter presented a short report on his visit to the Mission Indians, running through a list of villages visited and actions he had taken. He specifically emphasized the necessity of preventing further removals, explaining that there were twenty-three reservations in Southern California, containing over two hundred thousand acres, much of which did not lend itself to agriculture. He described the Morongo Reservation as key. If all intruders were removed and the government provided some sixty to seventy thousand dollars to find water, 175 families could be located there, with each family receiving a small farm of five acres; the remaining land could be used for dry farming. However, he reported, the schoolhouses he saw would be "a shame in Zululand, or to any other country."[79]

Returning home after the conference, Painter busied himself with lecturing, undertaking fourteen speaking engagements. He began on October 11, 1887, at Stockbridge, Massachusetts, followed by four November addresses in Great Barrington, at the Sedgwick Institute, the high school, the Congregational Church, and before a Ladies' Branch Association, presumably the Great Barrington branch of the Massachusetts Indian Association, a WNIA affiliate.[80] These addresses close to home made it possible for him to spend more time with Martha and young Charles. However, he did travel to Sheffield, Massachusetts, on November 15 to give a talk. Two weeks earlier he had written Welsh that he was still busy pulling his notes together for the investigative report on his tour to California and Indian Territory—it was already 219 handwritten pages. Finding it difficult to reduce, he thought it might end up 100 printed pages.[81]

The diversity of Painter's audiences was reflected in his December schedule. In Boston on December 7 he met with the Mohonk Conference Legal Defense Committee at noon, addressed the Massachusetts Indian Association at their annual meeting in the afternoon, and ended his day conferring with the Executive Committee of the Boston branch of the IRA. Later that month he spoke at Vassar College, "a much dreaded ordeal" during which he actually "had a delightful time," followed by a talk the next evening at the Second Reformed Church of Poughkeepsie. Next he set out for Concord, New Hampshire, to speak in the Unitarian Church, then addressed a late afternoon gathering of "Society ladies," which he described as a "splendid gathering." From there he went to Hartford, Connecticut. At month's end he was still reworking his report, especially the part about Indian Territory. He was scheduled to meet with Captain Hall, agent of the Kiowa and Comanche Agency, in Washington. "So please be patient with me," he wrote Welsh on December 31, "and if you get it later you will get it in better shape and worth much more to the I.R.A."[82]

The year 1887 had proved a busy one for Painter, especially so in dealing with the flawed Dawes legislation. At times he found himself defending part of it, while criticizing much of it, as well as walking a tightrope in support of Thayer's attempt to strengthen the legislation. Fortunately his lengthy tour of the Indian Territory and California had at least gotten him out in the field. The following year would be much different, as he faced a wider variety of smaller issues and less strenuous investigative tours.

▼ ▼ ▼

# CHAPTER 5

# DEFENDING AN AGENT, THE DAKOTA SCOUTS, AND A QUAKER EDUCATOR, 1888

In 1888 Painter faced a number of minor issues, each requiring his diplomatic, investigative, and lobbying skills. He succeeded in getting a competent Indian agent reappointed, restored annuities to Sisseton and Wahpeton Dakota scouts, and protected Menominee timber rights. Faced with the complex political machinery that ran Indian affairs, he worked to prevent the replacement of a successful Quaker school administrator and dealt with the complex issue of opening up lands in Oklahoma.

The year began with Painter's attendance at the annual BIC meeting on January 13, 1888, where he discussed his 1887 investigative trip to Indian Territory and California. President Cleveland and Secretary Lamar had asked him to report on the possible removal of various Oklahoma tribes—a removal he firmly believed that "the friends of the Indians should wisely resist." He echoed sentiments expressed earlier to Welsh and Davis and in his tour report, that the Indians were "taking root and have a right to stay there." It was only unfortunate that their schools were overcrowded and very badly managed, with personnel who did not represent "such phases of our Christianity and civilization as we wish to have introduced." He did note, however, that there were a few "honorable exceptions."[1]

As to his California trip, Painter informed commission members that he had accepted Cleveland's good intentions in ordering the removal of trespassers from Capitán Grande, but between its issuance and its execution there were many unreliable people, and the intent had not been carried out. He had also found illegal saloons. Apologizing for being driven to "this cranky position," he stated that it was impossible to do "anything with the machinery we have"—a reference to the unwieldy Indian Office. There was "no chance for this work of Christian civilization, except as the churches may do it," he concluded. Politics had to be removed from Indian affairs.[2]

Painter described his meeting with Cleveland before the signing of the Dawes Act, when he had assured the president that the IRA would work closely with him to ensure its success. The president had accepted the offer, stating he intended to move slowly. Two months later Painter had again visited the White House, and Cleveland asked him to provide a list of suitable allotting agents. The Interior Department used only two of his suggestions, however. Now Painter accused the president of moving faster than he had intended, presumably because of a "very great and urgent [pressure] from the frontiersmen to open up these reservations."[3]

Five days after the BIC meeting, Painter wrote Welsh that so far during this fiftieth congressional session, 131 Indian bills had been introduced in the House and 54 in the Senate. He personally was pushing the Mission Indian bill. He listed half a dozen pieces of proposed legislation, including Senator Teller's bill for compulsory Indian education, Senator Dawes's bill dealing with marriage between Indian women and white men, and Wisconsin Senator Philetus Sawyer's bill to sell timber on the Menominee Reservation. The latter he was determined to prevent, he informed Welsh on January 7. Later Painter would describe this bill as "an unqualified steal of Menominee timber." Based on the subject matter of the present proposed bills, Painter concluded that it was "evident that between Cranks, obstructive business rules, political fencers and general inertia we will have a long and utterly useless session of Congress."[4] The quality of the proposed legislation troubled Painter, and the quantity meant that he would be busy trying to defeat much of it. A week later Painter confided to J. B. Harrison, who covered the Philadelphia office when Welsh was absent, that he was overwhelmed. Dealing with the "chaos of the incoming administration," the "rawness and crudeness of the new [Indian] Committee in the House," and the "avalanche of new things being thrown into the seething whirlpool of uncertainties," he was "almost as raw and green as when [he] first came here." But he hoped "soon to be master of [himself] and on a level with the situation."[5]

Although Painter may have felt overwhelmed, the IRA praised him. Never before had the association received such attention from Congress and lobbyists as it had the previous year.[6] Washington insiders were now asking for his opinions and positions on their bills; and if it was negative, requesting suggestions. Painter was not only busy consulting with lobbyists and legislators; he was also engaged in defending a competent Indian agent, Edwin Eells, agent at the Puyallup Reservation in Washington Territory.[7]

### Eells's Defense

Originally appointed in 1871 by the AMA, Eells was described as capable, dedicated, and "undeniable [sic] competent" and was continually reappointed. Painter had first defended him in 1882, when the Washington Territory congressional delegate had favored another candidate. Now, six years later, Painter would again come to his aid. Describing a late January meeting with Indian Commissioner Atkins, Painter confided to Harrison that the commissioner was "more confidential than he has been of late, and said he was growing quite chary of dismissing men with the expectation of getting better when a man was doing well." Atkins informed Painter that he did not intend to turn out any good men simply for political reasons. With that opening, Painter asked if Eells had been reappointed. Atkins responded that he would be if he had anything to do with it. Replaying the scene for Harrison, Painter explained that he had taken "pains to get the facts before the President with reference to Eells in such way that if he is not re-appointed I should make it pretty hot for him before the public." Already Painter had presented a petition from the Indians, asking for Eells's reappointment, and had gathered reports from various inspectors who had visited the reservation. He also had conferred with Senator Dawes, receiving an affirmative vote from him. In confidence, Painter informed Harrison that he "was in very great favor with the president" but not so with the Indian Office.[8]

Painter learned that Eells's appointment was on hold because someone in the Indian Office had promised it to another. Eells, a Republican, was serving under a Democratic president with a Republican-controlled Senate. When Cleveland finally nominated him, Painter assumed the Senate would quickly confirm the appointment, but weeks passed with no action. Inquiring about the delay, Painter was informed that charges had been filed against the agent

Studio portrait of Edwin Eells, agent at S'Kokomish and the third director of the
Washington State Historical Society, 1904–1907.
*Washington State Historical Society, Tacoma, Washington.*

by the congressional delegate from Washington Territory, Charles Stewart Voorhees, whose father, Daniel Wolsey Voorhees, a senator from Indiana, had requested the nomination be postponed, leaving the agency's five consolidated reservations "in a state of almost complete disorganization." The delegate's aim was to "gratify a set of land grabbers" intent upon gaining as much of the Puyallup land as they could, an impossibility if Eells remained in office. In a March 5 letter to Welsh, Painter explained that he had called Atkins's attention to "the fact that a part of the scheme to get the farm on the Puyallup Reserve was the defeat of Eells' confirmation."[9]

On April 18, 1888, Painter wrote that Eells was in Washington, D.C., scheduled to appear before a Senate Committee on charges filed against him on March 22. The two men had spent the previous day conferring, giving Painter ample time to learn more about the agent. A week later Painter informed Welsh that Eells's enemies were moving to have Cleveland withdraw the nomination, "as they know they have miserably failed to show cause why the Senate should not confirm him." Although the *Congressional Record* had reported his confirmation the previous August, on April 13 Painter wrote Welsh that the report was a mistake. "His case hangs by the gills to suit the convenience of Voorhees who has gone to Indiana," Painter wrote in disgust. He had just appeared before the committee with the new batch of affidavits from Washington Territory, which "gave no new facts and add nothing to the case against him." He was also provoked with Dawes for allowing the confirmation issue to drag on, calling it "a case of unmitigated outrage." Over the next several years Painter's frustration with Dawes only grew, leading him to accuse the senator of ignorance on various issues. After almost nine months of official foot dragging, with Painter pushing every step of the way, Eells was finally reappointed, and he would serve as agent on the Puyallup Reservation until 1895.[10]

## The Sioux Bill

In addition to defending agents like Eells and opposing certain legislation outright, Painter at times had to work with lobbyists and congressmen to craft legislation for successful passage. One particularly thorny issue was the division of the Great Sioux Reservation, legislation for which had languished before Congress for six years. Although sympathetic to the Indians' desire to retain their reservation, Painter, Welsh, and the IRA believed that the Sioux, with their relatively small population, should not control an area four times the size of Massachusetts. But the reformers were also unwilling to approve the flawed 1882 Edmunds Agreement.

Back in the spring of 1884, at Dawes's insistence and with IRA support, Painter had visited all the Sioux agencies as chair of a Senate select committee and accompanied by its members. He had interviewed Indians, agency personnel, and members of the Edmunds commission. Then, with suggestions from the IRA and the Mohonk Conference, Dawes had drafted a new bill, which the IRA publicized in a pamphlet written in the Lakota language. On March 21, 1884, the IRA Executive Committee had resolved that the new proposed Dawes Sioux bill was "just and equitable in its provisions, and well meets the requirement of the case" and directed its passage. This legislation called for "just compensation," a million-dollar permanent Indian fund with 5 percent annual interest, allotment in severalty to those who were ready, and a requirement of consent by three-fourths of the Indian males. Half of the proceeds were to go toward industrial and other education, and the remainder was to be employed to "advance the Indians in civilized pursuits." The Mohonk Conference in its September 1884 proceedings had included an abstract of the bill, and the IRA printed twelve thousand copies of a pamphlet with the same wording.[11]

Now, on March 8, 1888, Painter informed Welsh that the Sioux Bill had passed the House the day before, and that he had "succeeded in getting most of the amendments [he] desired." Two weeks later he wrote that the bill had passed the Senate and would go on to conference for amendments. All of his amendments had been added. The previous month, in response to Welsh's question about his personal opinion, Painter had written that the bill ran "rough shod over the Indians in such way that none of us can foresee what evils may come from it which will more than counterbalance these immediate results which we seek." Without any consultation with the Indians, the Dawes Sioux bill became law on April 30, 1888. Painter, despite his misgivings, described it as "liberal, and even generous in its provisions," calling the land cession a redemption "from its condition as the refugee and bulwark of savagery." An assimilationist at heart, he envisioned "cultivated farms and homes sheltering a Christian civilization," which would influence the "neighboring savages."[12]

## Renville's Army Scouts

At times Painter worked directly with individual Indian leaders on specific issues. One such leader was Gabriel Renville, chief of the Sisseton and Wahpeton bands of the Eastern Santee (Dakota) Sioux.[13] In early 1888, Renville came to Washington to solicit Painter's assistance in securing restoration of the annuities of tribal members who had served as army scouts during the 1862 Dakota conflict. Describing Renville as "dignified, reticent, intelligent" and "straight forward and manly in his bearing," Painter remained impressed with "the quiet dignity and greatness of the man" even after numerous interviews. Renville was accompanied by his interpreter, Samuel Jerome Brown, who on his mother's side was part Dakota.[14] With Brown beside him, Renville displayed "an unruffled, dispassionate calmness which almost appeared to be indifference" as he detailed the great wrongs his people had suffered. However, at times Painter witnessed "flashes of lightning in his eye which revealed reserves of strength."[15]

Renville's people, the Sisseton and Wahpeton, who with the Mdewakanton and Wahpekute were known collectively as the Santee Sioux or Dakota, had in 1851 signed a treaty at Traverse des Sioux ceding 24 million acres in southern and western Minnesota in exchange for annuities. The Dakota then settled down on two twenty-mile-wide reservations along either side of the upper Minnesota River, where they endured a corrupt trading system and equally corrupt Indian agents. Seven years later, a month after Minnesota entered the Union, the Indians were forced to accept new treaties, ceding the northern half of their holdings, another million acres, in exchange for eighty-acre allotments and annuities. The politically corrupt leadership in Minnesota and the late arrival of the annuity money in 1862, combined with hardship and starvation, drove many of the Mdewakanton and Wahpekute to break into their agency warehouse and attack the neighboring Minnesota frontier. However, a large number of the Sisseton and Wahpeton served as scouts, assisting the U.S. Army in quelling the uprising. General Henry Hastings Sibley described Renville as "among the most trusted and reliable of the mixed-bloods" he employed during this time. He was so pleased with Renville's "fidelity, energy, and intelligence" that he appointed him chief of the scouts defending the frontier of both Minnesota and Dakota Territory.

He also praised Renville for his determined effort to save the lives of many whites taken captive in 1862.[16]

In 1863 Congress punished both friendly and hostile Dakota, abrogating their treaties, stripping them of their Minnesota lands, denying them payment of annuities for past land sales, and leaving them homeless and penniless. Finally, in 1867, a treaty established the Lake Traverse Indian Reservation in Dakota Territory for them. Renville was now seeking support to restore annuities for the former scouts. Impressed by the man's personal deportment and describing the service that he and his scouts had provided "at the peril of their lives," which the army had recognized "as of the utmost value," Painter drafted a bill for their relief. The day that Painter and Renville visited Commissioner Atkins's office was the very day that the chief of the finance department brought in a document for the commissioner's signature—a statement of accounts that Painter needed in order to complete his Indian scouts bill. Examining the statement, Painter learned that the scouts' annuities had been wiped out by extensive damage claims made by white residents relative to their property destroyed during the 1862 outbreak. "Poor Renville was dumb with amazement, as well he might be!" Painter later wrote, describing the accounting as a "remarkable system of book-keeping which wipe[d] out the dues of one man by charging against him damages inflicted by another." Meeting with Commissioner Atkins on Renville's behalf, Painter explained that because of their loyalty, the scouts and soldiers "should be regarded as friends, and exempted from the act of confiscation, at least of their funds." In the end, Atkins agreed and asked Painter to prepare a report to be incorporated into his answer to the House Committee on Indian Affairs. Hagan, in his IRA history, describes Painter's actions as a "good demonstration of [his] versatility as a lobbyist"; he not only drafted the original bill but also wrote the commissioner's report.[17]

To educate the public and urge congressional passage of this bill, in mid-August 1888 the IRA published three thousand copies of Painter's pamphlet *How We Punished Our Allies*, later reprinted in the October issue of *Lend a Hand: A Journal of Organized Philanthropy*. At Painter's request, WNIA president Quinton also reprinted sections of his pamphlet in the January 1889 issue of *The Indian's Friend*. The WNIA monthly had a large readership, with complimentary copies sent to Indian schools and congressional members.[18]

Gabriel Renville, ca. 1880–81. Renville sought help from Painter to restore
annuities for Sisseton and Wahpeton Dakota scouts.
*South Dakota Historical Society, Pierre.*

Despite this extensive publicity and Painter's testimony before the U.S.
Court of Claims, the bill languished in Congress. Although it passed the
Senate, it was held up in the House by Joseph G. Cannon, chairman of the
appropriations committee, who opposed the restoration of the annuities. On

January 31, 1891, Painter sent Welsh a prepared statement to be used as an appeal, which the IRA sent out as a flyer in February. This descriptive flyer concluded with an appeal to every citizen who felt "a sense of shame in view of these wrongs, and who [had] a touch of humanity," to join in a petition to the House, requesting its members to "perform this act of justice, and afford this means of relief to the Sisseton-Wahpeton scouts." The legislation finally became a law on March 3, 1891.[19]

### Menominee Timber

Sometimes Painter was forced to work aggressively to defeat legislation damaging to the Indians' cause; a case in point is his work on behalf of the Wisconsin Menominees. In 1887 Wisconsin Senator Philetus Sawyer, a wealthy lumberman from Oshkosh, had introduced a bill allowing local lumbermen to purchase Indian timber at a ridiculously low price. Indian consent was required, but Painter described the bill as a "plan of civilizing by sale of property as an old and tried expedient, which is always in high favor with the average Congressman." The Senate committee had deemed the legislation "as wise and good for the Indian." Writing Welsh on March 5, 1888, Painter accused Dawes of viewing "Sawyer [as] an Angel engaged in lumber business." At the same time Painter accused the Wisconsin senator of defrauding the Stockbridge Indians under a similar type of bill. "I have the proof," he wrote, "we may have to make an open fight." Two weeks later, on March 20, Painter wrote Welsh that he was in "a state of rage."[20]

The previous day Dawes had brought up the Menominee bill with an amendment striking out the clause requiring consent after falsely claiming that although the chiefs were in opposition, the rest of the Indians approved. Painter told Welsh that he and a Menominee representative had visited Dawes, informing him that the Indians had sent a unanimous petition to the Indian Office requesting that their lands be allotted. They strongly opposed loggers taking possession of their reservations, bringing in the very lowest class of white men to debauch their women, preferring to "take care of their own logs."[21] Painter was quickly reaching a point of exasperation with Dawes, not only over the Menominee issue but because the senator still had not pushed Eells's confirmation.

Supported by their agent, the Menominees had raised money to send a delegation to protest the bill, but it passed the day after the delegation arrived, giving them no opportunity to be heard. Painter testified against the bill before both the Senate and House committees, and on April 18, 1888, he wrote Welsh that he thought he had effectively headed off the Menominee "timber steal." Less than a week later he informed Welsh that he hoped President Cleveland would not approve the bill because he favored allotment instead, and would not allow "it to be done by an Agent representing the lumber interest."[22]

The final decision was taken out of everyone's hands. Robert M. LaFollette of Wisconsin, a member of the House Indian Committee, arranged for the bill to die in committee. Unfortunately that was not the end of the Menominees' problems. On November 20, Attorney General Garland decided that the "dead-and fallen timber," not needed or used for improvements, agricultural purposes, or fuel by the Indians, was the property of the United States, giving the Indians no right to cut and sell the timber on their own reservation.[23]

The previous winter the Menominees had sold $86,031.15 worth of this timber in Oshkosh. Painter now described this type of sale as immensely valuable to them; the Indians would benefit far more from cutting their own timber than from anything the Sawyer bill would offer. So Painter recommended the allotment of their reservation and the allotment of "so many feet per capita" of their pine trees, with a restriction preventing the cutting of immature trees. He concluded that the IRA must make sure that Sawyer's bill was either amended or defeated. In his formal report, he estimated there was 500 million feet of pine on the reservation, which would provide a great deal of dead and fallen timber to augment the Indians' meager earnings. Aided by Indian Office personnel, in January 1889 Painter drafted a bill to permit the Indians to sell this timber. Receiving the endorsement of Commissioner John H. Oberly and Interior Secretary William F. Vilas, Painter introduced his bill to Congress. On February 15, 1889, he visited outgoing President Cleveland in regard to signing the legislation, later informing Welsh that he thought it would "receive immediate and favorable attention." The bill became law within a short two-month period because of the behind-the-scenes activities of Painter and Welsh and the respect they enjoyed among government officials.[24]

In a letter dated March 5, 1888, Painter listed twenty-seven individual activities he had recently been engaged in, including committee and hearing appearances, conferences with officials, visits to Senate offices, preparations of statistical reports, examinations of cases brought to him, and bills he prepared in response. Had the IRA been able to employ a dozen competent men like Painter, it might have been able to properly investigate the problems of the more than 250,000 Indians who lived on 160 reservations. Painter was successful largely because of his easy access to Cleveland. For example, in late April he went to the White House, and the door keeper informed him that the rooms were full and his chance of seeing Cleveland was small. However, within a very short time the door keeper seated Painter near the president's desk, and Painter had his conference. "Certainly I ask for nothing more cordial or deferential," he informed Welsh.[25]

### The Oklahoma Bill

Not all of Painter's work was as pleasant as conferring with President Cleveland. He also had to please Welsh, who believed that when "Indians possess more land than necessary for their maintenance when living in a condition of civilization," it was desirable to open up surplus land for white settlement. Terms had to be equitable, with the legal transference of land carried out in an ethical manner. The land in question was the vast Indian Territory.[26]

The idea of a permanent Indian frontier had emerged after the acquisition of the Louisiana Territory and finally became a reality in the 1830s, with the removal of the Five Civilized tribes from the Southeast to the trans-Mississippi west. Initially their landholdings included much of modern-day Oklahoma, designated then as Indian Territory, with the exception of the extreme northeastern section, the home of several former Old Northwest tribes. The Five Tribes had been guaranteed a measure of independence and self-government. Neglected by the federal government, Indian Territory tribes had negotiated treaties with the Confederacy. At the war's end, they were forced to sign punishing treaties, stripping them of large portions of their land, upon which mostly Southern Plains tribes were then resettled (Comanche, Kiowa, Southern Cheyenne and Southern Arapaho, and Kiowa Apache). Thus the Indian Territory had become divided, with the Five Civilized Tribes in the eastern section on reservations established by treaties

and the Southern Plains tribes to the west, mostly on executive order reservations. As the country expanded, railroads petitioned Congress to open
up these western-most lands. The following decade brought the "Boomers,"
who relentlessly encroached upon Indian land, demanding that the 2 million
acres of the Oklahoma District ceded by the Creeks and Seminoles and not
yet assigned to any tribe be opened to homesteading.

Although the IRA did not play as large a role in the fight to defend this
land as "might be expected," writes Hagan, Painter, who had toured the
area in 1885 and again in 1887, was nevertheless called upon to bring order
out of chaos. Like Welsh, he was not opposed to opening up the immense
territory. In his 1887 pamphlet he had written that "the purpose to fill up
Oklahoma with settlers will never sleep, and ought never to sleep, until
it is accomplished."[27] However, settlement had to be orderly, with Indian
consent and compensation, and Painter strongly objected to the removal
of the Wichitas, Cheyennes, Arapahos, Comanches, and Kiowas. Instead
of treating the Indians "as chessmen to be moved as the white man plays
his game," he much preferred to absorb them or extend laws over them.[28]
Therefore, to ensure that any legislation impacting the Indian Territory met
IRA criteria, Painter conferred with numerous supporters, especially Illinois Congressman William M. Springer, chair of the House Committee on
Territories, who was proposing a bill to create the territory of Oklahoma. As
Painter later explained in *The Indian's Friend*, the Springer bill provided "a
territorial government for that homeless outcast, known as 'no-man's-land'
[the Oklahoma Panhandle] lying west of Cherokee outlet, outside the limits
or jurisdiction of any existing State or Territory." The bill also provided for
a commission (the Cherokee Commission) to negotiate with the Cherokees,
Creeks, and Seminoles for purchase of lands west of their current position
and to cancel Cherokee leases with cattlemen in the "Cherokee outlet."[29]

In reporting on Springer's bill, the *Kansas City Times* described the IRA's
views as "generally based upon sentimental considerations" as "a society
which more than any other controls and shapes the sentiment in the East in
relation to Indian affairs." Its recommendations had outlined government
policy, and its agents had "furnished the country at large with truer accounts
of the condition of the Indians than could be secured from any other source."
Because of the IRA's belief in reducing reservations, the reporter concluded

that the association would greatly aid in the Oklahoma crusade. Painter was quoted as favoring a territorial form of government but opposing the opening of the recently acquired Creek and Cherokee lands "without their consent and proper compensation" and the removal of the Southern Plains tribes occupying executive order reservations.[30]

In mid-March the *New York Tribune* criticized Commissioner Atkins for recommending for a third time in his last annual report the removal of the Cheyennes, Arapahos, Wichitas, and Kiowas from their present Indian Territory reservations into the Oklahoma District. The newspaper, describing Painter's vigorous protest against Atkins's stand, quoted Painter as saying, "[W]e ought by this time to have learned something from experience in regard to such removals." It was, Painter stated, "difficult to find a tribe whose removal has not proved to be a long step backward in their progress."[31]

Meeting with Springer and Iowa Congressman James Baird Weaver on April 23, 1888, Painter went over the proposed legislation, explaining what the IRA expected. Springer was emphatic "in his declarations that he [did] not seek or desire the disturbance of any Indian in regard to the land he occupies," wrote Painter.[32] However, the amended bill failed in the Senate.

Rumors had circulated on the House floor that the IRA had favored the legislation, when in fact the association had objected to it from the very beginning, Painter having described it as "at the wrong end of the business." On February 15, 1889, Painter wrote that some of his friends in Congress no longer supported him because he had been quoted as favoring the legislation. "Their fault finding only illustrated how little, even our best friends in Congress, know of things on which they take action," he informed Welsh. As a result of these unfounded rumors, the IRA was accused of robbing the Indians of their property in violation of treaty obligations. In April 1889, in defense of the IRA and to explain publicly "the exact object proposed by the 'Oklahoma Bill,'" Painter wrote *The Oklahoma Bill and Oklahoma*. He explained that the association did not oppose the establishment of a formal government, only asking that whatever form it took, it had to be "over the whole of the Indian Territory," not over a mere district. This bill, however, proposed a territorial government "only for the 'public lands,' to which no Indian has the shadow of a claim." In the end, Painter carefully amended the original bill to ensure that every "kind of right or claim" by the Indians was protected.[33]

While Springer's bill was pending in the Senate, Cleveland began negotiating with the Creeks and Seminoles to purchase their claims outside their reservations. As Painter explained in "Oklahoma," published in *The Indian's Friend*, although Springer's bill to create the Territory of Oklahoma had failed, "the body of land known as Oklahoma has come into our possession by honorable and liberal purchase." All that was needed now was a presidential proclamation and the opening of a land office, and that long-coveted land would be available, "not to the boomer, but to the law-abiding, home-seeking settler." Springer helped the situation along with an amendment to an Indian Appropriations Act; Cleveland signed the bill into law in March 1889, and settlers rushed in.[34]

### Defending a Quaker Educator

Several months after his April conference with Springer, Painter hurried off to southwestern North Carolina at the urgent request of Nimrod Jarrett Smith, principal chief of the Eastern Band of Cherokees.[35] On June 21, 1888, Painter wrote Welsh that this visit had been "well timed" and that he believed "good will" would come from it. The IRA published his sixteen-page report on the visit, the last half of which was reprinted in *The Civil Service Record* to reach a wider audience.[36]

Painter had also gone to North Carolina to learn why Commissioner Atkins had refused to renew Henry W. Spray's contract. Spray, a Quaker, had been superintendent of the Cherokee Training School since 1884. All reservation schools on the Cherokee Reservation were Quaker-run by this time, and each agent had reported on the excellent education they provided. Painter included in his report excerpts from their reports to emphasize that they were "authorized sources of information upon which the administration must, *per force*, it would seem, base its action when called to act in reference to the schools," not the whim of the Indian commissioner.[37]

Also curious about Atkins's reasoning for recommending the removal of these Cherokees to the Indian Territory, Painter paid him a courtesy call. "They have become mixed up in politics," was Atkins's reply. Painter later learned that until 1884 the Cherokees, as citizens of North Carolina, had voted Democratic, but that in the most recent election they had voted, almost to a man, for James G. Blaine, former Republican speaker of the House from

Nimrod Jarrett Smith, principal chief of the Eastern Band of Cherokee, 1880–1891. *Photograph originally in* Thomas Donaldson, Eastern Band of Cherokees of North Carolina *(Washington, D.C.: U.S. Census Printing Office, 1892), p. 1. Hunter Library Special Collections, Western Carolina University, Cullowhee, North Carolina.*

Maine. Some locals, believing that Spray, who had been appointed as school superintendent just two months before the election, was responsible for this political switch, saw an opportunity to remove not only him but the Quakers and the Cherokees.[38]

Painter was impressed with the reservation, describing the lands where half of the two thousand Cherokee lived as "fertile, broken, well watered, heavily timbered, [and] well adapted to agriculture." The Indians were civilized, interested in education, lived a well-ordered life, and possessed a desire for progress. He was also impressed with Spray's boarding school. "I do not think I have seen its equal at any other Government Indian school," he wrote. It achieved wonderful results and exuded "a wholesome religious earnestness, free from cant or sentimentalism," as well as providing healthy, abundant food to the children. Based on his observations and the agent's reports, Painter concluded that "there could be no question as to the approval and continued support of the Department, and of the satisfaction the Commissioner would feel in view of it." He was still at a loss to understand why Atkins would not support such a successful educational system.[39]

But Spray and local politics were not the sole issue. For more than half a century the Methodists had been in charge of the schools, and local whites viewed the Quakers as carpetbaggers. However, the Cherokees were pleased with them, holding a council in Painter's presence during which they voted unanimously to continue Quaker control. Painter also learned that the government had been complicit in Spray's removal, sending a special inspector to hold a council with the Indians to determine how they felt about their schools. The Indian Office had agreed beforehand that the inspector would report against Spray, no matter what the Cherokees decided.[40]

Painter described Atkins's approach as "a strong side-light upon the theory and methods of the Indian Office as it has been conducted in the management of Indian schools, and Indian affairs generally." The present management of Indian affairs was "in the hands of those who have power to sacrifice" all the good that could be done "in order to reward political friends, or further purely personal and partisan ends."[41] This liberal use of the spoils system was a particular concern for Welsh, who was an enthusiastic supporter of extending Civil Service authority over the Indian service. He was especially critical of Secretary Lamar, whom he accused of "dreamy acquiescence" in sprinkling

Indian agencies with numerous appointees from Tennessee and Mississippi. Commissioner Atkins and his assistant, Alexander B. Upshaw, were both from Tennessee, and according to the IRA they "regarded the Indian reservations as a green pasture where their political herds might comfortably browse and fatten." Painter, who had witnessed the poor quality of teachers during his 1887 tour of the Indian Territory, had joined with the IRA Executive Committee in November of that year to urge President Cleveland to extend Civil Service rules to the Indian service.[42] As late as August 18 Painter was still dumbfounded that the Indian Office had sent a special inspector specifically to report against Spray. Since most of the school buildings on the reservation were Quaker-owned, however, their removal was more complicated.[43] The issue became less important when Atkins resigned on June 14, 1888, to make an unsuccessful run for the Senate from Tennessee.[44]

Painter's experience in North Carolina had reaffirmed his beliefs about the complexity of the machine running Indian affairs. Indian interests were sacrificed by "overshadowing and antagonistic interests" that received primary consideration. While whites benefited, Indians were torn from their homes "and planted elsewhere, or even cast adrift." No existing laws could be invoked on their behalf, and they had no voice in the management of their own affairs. The Cherokees, Painter noted, funded their own day schools, and therefore the order to close the schools "ought to set the American people to a serious consideration of the kind of despotism we have placed over more than a quarter of a million of people, in the effort we are making to qualify them for citizenship in our free Republic."[45]

Painter returned home in early July, in great pain from a cold in his ear. Under a physician's care, he informed Welsh that he was hearing a "whole forest of Crickets and Katy-Dids singing." By mid-month he was well enough to give an address in Williamstown, Massachusetts, attended by the president and professors of his alma mater, Williams College. He remarked to Welsh that "there was manifestly considerable interest created" by his talk. Five days later he spoke before the Great Barrington Association, which had not only raised over one hundred dollars during the year to support a student at Hampton but had donated money to the WNIA hospital on the Omaha Reservation. In an early September letter, Painter listed five upcoming speaking engagements in Massachusetts and New Hampshire and a trip to Boston to confer with members of the Boston Indian Citizenship Committee. He also informed Welsh that immediately after the Mohonk Conference, he intended to set out for Minnesota and Dakota and perhaps pay a visit to the Oneidas and Stockbridges of Wisconsin. From there he would probably go directly to Washington Territory and Oregon.[46]

## Lake Mohonk

The first agenda item of the annual Mohonk Conference, held in late September, was Indian education. Painter reported on his recent trip to the North Carolina Cherokees and their unique educational experiences. Then the keynote speaker, Dr. Lyman Abbott, presented a paper, which was then referred to a committee, with Painter as a member, that would write up resolutions for conference action.[47] When proceedings resumed, Painter read the committee's resolutions, which included the creation of a commission composed of three eminent educators to not only control Indian education but to urge Christian churches "to put forth efforts persistent and sufficient to bring [the Indians] under such religious influence as shall give value and permanence to this educational work." Painter also recommended that this new commission implement some provisions of the Dawes Act. Finding nothing impractical in Abbott's plan, Painter hoped that the time had come to "make a persistent, a determined, and unremitting effort to have a change made" in the way the Indian Office operated its educational system.[48] Yet again Painter's proposals would come to naught.

Thayer, chairman of the Mohonk law committee, was next on the agenda. He stressed three points: his committee's proposal to extend courts and a system of laws over the reservations; a substitute bill—the Morgan bill; and other general suggestions to improve the Indians' legal status. Painter controlled the discussion, reminding attendees that it was crucial for the Indians in the Indian Territory to have some access to a court system—it was three hundred miles from the center of the Territory to the nearest court. Anarchy prevailed on some reservations; these were "not places in which people whom we wish to become civilized should be kept."[49]

As an example, he referenced the legal difficulties of the four bands of Dakotas, who had been left penniless after the Minnesota uprising and the resultant confiscation of their lands and annuities. A member of the delegation brought to Washington to enact a new treaty on their behalf had been kidnapped and hanged from a tree on the Virginia side of the Potomac River. Chief Renville had been ill treated during his recent visit to the capital, and Painter had learned that the Indian Office had used the scouts' annuities to pay damages to white victims. The time was coming, he declared, "when these Indians will demand an overhaul of their accounts with the Government, and the statements of the Bureau must be examined and settled in the courts." At the conclusion of the open discussion, Rev. William Hayes Ward resolved that the conference recognize the necessity of protecting Indian rights and moved to establish a general judicial system to be extended over all Indian reservations. Because a proposal for such legislation already existed in the form of the Thayer bill, the conference attendees agreed to do all they could to ensure its passage.[50] The bill, however, would continue to languish in committee.

On the second day of the conference, Painter wrote Harrison that he was being kept so busy serving "as a bureau of information" that he had no time to "enjoy the beauties of this most beautiful place." Painter had just learned that John Oberly had been nominated as Indian commissioner to replace Atkins, who had resigned the previous June. With a newly appointed superintendent of schools and Oberly's appointment, he expressed the hope that "we will have efficiency in the service now." He was almost inclined to go immediately to Washington and consult with the new commissioner before setting out on his investigative tour. The discussion of schools and laws for the Indians was going along fine, prompting him to conclude that his "radicalism of last year seems to be the prevailing sentiment now."[51]

On September 28, during the final session of the proceedings, Henry Oscar Houghton, a prominent publisher and treasurer of the Boston Indian Citizenship Committee, offered a resolution for a new position—a paid secretary for the conference to promote its policy of "religious, educational, industrial, and secular interest of the Indians." Duties would include gathering pertinent information, presenting legislation before Congress, and assisting the Indian Office. Frank Woods, also of the Boston Committee, remarked that the conference already had such a person in the "unpaid services" of Painter, whom he described as starting "movements for the benefit of the Indians." The resolution was referred to the conference's Executive Committee.[52]

On October 2, 1888, Painter informed Welsh that the Mohonk Conference had passed a resolution providing for a paid Washington agent whose "duty it should be to watch Roman Aggression, and all matters relating to Indian interests, to the executive committee with power to act." The "Roman Aggression" was a reference to what Painter and others thought was the "disproportional influence the Catholics were exerting in Indian education." According to Hagan, like many of the evangelical Protestant reformers who dominated the Indian reform movement, Welsh had "latent fears of the Roman Catholic Church." To assuage his fears, Painter had come up with a better alternative. He could take over the job with a bit of juggling on the part of the IRA. Painter noted that this proposed position only required the gathering of facts, a diligent eye on the government, and a "medium through which the various Churches could deal with the Department"—tasks he was already completing for the IRA. The conference wanted him to take the new position, but he preferred not to leave his IRA post and was well aware that Welsh thought he "must not be considered in the case."[53]

Suggesting they test the idea for the winter, Painter requested of Welsh a clerk and an office, enabling him to "give this saved time to such things as I think you can with advantage undertake to do," he wrote. "Most of the things you wish done are the things I am now looking after," he continued. "I think if they would give me what would be fair for the increase of work, and then relieve me of my clerical work by furnishing a competent clerk, it would enable me to do better work for you, and give me time for their work also." Painter suggested that Welsh contact Houghton. "If it should seem best 'all round' that this plan should be carried out then it may be best for me to go to Washington immediate after the 1st of November."[54]

The idea never came to fruition. According to Hagan, it is clear that both Dawes and his wife, Electa Allen Sanderson Dawes, did not favor the idea of Painter in such a role. General Whittlesey and others also weighed in, opining that it was undesirable to put the conference "in a position of antagonism" toward the Catholic Church.[55]

### A New Tour

At the conclusion of the Lake Mohonk meeting, Painter set out for his investigative tour, first to the Sissetons, then on to the White Earth Indian Agency in Minnesota to visit various Chippewa bands. Next he traveled to neighboring Wisconsin to confer with the Menominees, Oneidas, Stockbridges, and Munsees at the Green Bay Agency, and then to the Omahas and Winnebagoes in Nebraska. Although Commissioner Atkins had specifically requested that he look into a situation at the Omaha Reservation, Painter left no detailed explanation of his activities there, or on any of the other reservations.[56]

From the skeletal details Painter provided in his sixth annual report, it appears that the issue facing the Omahas, and probably the other tribes he visited, was simply a lack of understanding of their legal rights now that they were considered citizens under the Dawes legislation. The failure to pass the Thayer bill had turned this issue from a "very grave condition" to an intolerable one, Painter noted. At a conference at Gabriel Renville's home, the Sissetons asked about their relationship to their agent—specifically, what kind of powers he had over them. Painter tried to explain that their condition was "similar to that of a tadpole which has developed legs and [had] not dropped his tail." In other words, they were in a transitional stage, and as long as they retained a tribal interest and remained on a reservation, they had to "submit to some things that other citizens will not have to suffer. You will get rid of the Agency system and Bureau interference just as soon as you dispose of all tribal property."[57]

Their solution, however, was to ask the Dakota territorial legislature to create a county out of their reservation, enabling them to elect county officers and manage their own affairs. Intrigued by the concept, Painter wondered if it could be used as a remedy for the Omahas and Winnebagoes, who had found their rights to tribal property as individuals on both allotted and unallotted reservations problematic, especially as common property was becoming limited. The situation among the Oneidas was also "alarming" and "full of danger." The more progressive Indians were fencing in, using more land than their share and becoming "fierce and earnest in their opposition to allotment under any bill," while local whites were pushing allotment through their congressional representative, a member of the Committee on Indian Affairs. Painter feared for the future progress of these Indians.[58] He was back in Great Barrington in time for Christmas dinner with Martha and Charles, who was home from his studies at John Hopkins. Painter already had made plans to give addresses in New Britain, Meriden, and Waterbury, Massachusetts.[59]

In 1888 Painter had dealt with a wide range of issues involving different tribes, acting at times in a more direct and personal manner, as when he met with and worked on behalf of a competent Washington Territory Indian agent and a Quaker educator, each facing possible removal. He used his extensive lobbying skills to push legislation through Congress to restore the annuities of former Dakota scouts, and he protected Menominee timber rights. Unfortunately, his investigative tours were short and under-reported, leaving almost no details of those accomplishments. During the upcoming year he would face two major issues, the proposed removal of the Southern Utes and a long, futile effort to locate a permanent homeland for the Chiricahua Apaches.

# CHAPTER 6

# OPPOSING UTE REMOVAL AND SEEKING A HOME FOR THE APACHES, 1889–1890

On January 17, 1889, Painter attended his sixth BIC meeting. On the agenda was the removal of three bands of the Southern Utes from southwestern Colorado, near Durango, to a new reservation in Utah Territory. Rev. Thomas S. Childs of the Presbyterian Board of Home Missions, a member of the Southern Ute Commission appointed by President Cleveland, addressed the removal, an issue the IRA had successfully opposed in 1886. Aware of the association's stand, Childs explained that the Utes were willing to leave Colorado. The "feeling that removal of the tribe involves injustice," he clarified, did not necessarily mean "that it is a crime or injustice." During the discussion period Child warded off questions from both Painter and Welsh. Learning that the proposed reservation in Utah was on public land, Painter inquired why it had not been homesteaded. Childs responded that it had no special value, except for grazing, to which Painter retorted: "[T]hen the Indians must continue tribal?" Yes, agreed Childs, they would continue "living by pastoral work, which is much better than what they are doing now," which was living like paupers. Painter reminded the conference that during a visit to Colorado, Commissioner Atkins had conferred with the Utes, learning that with a few exceptions, they were opposed to the removal. Atkins, Childs countered, had actually found the Indians about evenly divided. Welsh then asked: if the main reason for removing the Utes was settlers' demands for land, would not that same situation occur in Utah? In the end, the conference opposed removal unless it was advantageous to the tribe, to which Child responded that it was, for his commission had located a far better reservation to which most of the Utes were willing to remove.[1] The following October Painter would pay a visit to the Utes to see for himself.

Welsh believed the Utes' willingness to move was based on "ignorance and susceptibility to bribes." His cardinal rule was that removal and the breaking up of reservations should not be done to suit the conveniences and needs of white settlers, especially if Indian-held lands could afford homes and self-support. To strengthen its opposition to the removal bill, which had passed the Senate, in February 1889 the IRA published Painter's fifteen-page pamphlet, *Civilization by Removal!: The Southern Utes.* Copies were sent to members of the various committees on Indian affairs of both congressional houses. The Ute removal would prove to be one of the most challenging issues Painter faced. His actions would be thwarted continually, especially by the chairman of the subcommittee on the Ute bill, who repeatedly failed to notify him of meetings or hearings, prompting him to write Welsh: "I can assure you I have never had to fight the Devil quite so manifestly as pure unadulterated evil as in this Ute matter."[2]

This particular BIC meeting had been awkward for Herbert Welsh. Childs was a friend in whose home he had been a guest. Furthermore, Childs was knowledgeable about the situation, having served from late July to early December 1888 as secretary of the Ute Commission, which had two other members, the Hon. J. Montgomery Smith and Major R. B. Weaver. They had negotiated treaty modifications with the one thousand Mauches, Capotes, and Weeminuches still living on their 1.1 million-acre reservation in southwestern Colorado, conferring with the local citizenry, crisscrossing the reservation, and escorting a handful of Utes to southeastern Utah Territory to examine the new reservation. Their final report had been received by the Interior Department just days before the BIC meeting.[3]

On February 9, 1889, in strict confidence, Painter revealed to Welsh Childs's reason for taking such a strong stand on Ute removal. He had been privy to a letter from a government employee, revealing that Childs had recently been elected president of a land and water company in Durango that was taking over the old Ute Reservation. And he had put considerable money into the company. However, there is no evidence that Painter ever used this information. On February 8, he informed Welsh that the pressure upon him had been "constant and overwhelming. We never have had such activity in Indian legislation since I have been here and I have never had so much writing to do." He had "struck richness in Childs' accounts" and was busy including much of the information from the Ute Commission's report into his own pamphlet.[4]

In *Civilization by Removal*, Painter characterized the proposed legislation as a repetition of the often-tried "expedient of civilizing Indians by removing them" to other lands that did "not present so great temptations to Anglo-Saxon greed." With his usual attention to detail, he had researched agents' reports as far back as 1882, chronicling positive changes along the Utes' road to civilization and concluding that Colorado had simply determined there would be no Indians within its borders. The proposed new reservation, three times larger than the former one, was barren and parched land in Utah Territory, more suitable to grazing. Painter was displeased with "the theory that we must make herders of them as the natural and necessary preliminary step to their becoming civilized citizens." In actuality, the Utes were hunters and gatherers, showing little interest in farming and a willingness to move. But the IRA, certain that it had the best interests of the Indians at heart, opposed removal, believing it delayed the Utes' adoption of farming.[5]

Painter accused the Ute Commission of securing "*the consent of the Indians to remove, and not primarily to discern*" their wishes. They were to be removed from good land where during the last eight years they had been making encouraging progress only because "there is annoyance from the whites who wish their lands, we beg leave to differ," retorted Painter. While his pamphlet was still at the printer, a copy of the commission's report had been given to Congress, enabling Painter to revise the pamphlet to include statements from a Ute named Charlie, who explained to the commission that two years previously about half of his people had wanted to move but lately they had started to do some farming. "Here it is good for farming, and out there it is good [only] for raising cattle and sheep," he was quoted as saying. The commission had worn the Utes down, and in the end they had agreed to move. Then Charlie remarked that future government officials would not come to Utah Territory and say "*Get out of here, Utes; you have got too good a land!*" Painter concluded that the Utes could be civilized more "cheaply, honorably and satisfactorily" on their Colorado lands.[6]

Childs immediately cried foul, accusing Painter of "misrepresentations and false statements."[7] He also accused Painter of a dishonest connection with the Pittsburg Cattle Company, which had provided him with transportation during his tour of the Ute Reservation. Painter responded immediately, willing to make corrections and asking Childs to identify specific false statements. Instead of writing Painter directly, Childs then sent an accusatory letter to the *Durango Herald*, which was later repeated as an editorial. When Painter learned of this letter months later, he asked Welsh, as "his chosen medium of communication," to tell Childs how much he regretted the situation, and that he was willing to make a public apology.[8]

## Commissioner Oberly

On the issue of Ute removal, Painter and Welsh nominally had the support of the incoming Indian commissioner, Thomas Jefferson Morgan. Although pleased with this choice, both Painter and Welsh would have much preferred that John Oberly be reappointed. However, Grover Cleveland's loss to Benjamin Harrison in November of 1888 meant a shift from Democratic to Republican control and all new appointments. Cleveland had expected to be re-elected when he appointed Oberly the previous September, but only a month after Oberly took office on October 10, 1888,[9] both the president and his party were defeated at the polls, making Oberly's tenure one of the shortest on record. Painter had described the "demoralization of the campaign" as bad, "but the paralysis resulting from the election was worse." Painter noted that Oberly had been willing to take on what seemed a hopeless task: "to lift the Indian Service out of the low estate into which it had fallen under the administration of the past four years." Since then he had performed his job with a good natured "but quiet determination . . . to do the utmost that can be done to administer his office first of all with reference to the best interests of those committed to his care as wards of the nation." Closely studying Oberly, Painter conveyed to Welsh his appreciation of the "difficulties under which he [had] so far labored," concluding that he had "confident hopes of an improved service if we can only have him [Oberly] continued in office."[10]

Aware of Welsh's interest in Civil Service reform, Painter reminded him in a letter dated January 28, 1889, that on March 4 control of the government would change. He assured Welsh that with the new administration the "spoils system shall come to an abrupt conclusion, and that honesty, fitness, and efficiency" shall be "the sole reason" for appointments or retention, especially that of Oberly. Describing the Indian commissioner as *able, honest, efficient*," and sympathetic to those who had the best interest of the Indians at heart, Painter urged Welsh to lobby on Oberly's behalf, listing half a dozen reasons why he should be retained. Oberly's removal simply because he was a Democrat was "a declaration that other considerations than the interest of the Indians are to be made controlling in the administration of the office." Previously one of Cleveland's three Civil Service commissioners, Oberly was "fully and irreconcilably committed" to applying the Civil Service reform principles to the entire Indian service; his retention would be a positive declaration by the new administration that the spoils system had ended in regard to Indian affairs, reasoned Painter. On April 5 he informed Welsh that Dawes, accusing them of neglecting their "legitimate" Indian work, was critical of both the IRA's and his efforts on Oberly's behalf.[11]

Oberly, who had continually made himself available and responsive to Welsh, already had his support. In a January 26, 1888, letter to Painter, Welsh noted he was already "writing in every direction"—to Senator Dawes, to IRA branch members, to major newspapers, and to a network of religious journals. He had even written an eight-page pamphlet and sent hundreds of letters to reformers, urging them to write their congressmen and to circulate pro-Oberly petitions. Members of the Mohonk Conference and prominent Bostonians, including Rev. Samuel Longfellow, responded. In early 1889 Welsh sent petitions to Quinton to distribute to her members, thanking her in a February 4 letter. Quinton herself was pro-Morgan, but she distributed the petitions and also printed one of Welsh's letters in *The Indian's Friend*, thanking him at month's end for the excellent article and explaining that she had taken the liberty of leaving out a paragraph.[12]

In mid-March 1889 Painter wrote that he was "more and more convinced that [Oberly's] record in politics before he became an official here in W.[ashington] is clean and honorable." As late as May 18, Painter had no news of an appointment, and was feeling hopeful that Oberly would remain in office. "My reasons?—chiefly a prophecy of my bones," he had informed Welsh. So far, he noted, there was "nothing going on in Indian Affairs but routine work."

In the end, however, Oberly was replaced by Morgan, an ordained Baptist minister, currently the principal of the State Normal School at Providence, Rhode Island.[13] Welsh informed incoming President Harrison that the IRA found Morgan, who would assume the position in late June, acceptable. Executive board member Philip Garrett was pleased with the appointment, writing Morgan that he wished to "express the extreme gratification" at his confirmation. Garrett viewed it as a "signal triumph on unworthy & sinister opposition."[14] Quinton, who had known Morgan and his wife for twenty years and had "the deepest interest and anxiety for his confirmation," had informed Welsh in early December that she and her association had been working diligently on his confirmation.[15]

As the transition from Democratic to Republican continued, Painter again complained to Welsh about Senator Dawes's actions, especially relative to the Ute bill. "Dawes will be regarded undoubtedly by the new administration as fully informed, and superlatively honest," wrote Painter on March 1, 1889. "When he says that these outside philanthropists & cracks do not know what he knows from his position," Painter continued, "there is danger that it will be accepted as true by officials who wish for a justification in turning all rascals out." He warned that more danger menaced from this situation "than from any other source." He complained that currently Dawes was refusing to listen to facts about the education appropriation bill in the House.[16]

### A Visit to the Utes

In October 1889, following his attendance at the Mohonk Conference, Painter set out for Pueblo, Colorado, to tour the Ute Reservation. He had informed Welsh in late July of his intention to do so, writing that although it would be a difficult trip, "it must be made if we are to act intelligently in this matter." Reluctant to go any earlier, he explained to Welsh that the previous tour had taken a physical toll: "I found myself quite used up by the banging I had on that southern trip." He continued, "[M]y mind & spiritual faculties seemed in a comatose state for some time after I got home, and my physical process much exhausted." So far he had made a fight against the Ute removal in general, but now he needed more facts, so this trip was crucial.[17]

On October 14 Painter headed for the Ute Agency, where he spent two days—one devoted to the issuing of rations. This gave him an opportunity to personally confer with the Indians, whom he described as seemingly unanimous in their desire to move. From there he headed to Durango, where local businessmen turned out to honor him. After spending three days at Fort Lewis, studying military maps to learn more about the proposed Utah reservation, he took the train to Montrose, where in a public meeting, he listened to the concerns of local citizens opposing removal. Weeks later, in a December 18 letter to a Mr. Raymond, Painter explained that the citizens of Montrose had wanted him to understand that the proposed reservation was not suitable if the intent of the government was to civilize the Utes. Then for the next ten days, in the company of J. M. Cunningham, manager of the Pittsburg Cattle Company, Painter traveled three hundred miles in a spring wagon to inspect the proposed reservation.[18]

Although later describing this trip as "very hard *sledding*," he would be glad he had gone. Forced to spend three nights bunking with cowboys, Painter spent another night on the floor before the fire in a Mormon cabin, and then twenty hours at a railroad section house with thirty section hands and cowboys. Accepting the kind and generous hospitality extended by both sides, he later assured Raymond that he acknowledged "no obligations to either to take their view of the situation." From questions and personal observations, Painter learned that the Indians would not be the only ones to lose from the move. He placed the monetary interest of the cattlemen grazing their herds on the proposed new reservation land at $1,137,750—the destruction of which deserved some consideration. "The whole thing is even worse than we had thought it," he informed Welsh, asking him to write Indian Commissioner Morgan and "beg him not to make the mistake of his predecessor and recommend the removal but to protest against it with all his might.[19]

As he crossed the proposed Utah reservation, Painter learned that only some five hundred out of the 3 million acres were fit for agriculture. During the mid-December IRA annual meeting, he would describe the reservation as totally unfit, for it lacked water and pasturage. Two years later the IRA would sponsor another investigative tour by younger men who spent their time on horseback; their conclusion was the same as Painter's. Both IRA tours were provided with transportation, guides, and housing by the Pittsburg Cattle Company, which grazed cattle on the proposed new reservation land and had an interest in keeping the Indians out, providing fodder for the opposition.

Painter, aware of the danger of this familiarity, explained that the association accepted all help to learn the truth.[20]

## Debating the Ute Bill

The *Durango Herald*, a supporter of Ute removal, described Painter's "cunning art of the lobbyist" as the reason for the bill's failure in the House. "We should counteract the poison of Painter that is being instilled in the minds of United States Senators and Representatives," wrote the reporter.[21] In early December 1889, Painter informed Welsh that he thought some steps should be "taken at once to stir up public sentiment against the removal of the Utes," explaining that he had been invited to speak on the subject at Germantown the following week and would be going to Brooklyn and New York as well.[22]

During January 1890 the activity intensified. On the seventeenth Painter informed Welsh that the bill was set to appear before the Senate committee in a couple of days. Later that month he described his testimony before the committee as lasting seven hours. He felt "abused and vilified by Honorable Senators and Drs. of Divinity and other Colorado magnates." He wrote Welsh that "the aggressions of Senator Teller and others upon myself personally and especially with relation to our work have been of such character that I am in some doubt as to what course I shall pursue." For the previous five or six nights, sleep had "been almost nil." On the morning of January 29 he appeared before the House Committee for several more hours totally unsupported, facing a large group in favor of the bill. Two days later in the House's committee room he met with some Durango residents, later informing Welsh he had "the pleasure of expressing" his views "in regard to the methods which some of them have seen fit to use in urging the removal of the Utes." They were "a somewhat peculiar people," he noted.[23]

Also in January, the IRA published Painter's pamphlet *Removal of the Southern Utes*, which detailed the arguments for removal most often given by the bill's supporters. These included the burden the Utes placed on the town of Durango—"a bar to its progress." The Utes were crowding the whites, and therefore their removal would "remedy all these evils, give them a home not coveted by white men, where their presence would injure no one." To gain broader support, Painter revealed that Colorado residents who bordered the new reservation protested this move and had sent in eight hundred petitions to that effect. They were joined by protesting residents of Utah Territory, who viewed "this as a wrong to be inflicted upon that territory to gratify Colorado." Furthermore, a band of renegade Paiutes occupied the intended new home; already there had been a fight between them and a band of Southern Utes. Cowboys willing to defend their grazing rights in Utah gave fair warning that military protection would be necessary to protect the Indians. Finally, some 330 bona fide miners and claim owners already occupied this proposed site, despite the Ute Commission's assurance that the government had possession of all the land.[24]

Meanwhile the debate dragged on. In March 1890 Painter again expressed his growing frustration with Dawes, describing him as dishonest and juggling with the IRA over the Ute bill. The senator claimed that for the past ten years the Utes had regressed in their Colorado reservation; all agents' reports, however, contradicted him. Painter accused Dawes of "making the failure of the Government to fulfill its promises a reason for removing them [the Utes] to lands on which it could never fulfill its promises." In response to Welsh's query about what the IRA's next move should be, Painter recommended amending the bill to provide "equitable compensation to all whose interests will be destroyed or affected by the removal." Provisions needed to be added to ensure that the "work of civilization among these Indians in their new home" was facilitated. This should include the construction of water storage facilities, irrigation projects, new agency buildings, and an army post. He assured Welsh that some senator would question "what it is all for," and he concluded, "I do not believe that any bill can be passed meeting the necessities of the case and the obligations involved if they are not fairly presented."[25]

Painter continued his efforts to defeat the bill, drafting a minority report in May 1892 for dissenting members of the House committee to present. The IRA in its annual report explained that this case was precedent-setting. If this bill were allowed to become law it would be a "very clear invitation to land grabbers elsewhere that Indian reservations are to be had for the asking." The issue would not be resolved until February 1895. Colorado had renewed its pressure upon the Utes the previous year, and although the scheme to remove them to Utah was eventually abandoned, supporters had gotten legislation introduced into Congress forcing the Indians to take their allotments on the less desirable part of their Colorado reservation. Despite Painter's best efforts, his amendments only slightly improved the legislation by allowing each Indian to either take an allotment in the eastern part of the reservation or join other Utes in the western area, holding land in common.[26]

The IRA had sent out over twenty thousand pieces of mail to protest Ute removal, as well as reports written by both Painter and Welsh, articles to friendly newspapers, statements of two to thirty pages printed in lots of fifteen hundred, and hundreds of letters written by Welsh. Literature was tailored to each audience: congressmen received one mailing, while bishops of the Episcopal and Methodist churches received a different one. Welsh continually rallied his allies.

On February 21, 1892, he requested support from Quinton, who responded: "This Ute matter makes every drop of one's blood boil with indignation & chill with grief by turns." She continued: "Was anything ever more manifestly wicked & foolish" than imprisoning "in perpetual barbarism a thousand souls!" As she had done in the past, she rallied her members, sending out letters and official WNIA leaflets to various branches and elsewhere.[27] Two years earlier her article protesting the Utes' removal from Colorado had been published in the March 20, 1890, issue of the *National Baptist*, reprinted by the WNIA as *The Ute Question*. Here she contended that the removal "would shift the evils and burdens complained of by Colorado to the unwilling shoulders of the people of Utah." She wondered if in Christian America "another native tribe of men and women can be despoiled of their rights, robbed of their homes and be driven from good land where self support and civilization with honest effort on the part of Government can be achieved to a mountain desert where civilization and civilized self support are impossible, and where a war of extermination is inevitable?"[28] Quinton's article was reprinted in the May issue of *The Indian's Friend*.[29]

## A Home for the Apaches

The struggle to save Ute lands was only one of many long-term issues Painter handled. In early May 1889 he called upon Acting Secretary of War John M. Schofield about the future of the Chiricahua Apache prisoners of war currently held by the army at Mount Vernon Barracks, Alabama. The decades-long Apache wars in the Southwest had ended in 1886 with the capture of Geronimo and his followers. Irate Arizona Territory citizens had demanded their removal, and the government sent them to different army facilities in Florida; most of the men, women, and children, some five hundred in all, initially went to Fort Marion in St. Augustine, while a smaller group of adult men, including Geronimo, went to Fort Pickens in Pensacola Bay. Partially because of Welsh and an IRA campaign, the groups had been reunited in 1888 at Mount Vernon Barracks, twenty-five miles north of Mobile Bay.[30] Welsh had taken a special interest in their welfare after meeting John G. Bourke, a captain of the Third Cavalry, then a member of General Crook's staff during an IRA-sponsored southwestern trip in 1884. Bourke transferred to Washington, D.C., at the same time the first Apache prisoners were moved to Florida, and he and Welsh cooperated to improve their circumstances. Welsh, who made an investigative tour to Fort Marion in 1887, would spend the next eight years on this project, draining IRA resources and consuming much of Painter's time.[31]

Painter had begun organizing Welsh's trip to Fort Marion in early February 1887.[32] On the eleventh, he informed Welsh that his long wait in the anteroom of Secretary of War William C. Endicott was "duly rewarded with a very long interview with that fierce divinity, who cooed as gently as a sucking dove." Endicott was willing to provide Welsh with a letter to the military officials in charge of the Apaches, granting permission to investigate their condition. However, new complications had emerged. Some people had begun to complain about the separation of Apache families, with children being sent off to Carlisle Indian School, while others complained about the "crowded and unclean condition of the Indians." Endicott reminded Painter that the government wished to educate the children but could do nothing with the adults. The IRA agent found this odd, since Captain Pratt had started his educational program with warriors from the Southern Plains tribes at Fort Marion in the mid-1870s. Painter had also inquired about "the breach of good faith by which Chato was brought on here under promise of a safe conduct." Chato, one of General Crook's Apache scouts, had been imprisoned along with the hostiles. As an assurance of the IRA's well-meaning intentions, Painter reminded Endicott that the association "had no sentimental views of the Indian question." Endicott responded that he knew both the association and Welsh "had very sound & practical ideas of the subject."[33]

Cabinet card studio photo of Chato (c. 1888–94), while a prisoner of war
in Mount Vernon Barracks in Alabama.
*Smithsonian Institution, National Museum of the American Indian, Archive Center,
Suitland, Maryland.*

In mid-March 1887, Welsh wrote Painter requesting more details, specifically, why the nonhostiles had been included in the roundup, removed from their San Carlos Reservation, and confined at federal military installations. He complained that now these able-bodied men were idle, being taught no trade or useful occupation. Were they being trained "systematically for pauperism at Government expense?" he queried. Welsh was most concerned with Chato's detention. Along with fellow scouts Martinez and Kieta, he had walked into Geronimo's camp and encouraged him to surrender.[34]

After conferring with Commissioner Atkins on March 18, 1887, and gathering information from the chief clerk of the War Department and from Secretary Endicott, Painter informed Welsh that the Indians' removal had been demanded by Arizona's citizens. Chato, who was "regarded as the most influential," had been invited along with fourteen other Apaches to Washington to talk about their possible removal to another reservation. Because of his reluctance to leave San Carlos, government officials decided they could not allow his return to the Southwest. "So the others were carefully rounded up while he was detained here at Carlisle," Painter explained. The removal was a military precaution. "I think there is no pretense that there was danger of an outbreak on his [Chato's] part, or that of his people except in view of the purpose to remove them," Painter noted. "So far as the Indians who were not hostiles are concerned this action was based on what was feared might be done by them, and not at all on what they had done."[35]

Ten days later President Cleveland informed Painter there had been insufficient time to separate the guilty from the innocent ones before removing them to Florida. "There was an urgency about it that did not admit of delay," but now that they had been moved, Cleveland did not think "there was such a crowded condition down there as to endanger health."[36] The Indians would have disagreed; even the commandant at Fort Marion said there was no room for more. Their temporary home at Fort Marion was a small fortress in a hot, humid climate—very different from their six-hundred-square-mile reservation in the dry Southwest. In early April 1887 Painter had expressed to Interior Secretary Lamar his fear that the Indians were overcrowded, and with hot weather coming, "if sickness broke out among them the Country would cry out against it." Lamar agreed to bring the issue up before his next Cabinet meeting.[37]

To secure a permanent home, Welsh had to repair relations with the well-heeled Boston Indian Citizenship Committee, still smarting over the failure of the IRA to sufficiently support its Thayer bill. The committee had agreed to find funding to purchase a home for the Indians. In the meantime Painter continued to work closely with Secretary of War Endicott, conferring with him in May of 1888 and again the following February, when he informed Welsh that the Apaches were "not in utter illness as they make their homes and cut wood." All parties involved had agreed that it was impossible to return them to San Carlos but that "adequate attempts to Christianize and civilize" them must be continued. Painter was so consumed with this and other IRA business that he was unable to take time off to attend his brother's funeral.[38]

In late May 1889, Painter conferred with General Schofield. Then, early the following month, acting for Welsh and the Boston Committee, he again met with the general, who agreed to assign an officer to accompany Painter to the Southeast to look at potential homes. On June 7, 1889, Painter informed Welsh that he was ready to go, hoping that Captain Bourke would be the general's choice. To better his chance of being selected, Bourke had written Welsh in May that he was "desirous" of being included. "There is no man in the world better acquainted with the Apaches and all that pertains to this matter of their unjust incarceration than I am," he wrote. "I may without the slightest suspicion of egotism claim the right of being assigned." Painter, whom he described as "an excellent man for such a position," had visited him that morning to inform him he would be glad to have him come and had agreed to write Welsh "a note on the subject by the first mail." The permission was granted, and Painter and Bourke were assigned to inspect the Sherwood Farm near Hampton, Virginia, which Welsh had visited earlier at General Armstrong's insistence,[39] and an eight-thousand-acre plantation near Wilmington. If neither were acceptable, they were to continue their search. Painter was dreading the fearful summer heat they would have to face.[40]

On June 18, 1889, Painter and Bourke left Washington. They followed Schofield's recommendation, conferring first with the Apaches at Mount Vernon Barracks. Chato spoke first, expressing an interest in farming. His people had successfully raised watermelons in Arizona. But he also wanted pasturage for hay, timber for cordwood, and cattle and sheep. The others agreed. Born and bred in the mountains, they also preferred a cold country where it snowed. They asked that a delegation of their people be appointed to examine any lands selected, a request that was never granted.[41]

Painter and Bourke investigated along the Georgia and Florida border and the Florida and Alabama border before entering the Eastern Cherokee Reservation in North Carolina, which Painter knew well. Bourke, in his report to the adjutant general of the army, described the reservation as incredibly beautiful and "picturesque beyond description" and its residents as attaining "a high degree of advancement." Quaker School Superintendent Henry Spray was confident that the Society of Friends would take the Chiricahuas in hand. The agent and Chief Nimrod Jarrett Smith assured Painter that the Cherokees would most likely sell the Apaches a tract of land. However, first a council had to be convened. Bourke saw possibilities in the area, with nearby Ashville, a tourist mecca with forty thousand visits the previous year and a new railroad pushing through providing a potential market for Apache produce.[42]

The third location, Bear Garden, North Carolina, north of Wilmington, was least desirable—a soggy, virgin forest with "weird and peculiar" scenery of cypress and gum tree swamps. Bourke described their fourth location, the eight-hundred-acre Sherwood Farm, as too small but nevertheless a beautiful property, with fertile soil. The nearness of the Hampton School was also an advantage. In his report of July 5, 1889, Bourke recommended either the Sherwood Farm or the Cherokee reservation, confident that within three years the Chiricahuas could become self-supporting and law abiding. Based on their information, Secretary of War Redfield Proctor concluded that the Cherokee Reservation was the best. However, the local North Carolina press voiced objection, joined soon by the state governor and local residents, all decidedly adverse to this move.[43]

By late July Painter had not yet received Bourke's report, informing Welsh that the Boston Committee would not act until it was received. "It remains to be seen whether the Com. will provide the means to purchase a home," Painter wrote. "If they do not they will have failed in the only thing they have *really done* about it." In early September Painter informed Welsh that the committee was prepared to make an offer if he and Bourke decided either on the farm near Wilmington or the Sherwood Farm near Hampton. Because

John Bourke, captain in the Third Cavalry. Description reads "only known photograph of him in civilian dress; may have been taken in Chicago in 1893 when Bourke was assigned to the Columbian Exposition."
*Nebraska State Historical Society, Lincoln.*

they had recommended the Cherokee reservation, and officials in charge of the decision making were scattered during the summer, "it was difficult to take any action" immediately. However, he informed Welsh, the Boston Committee would act soon, "and an offer is to be made to the Cherokee for a part of their land. I rather think the Committee will redeem the quasi promises they have made."[44] In the end it was not the Boston Committee that made the decision.

In his annual report Painter wrote that the North Carolina governor had finally withdrawn his opposition and that local residents were "earnestly" in favor. On March 13, 1890, Painter informed Welsh that he had received a letter from a prominent politician and businessman living near the reservation, explaining that the opposition had largely ceased and that he wished the plan would be carried out. Painter was working on a proposal when General Crook suggested to the secretary of war that the Indians be moved to Fort Sill, in the Indian Territory, purchasing land from the Kiowas and Comanches. Writing Welsh on March 11, 1890, Painter described Crook's recommendation as "unwise and ill used." There was immediate opposition, especially from General Miles, who had been in charge when Geronimo and the Chiricahuas formally surrendered. All opposition failed; the Apaches were removed to Fort Sill in October 1894.[45]

### Lake Mohonk

For Painter, fall meant the congenial atmosphere of the Mohonk Conference, which began on October 2, 1889. His address centered on problems still remaining two years after the passage of the Dawes Act. For one, the twenty-five-year trust period meant an Indian who had received his allotment still had "only the rights of a tenant" and was unable to sell his own timber. For another, citizenship did not mean a reprieve from the government agent. Chief Renville, now a citizen with an allotment, had inquired of Painter: "What is the relation of an Indian agent to a citizen of the United States and to his property?" A man claiming to be their agent was exerting the same control as was "exercised when they were Indian wards," explained Renville. Painter could only respond that the Dawes legislation was a partial measure, putting the Indian in "a most anomalous position in the extreme, and full of peril to himself." Many Mohonk attendees expressed disappointment with this flawed legislation. They were reminded of Professor Thayer's warning of unforeseen problems. His original proposal, reworked by the conference and by the best legal talent that could be found, still languished before a subcommittee, largely because of Dawes's opposition.[46]

The coming year brought Painter an ever-expanding and onerous workload, strengthening his convictions that the Indian service needed reform. He had never seen a time "when the politicians have had such an absolute disposal of position, in the Indian service at least, as now." The civilization of the Indians should not be placed at "the mercy of mere party success," he stressed. Because of flaws in the Dawes Act, Painter was forced to write or support bills to provide for leasing of Indian lands, equal allotments to each Indian, and recognition of children born of Indian marriages. He took the time in the spring of 1890 to prepare a leaflet on the value of Indian education in support of Indian Commissioner Morgan's efforts to increase congressional appropriations for education, and although he continued to hold off the passage of the Ute removal bill, he never personally had a say in a permanent home for the Chiricahuas.[47]

On January 22, 1890, Painter attended the nineteenth conference of the BIC with other representatives of missionary boards and Indian rights associations. Conference proceedings reveal minimal participation on his part. The following day he informed Welsh that he was attending Senate committee hearings on the Ute matter, which was still dragging on. Late in assembling, the committee only had time to hear those in favor of removal. They were, however, meeting again on Saturday morning, and Painter doubted if those opposed to removal would be in attendance. Painter was still concerned because President Harrison's nominee for Indian commissioner, Thomas Morgan, had not yet been confirmed. "Of course, all delay in this matter gives cause for some anxiety," he informed Welsh, "though we think his [Morgan] confirmation is certain."[48]

### A New Commissioner

When Thomas Jefferson Morgan was confirmed, he entered the office with two decades of experience. Like Painter, he was an ordained clergyman, and since 1872 he had been actively involved in education. He almost immediately turned to Painter for support of his educational program. On March 6, 1890,

Painter wrote Welsh that Morgan had asked him to rally cooperative forces to secure enlarged education appropriations. Morgan had also requested suggestions for the issuance of Indian supplies "to minimize the Indian's loss of time in securing his rations." Finding this request "of the greatest importance," Painter described Morgan as showing "an unusual grasp of the problems with which he has to deal."[49]

To support Morgan's efforts to increase educational funding, Painter wrote a lengthy letter to Bishop Walden Perkins, a Kansas Republican who served as chairman of the Indian Committee for the House of Representatives. On April 18 Painter informed Welsh that every time he returned from an interview with that committee, he experienced "a more intense feeling of utter disgust." The members could be reached only through "the public print." Therefore, with few changes, Painter had the IRA reproduce his letter to Perkins. Published on April 30, 1890, as *A Plea for Enlarged School Work*, the letter aimed to dispel rumors that Indian students educated at Carlisle and Hampton were failures, a misrepresentation that stood in the way of increased appropriations. The pamphlet explained that beginning in 1876 there had been a large annual increase in funding, but the passage of the Dawes legislation in 1887 had resulted in a 2.6% reduction. Although Painter did not spell it out, apparently some congressional members had assumed that the passage of the severalty legislation had solved the Indian problem, when in fact it had simply opened the door to citizenship, which required even more education. Painter concluded that the Indian problem must be solved "either by death or by the schoolmaster." The path out of savagery he believed led "through the school-house."[50]

To emphasize the successes of Indian education, Painter presented a statistical analysis of 293 Hampton students collected by General Armstrong. Sixty-one were deemed excellent and twenty-five unsatisfactory, with the remainder either good or fair. Most were currently employed, sixty-three working their own farms, thirty-five continuing their education, and forty-two girls married and living at home. Rather than continue the old system of "supporting them in ignorance and idleness," Painter respectfully recommended that the educational work be enlarged to include all Indian pupils. Using the analogy of a father who had ten sons, he explained that it would be best to educate all ten of them, rather than only one, giving the others "encouragement to live in ignorance and idleness" so they destroy what good the one is doing. There was no need to tentatively experiment, he wrote; if the answer is yes, than "let us take it up strongly, wisely, adequately, and do it, for thus alone can it be done economically."[51]

In June, Painter had written Welsh that Morgan was most anxious about the education funding and had asked him and the IRA for support. General Whittlesey suggested that a copy of Painter's pamphlet be given to each senator, and Painter asked Welsh to write a brief printed note to accompany each one. The pamphlet and Painter's lobbying resulted in a large increase in educational appropriations, prompting Painter to describe it as the "chief item of interest in legislative action of a favorable character" and winning him praise from Morgan when the Indian appropriation bill became law on August 20.[52]

### The Sac and Fox Reservation

Usually the fall found Painter and Martha enjoying a three-day respite at Lake Mohonk, with Martha visiting with the other wives while her husband enjoyed spirited discussions with fellow reformers. Unfortunately, in 1890 Painter spent part of September and half of October on the Sac and Fox Reservation in Kansas, overseeing an investigation at the request of Commissioner Morgan.[53] Tying up loose ends before his tour, on September 19 Painter informed Welsh that for the last several days he had been kept busy in Washington, visiting the House Indian Committee to urge the passage of the Mission Indian and Sisseton Scout bills. He had also visited Robert V. Belt, acting Indian commissioner, who agreed to give the Sisseton matter a push. Wishing Welsh a pleasant and profitable conference and regretting that he would not be attending, Painter headed for Kansas to investigate the Murphy family, who demanded to be enrolled as adopted members of the Sac and Fox tribe.[54]

This family was so large that it claimed fully one-fourth of all tribal lands. Initially, Special Agent George W. Gordon had investigated, reporting against the Murphys on September 23, 1889. Political pressure from Nebraska senators had been exerted, and Gordon's findings were set aside, prompting Painter to write that "the precedent of the office was disregarded, the express stipulations of a treaty were violated, and these claimants ordered enrolled."

Morgan, reasoning that the family was part Indian by common consent and that it was important for all Indians to receive some land, had authorized their enrollment in July 1889. Painter strongly questioned this action, for it kept the Sac and Fox "in condition of uncertainty and unrest for a whole year subjected to a great burden of expense" just because certain politicians tried to control matters that "belong exclusively to the executive department."[55]

Informed by Inspector Benjamin H. Miller that the new investigation on the Murphy claim was to begin on September 18, 1890, Painter made a hasty trip to Nebraska, arriving that night to meet Miller, whom he described as "a clever, honest fellow, but not a particularly able man." Because Interior Secretary John W. Noble had ordered Painter to give the fullest latitude to the Murphy clan, their three lawyers, and witnesses, Painter and Miller spent from September 19 to October 21 listening to all of the evidence, which when stenographically reported, covered over one thousand pages of testimony, costing the department somewhere between seven and eight hundred dollars.[56]

In early October, Painter described the investigation as "very complicated," adding that he was dragging along "wearily." He had dreaded the assignment ever since August, when Morgan first asked him to be present. At that time he had described it as "a very disagreeable job and under disagreeable circumstances."[57] Now Miller was giving the claimant's attorneys too much latitude, complained Painter. Every morning they left the Union House in Falls City, Nebraska, at seven o'clock for the eight-mile drive, returning back to their hotel before six. In his next report, on October 20, Painter informed Welsh that Miller had issued nine subpoenas for more witnesses. "It is one of the most mixed cases I have ever known," he wrote, believing it part of an organized effort by some local citizens to drive the Indians to the Indian Territory. It was too late for that, however, since the allotting agent had already completed his work. Painter was anxious to get back to Washington to push the Sisseton bill, for if it failed "there will be great suffering among these people." He also needed to be present to oppose the Ute removal bill, "for it is the hope of the Durango people to get it up if such opportunity occurs."[58]

At the conclusion of the investigation, Painter informed Welsh that Miller reported to the Interior Department that the Murphy family were not Sac and Fox and therefore had no tribal rights to property. Painter concurred "fully & unhesitatingly," sending in his own observations. Incensed with the actions of congressmen who set aside the findings and reports of government inspectors and ignored the agent's recommendations, he described the situation as intolerable.[59]

Four years later, with a new administration and strong political influence from the two Kansas senators, the family renewed their petition. The request was granted by the Interior Department, followed by a strong protest from the Indians after several family members took possession of some of the best reservation land already under cultivation. A second long investigation by Inspector Miller and Painter followed, with the same results. However, the Murphys took refuge on the surplus, unallotted land and with senatorial influence were granted a new investigation. Hoping this would be the last of the case, Painter wrote that "because of Senatorial interference on behalf of men who have not one scintilla of right to a share in this property," the Indians had been kept in a constant turmoil and forced to bear "a heavy pecuniary expense to defend themselves against the loss of fully one-third of their entire property." Ultimately political pressure prevailed, and a bill compelling the family's enrollment was introduced. The family also filed a suit in the U.S. District Court, resulting in eight thousand dollars in legal fees for the Sac and Fox. A disgusted Painter concluded in his 1894 report that no one could "doubt that briefless shysters will instigate suits all over the country, and Indians be induced, by fear, to employ counsel for defense," knowing that the federal district attorney will not give adequate defense.[60]

## A Return to the Indian Territory

Leaving the Sac and Fox Reservation in late October 1890, Painter toured the neighboring Iowa and Pottawatomie reservations, finding the Iowa school buildings in need of repair. In a civilized community, he reported, the dormitory would have been condemned. He toured Haskell Institute, which earned his high praise, and then headed for the Indian Territory. His last visit had been six years earlier, and to his pleasure he found great improvement in Muscogee—wooden shanties replaced by comfortable block houses, a fine hotel, and a girls' school efficiently run by a Miss Robertson. He described her young Creek and Cherokee students as "the founders of homes such as in time will redeem this territory from its semi-barbaric condition." He was displeased with the local justice system, blaming Congress for bungling the

legislation of U.S. courts when they created the Territory of Oklahoma. Under
territorial laws, a citizen of any of the Civilized Tribes could become a U.S.
citizen without forfeiture of any Indian rights of citizenship. A number of
Indians had done so, thereby removing themselves and their property from
under the protection of Indian law. The Choctaw had disenfranchised those
of its tribal members who had taken this path. Painter was concerned with
the inevitable conflict that would arise between the two legal systems.[61]

Painter found much to praise during his visit to the Modocs. They had
adjusted well, even on Quapaw land, which Painter had originally described
as "the malaria plains of the Indian Territory" and where many Modocs had
died following their removal from California and Oregon. He found them to
be quiet and dignified, the Quakers having done an excellent job of Christianizing and civilizing them. At the Osage Agency, Painter investigated a
claim that students returning from Carlisle had readopted their old way of
life almost immediately; none could speak English. He easily contradicted
this claim, which had originated in an unidentified New York newspaper.
There were no returning graduates from Carlisle among the Osage, and those
who had attended other off-reservation boarding schools did speak English.
He did find, however, a deterioration of their condition since his last visit,
blaming it on the quality of government employees. In Arkansas City, Painter
encountered Commissioner Morgan and his wife and accompanied them
to Chilocco Indian School, which he found much improved in cleanliness.
Morgan was on an official tour of reservation schools in the Indian Territory
and in Southern California, with the goal of locating a site for an Indian
training school among the Mission Indians.[62]

Painter was disappointed when he arrived among the Southern Cheyennes
and Southern Arapahos, finding no visible change in their progress since his
visit three years earlier. Farms were neglected, partially, he later explained to
Welsh, because of a Messiah dance (Ghost Dance) such as one he had witnessed at Fort Reno. Desperate to save their nomadic way of life, the Indians
had turned to Jack Wilson, or Wovoka, a Paiute who taught them a dance
that, with regular performance, would cause the whites to disappear and
the buffalo and ancestors to return. During his visit, however, Painter found
no "cause for alarm." What he did find was neglected farms, an abominable
government school among the Cheyennes, and a painful and discouraging

"lack of facilities for doing good work." The bright spot was the Mennonite school, which was doing first-class work.[63]

Painter left the Indian Territory on November 6, planning to take a hack to the Osage Agency. In a letter sent from Baxter Springs, Kansas, he complained of bowel troubles, blaming his condition on the local water. During the eighteen-mile drive that day, he had suffered greatly from the jostling. Earlier in the week he had endured a sixty-mile drive over some of the roughest roads he had ever attempted, forcing him for the next two and a half days to eat "only a little thicken milk or a glass of milk and a few mouthfuls of corn bread."[64] His investigative tours were taking a toll on the fifty-seven year old lobbyist, whose letters began to reflect more health issues. Despite his infirmities, Painter had on this tour visited more than a dozen reservations, all of the reservation day schools, and the industrial boarding schools at Lawrence and Chilocco, at the latter finding a vast improvement in the personnel.[65]

## An Unforeseen Uprising

After almost two and a half months in the field, Painter, who had taken a bad cold and developed a severe abscess in his middle ear, finally reached home in time for Thanksgiving dinner. On November 28, he informed Welsh that his wife had not forwarded Welsh's latest letter, which had suggested the "propriety" of going to Dakota Territory to look into the probabilities of an outbreak among the Sioux. "I do not believe, or have I believed that the Indians contemplated an outbreak," he now wrote. He was not anticipating one unless white citizens and soldiers engaged in "foolish behavior." He compared the dances and attendant frenzy he witnessed with "the excitement of a Methodist Camp Meeting." He saw only Indians dancing and whirling around "until they [fell] in a swoon in which they have visions of Christ, of their dead, of the coming good time which is soon to come to them." On his earlier visit to the Cheyenne and Arapaho Reservation, he had found the Indians "as they had been for months in the full frenzy of this religious Craze, and after investigation, having all [his] impressions in regard to it fully confirmed, [he] decided that there was no need of [him] going" to Dakota. By this time, his ear, which had been troubling him for the past two years, was so painful that he was fearful he would end up with an abscess. He was in no condition to investigate the situation among the Sioux, although he later wrote that had he received Welsh's letter and if he "felt equal to the task," he would have gone.[66]

On December 2 Painter again reassured Welsh that "the danger of an outbreak lies with the whites rather than with the Indians," although he prefaced his statement with a disclaimer that no one could tell what an "individual much less what a whole people under increased religious excitement may do." He concluded that "no one who knows anything of the present religious craze, its origin and its hopes for issue will entertain the slightest apprehension that it will provoke an outbreak." However, to reassure himself, on December 13 he met with both the adjutant general of the army and with Indian Office officials and found no serious apprehension among them that there was trouble. He was satisfied that no one need investigate. The army had put on a drill, and various commanders had gotten together, which he thought "a good thing to do." He informed Welsh that IRA President James Rhoads should feel assured that "no harm [was] coming to the Indians," or to the IRA. Painter's opinion never changed. In a March 1893 pamphlet he would write, "in all this there was no threat or danger of outbreak, for explicit as was the assurance that the whites were to be destroyed was also the command that they were to do no violence themselves, even if they were wronged by those who were doomed to speedy destruction."[67]

Painter was not the only contemporary observer who held this opinion. Elaine Goodale [Eastman], the first supervisor of education for the Sioux, had initially visited their reservation in 1885. Years later she wrote that she had ignored the scaremongers and set out with her camp outfit on a second inspection tour of the dozen or so camp day schools. One evening in November she had joined a group of spectators, the only non-Indian, and witnessed a dance performance. In her memoirs she explained that none of the missionaries, who knew the temper of the people, "had the least fear of an uprising. We who loved them moved among them as freely and with as much confidence as ever."[68]

No one could have anticipated what happened next. Like other Plains tribes, the Sioux were faced with the destruction of their nomadic way of life and forced to live on small reservations, and so they had adopted the Ghost Dance. As the frenzy increased, Daniel F. Royer, the inexperienced, newly appointed agent at Pine Ridge, demanded more troops. Their arrival exacerbated the situation, sending many hundreds of Sioux to the Badlands. Then, on December 15, 1890, two days after Painter's reassuring letter to Welsh, Hunkpapa Medicine Man Sitting Bull was killed by Indian police while being arrested. Two weeks later, on December 29, members of the Seventh Cavalry fired into a camp of Miniconjou Sioux at Wounded Knee, killing hundreds. This escalating crisis among the Sioux had gone virtually unnoticed by the IRA until that November. Welsh later attributed much of the unrest to the spoils system and its appointment of inexperienced agents, a lack of education, and the government's failure to fulfill obligations of the agreement that had reduced the Great Sioux Reservation.[69]

James Thayer weighed in on the massacre in a letter to the editor of *The Nation*, reprinted in *The Indian's Friend*. Continually promoting his courts bill, he described the "shameful, dreadful business" of the massacre as the "natural fruit of the blundering mismanagement and corruption which always have been and always will be inevitable in undertaking to govern Indians *without law* by a set of politicians at Washington." He queried: Why should the country "be carrying on 'war' with a handful of people—people who are absolutely under their control?" And why were these people not "incorporated into our political system a long time ago?" He concluded that "the whole miserable system of governing the Indians and administering their property without the ordinary legal responsibility should end at once."[70]

Over the previous two years Painter had faced new challenges, including a protracted struggle to prevent the removal of the Southern Utes. He had also faced failure. Despite his tours of potential homes for the Chiricahua Apaches, it would be military officials, not Painter, who made the decision. He had also been unsuccessful in thwarting the Murphy clan's assault on Sac and Fox lands. The next year, 1891, would be unlike any other in his decade-long employment with the IRA. Instead of his usual work—lobbying before Congress, interacting with Indian Office officials, and dealing with potential removals or timber rights—Painter would spend almost the entire year in Southern California as a member of the California Mission Indian Commission, surveying isolated Indian villages and making decisions that forever altered the lives of these Indians.

# CHAPTER 7

# THE CALIFORNIA MISSION INDIAN COMMISSION, 1891

In early June 1891, Painter informed Interior Secretary John Noble that during the surveying undertaken by the California Mission Indian Commission at San Jacinto, he had discovered an Indian family, headed by one Mariano Leon, living in a canyon off the reservation. "They had a good spring, some excellent land, vineyards 15 years old, fine peach orchards, and other fruits" and had lived there for decades. "I am having a supplementary survey made," Painter concluded; "his home, and the labors of these years must be secured to him." This discovery was one of many that he made during his almost year-long commission work, which required him to travel long distances under difficult conditions. In an August 10 letter to Indian Commissioner Morgan he wrote, "I reached here on Sat. evening, being the 22nd day of continuous travel, during which time I traveled some 500 miles by wagon and horseback." For seven nights in a row he had slept on the ground rolled up in his blanket.[1] The California Mission Indian Commission was successful only because he endured such hardships, staying behind when the other commissioners temporarily returned home. As a result at least thirteen new executive order Mission Indian reservations were created; most of which still exist today.[2]

Painter's year had begun with his attendance on January 8, 1891, at the annual BIC conference with the secretaries of religious societies. During his short address he spoke of the importance of "compulsory education as indispensable to qualify" Indian children for citizenship while condemning the continuation of the reservation system as one of the strongest impediments to this goal. "The work can be done when you get them away from that, but then you thrust them back into these conditions and much of the work seems for a time to be lost"—a reference to the complaint that after leaving boarding school many students often returned to their "tepees and blankets." "We must have a system that will take this out of the control of politicians and make it a civilizing bureau," he concluded, preaching another of his goals, that of making the Indian Office a separate entity.[3] Several weeks later he noted there was no question but that it should be reconstructed. It was too "cumbersome at present, beyond any reasonable degree of efficiency."[4]

Five days later Painter wrote Welsh that the BIC had "urged & petitioned the President [Harrison] to extend the Civil Service rules over the Indian Department." Although both men favored this reform, Painter noted it was doubtful whether the president could do so with the position of Indian agent, although he could certainly apply such rules to other employees and could "require that these shall satisfy him of their fitness before he nominates them." Therefore, Painter advised Welsh to appeal to friends and organizations, encouraging them to visit the president and overwhelm him with letters and petitions. Painter also lamented that the current amount of work dumped on him had become discouraging, especially because he could not find a typewriter or a stenographer.[5] This was not his only concern. At month's end, he wrote that the temper of both houses was "getting to be quite ugly, politically, and it begins to look as if nothing would be done and a called session would be inevitable."[6]

### The Mission Indian Bill

Education and remodeling the Indian Office was pushed from Painter's concerns on January 12, 1891, when Congress passed the "Act for the Relief of the Mission Indians in the State of California."[7] For years he had closely watched its annual submission. The previous March he had described its fate in the hands of the Senate and Senator Dawes, whom he had accused of unwisely striking out amendments that both he and the Indian Office had suggested. Dawes had fallen back upon the original bill, "counting for naught events that have transpired since its introduction and necessities which grow out of the relations which Indian reservations and Indian property sustain to the interests of the whites," complained Painter. In mid-December, Painter had informed Welsh that the Mission Indian Bill passed and that Frank Lewis had been notified of his appointment as special counsel. "I took up the case of these Mission Indians in 1885 when it had greatly defaulted and had been abandoned," Painter reminded Welsh, and he wanted to be appointed to the commission that would implement the legislation. "I feel that it is due me, and the memory of Mrs. Jackson whose work I took from her hands, that I have such a place." He believed that the Boston Indian Citizenship Committee would support him.[8] On January 20, he informed Welsh that Secretary Noble had queried him on the intent of the Mission Indian bill and what he knew about these Indians, and that Commissioner Morgan wanted him appointed to the commission. Days later he wrote that Noble had sent for him for a two o-clock meeting, and he presumed that meant Noble had accepted the commissioner's recommendation. Painter volunteered that General Whittlesey, Noble, and the Boston Committee were all "very urgent" that he go. "I confess to a feeling, that under the circumstances, I ought."[9]

The legislation called for the appointment of three disinterested persons to the Interior Department's California Mission Indian Commission to select reservations for each band or village of Mission Indians, to include their actual lands and villages where practical. Upon completion and acceptance by the interior secretary, patents were to be issued to each reservation to be held in trust for twenty-five years. At the discretion of the interior secretary, reservation lands could be allotted to those Indians found capable. Painter was appointed as disbursing officer, with fellow commissioner Albert Smiley, who had made his first visit to the Mission Indians in 1884 for the BIC, as chairman.[10] The third member, Joseph B. Moore, was a judge on the Sixth Judicial Circuit Court from Lapeer, Michigan.[11] According to the *San Francisco Chronicle*, including a lawyer had been deemed essential because much of the commission's work was "of a legal nature."[12]

Commission members were to be paid eight dollars per day when employed, along with necessary traveling expenses. Painter explained to Welsh that this was about equal to his current pay from the IRA. "Of course there is no pecuniary inducement for me to go," he noted, "except my great desire to see this work rightly done." He concluded: "I simply go at government expense to do what I would probably have gone at our own (IRA) expense to *look after*." He wanted to take Martha with him and inquired of Welsh if it would be unreasonable for him to ask for his IRA salary to continue.[13] In the end Painter went to California alone.

Judge Joseph Moore, lawyer in Lapeer, Michigan, and member of the
California Mission Indian Commission. Photograph by Century
Publishing and Engraving, Chicago.
*Michigan Historical Collections, Bentley Historical Library,*
*University of Michigan.*

On January 24, 1891, Painter described his physical condition as somewhat
dilapidated. His gymnastic rubber strap had slipped, and the end had struck
the corner of his eye. He was less concerned about his eye injury, however,
than he was about missing the upcoming annual IRA meeting because of
his recent appointment. If able to attend, he would confine his remarks to
his field observations and to the deterioration of the Washington system that
controlled the Indian service. He was pleased to announce that the House
committee's appropriation bill included an increase of fifty thousand dollars
for school purposes, with an additional one hundred thousand dollars to
enlarge and improve the Chilocco School and the building of a new Indian
boarding school in Phoenix. Most importantly, Interior Secretary Noble had
expressed himself as being in "favor of making the Bureau independent,

of his Department." That same day when writing of Noble's plan to Henry Pancoast, head of the IRA Law Committee, Painter commented that he hoped "we sentimentalists and philanthropists may stand along with these practical statesmen and politicians" and cooperate in some sort of reform of the administration of Indian affairs.[14]

On January 28 Painter wrote that he had received his commission and instructions, and because he was not expected to report to San Francisco until February 23, he could finish up several projects and attend the annual meeting. Partially because President Harrison had signified his willingness to consider extending the Civil Service rules to the Indian Office and Secretary Noble was ready to cooperate to make the Indian Office more independent, Painter proposed that a conference be held in Welsh's office in Philadelphia on February 5 or 6 with members of the IRA, the BIC, the WNIA, and the Boston Indian Citizenship Committee to make a plan of action to "secure one or two points, vital to the reform which we are seeking." Particularly eager to hold this conference, he referred to it in both his January 30 and January 31 letters, indicating a time of three o'clock for the meeting. No further reference to it was made; it is unknown whether such a meeting was ever held.[15]

Before leaving for California, Painter addressed another crisis. In late January, Joshua Davis inquired about the fifteen hundred Sissetons (Dakota) of North Dakota who were starving. He needed the details before he began a formal appeal for money. Painter assured him that the commissioner had sufficient money for their temporary relief. Already three thousand dollars had been sent, with seven thousand still available. The "practical thing to do, and most urgent," Painter later informed Welsh, was to "stir up the public mind in this point" and bring pressure to bear upon the House to take up and pass the Sisseton-Wahpeton scout bill.[16] Painter had been working on behalf of these scouts since 1888, when Gabriel Renville first visited him in Washington, but this more serious situation had only recently been exposed by former cavalry officer Henry Guy Carleton in a January 23 *Chicago Daily Tribune* article. Carleton had been commissioned by the *New York World* to comb through official records and interview various individuals to learn the cause of the present distress of various tribes, including the Sioux, whose rations had recently been severely reduced. While he was conferring with Commissioner Morgan, a dispatch arrived from the office of North Dakota

Congressman Henry C. Hansbrough, imploring that food be provided for the Sisseton Sioux near Watertown, South Dakota. Their crops had failed, and they were "starving and turbulent." Carleton had just learned that, from an agreement of December 12, 1889, the government still owed the Indians money for sale of their surplus land.[17] It is unknown whether Carleton's article had any impact, but on March 3, 1891, after years of lobbying by Painter and the IRA, Congress finally passed a bill for the relief of the Sisseton-Wahpeton scouts.[18]

### The Commission

As members of the California Mission Indian Commission, Painter, Smiley, and Moore faced an immense task. Not only were they ordered to create new reservations for some one thousand Indians, but they were obligated to visit the twenty existing reservations to ensure that all lands described in the original executive orders had been included. They also had to visit all villages, estimated by Mission Agent Horatio Rust at thirty-seven; appraise the value of the settlers' improvements on Indian lands; define the boundaries of those occupying lands on confirmed private grants and locate vacant public lands upon which to settle them; and arrange a complicated exchange of lands for those Indians living on lands granted to the Southern Pacific Railroad by the federal government.[19]

Working with a surveyor, the commission was to define boundaries of selected tracts and check previous surveys at the local land office. Because this commission was not being paid as much as those in the past, Painter informed Morgan that he was fearful that the ten-thousand-dollar appropriation would soon be exhausted and the work left unfinished. He reminded Morgan there were twenty reservations to survey, as well as "isolated tracts of land claimed by Indians under old Mexican grants," and new lands to select.[20]

Secretary Noble had suggested that the commissioners gather in San Francisco on February 23, but unusually heavy rains had caused washouts and destroyed railroad tracks in Southern California, making it impossible for Smiley to come up from Redlands, where he had recently retired. Instead Painter and Moore traveled to him, and on March 6 they held their first formal meeting; according to Smiley's *Account*, Painter had dined the evening before at the Smiley residence. The commission's first visit was to the village of San Manuel, near San Bernardino, where they investigated the claim of

Map of Mission Indian villages. Map illustration by George W. Ward.

one Paul Wiese. On April 3 Painter wrote Welsh that they had secured a section of public land for six or eight Indian families—land they had been living on before being driven away and their homes burned. During their survey the commissioners had discovered some eleven unclaimed acres adjoining this section.[21]

Months later they revealed more details about what they found in San Manuel. The land in question was broken and mountainous, with timber and pasture and only about thirty acres of arable land. Eight families had lived there for some thirty years in comfortable homes surrounded by a small orchard of grape vines and fruit trees watered by a spring. In 1888 a settler named John Smithline took forcible possession of part of their land, burning their fences and corrals and threatening to shoot them if they returned. Two years later he sold his claim for $150 to Wiese, who was living there at the time of the commission's visit. Wiese agreed to give up possession, and the commissioners recommended paying him two hundred dollars for his improvements. They had the section surveyed, requested the inclusion of 11.58 acres, which they declared "free from objection," and recommended the combined area be set aside as an executive order reservation.[22]

On March 16 the commissioners informed Noble they were facing a complicated situation at the Morongo Reservation near Banning. In their April 1 report, they described driving around the reservation for three days, exploring its canyons and water sources, before holding a conference with a number of Indians on March 16. In the canyon above the village of Potrero, located at the canyon's mouth, a number of white settlers were residing on odd-numbered sections, claiming that the land belonged to the Southern Pacific Railroad. They had developed water rights deemed essential for Indian use. The commissioners listed Richard Gird, John G. North, and C. F. and Margaret Jost as the most important claimants.[23] In their December 19 report, they explained that the Josts had settled there some years ago and had made valuable improvements. Gird and North, also acquiring their interest some time before, had built irrigation ditches at the upper end of the canyon, planting alfalfa and putting in an orchard. Although all parties had since been evicted, Gird and North had commenced a suit to recover damages and determine their rights to both water and land.[24]

The Banning Water and Improvement Company, through its president, Charles O. Barker, had options on these Morongo claims and was willing to trade them for even sections of desirable barley land within the reservation. Barker's scheme, if he could accomplish it, would "put the reservation all together & would supply it with an adequate amount of water for all purposes including irrigation." Although the commissioners did not think that proposition was fair enough for the Indians, they believed it desirable to make some sort of arrangement along those general lines. Doubting their authority to exchange lands, they requested instructions from Noble, by telegraph because of time constraints. If they had the power to compromise and exchange, they had no doubt of "their ability to so arrange the Banning Reservation as to make a permanent & satisfactory settlement." On April 1, Acting Indian Commissioner Robert Belt responded that the Mission Indian Relief Act gave them "ample authority to effect the change suggested" and that past executive orders had set aside lands that were not occupied or needed by the Indians, while other lands which they actually occupied had been excluded.

Mission Indian Camp at Palm Springs, California.
*A. K. Smiley Public Library, Redlands, California.*

Their job was "to ascertain exactly what lands the Indians do occupy and need, what they do not occupy or need, and to include the former, as far as possible . . . and to exclude the latter."[25]

Awaiting Noble's instructions, the commissioners drove through the Morongo Reservation across the desert to Agua Caliente (today's Palm Springs), which they toured with considerable care, gathering information about the valuable hot spring and holding a conference at the village with Captain Jose Rafael and at the nearby village of Rincon with the local captain and his small band. They then headed to Indio to confer with the local Indians. No one showed up because the Indian messenger had failed to send out notification in sufficient time. Based on their current information, the commissioners thought it best to confer with Special Counsel Frank Lewis and attorney Shirley Ward in Los Angeles before heading to San Diego. To become thoroughly acquainted with the terrain and the village condition, on March 24 they traveled by rail to Lakeside, switching to a wagon. For the next five days they journeyed over mountainous roads to Capitán Grande, the Santa Ysabel grant, and then on to Warner Ranch to visit the villages of Agua Caliente, Mataguay, and San Jose. From there they drove south to Santa Ysabel and Mesa Grande reservations, and finally Sycuan—all villages identified by Helen Hunt Jackson and Abbot Kinney in their government report of 1883. The commissioners informed Noble they had "endeavored to learn all [they] could at these various places with a view of taking intelligent action."[26]

On April 3 Painter informed Commissioner Morgan that Smiley, Moore, and Lewis, along with the interpreter/driver, had set out on a week-long, two-hundred-mile carriage ride over rough roads to visit Soboba, Cahuilla, Pechanga, Pala, Pauma, Rincon, and La Jolla, as well as the Indians living near San Luis Rey. At the tour's end, they intended to consult with Agent Rust. Painter had remained behind not only to complete a report but because he was already familiar with these villages, and the carriage was too small. Furthermore, they had agreed to divide the work to save time and money, with Painter charged with locating a reliable surveyor and holding an Indian council in Indio.[27]

Completing his tasks, Painter headed for the desert, where on April 7 he met with thirty-six representatives from Torres (Torres-Martínez), Cabezon, and neighboring villages and camps. He described them as "jubilant with the hope that they [were] to have lands assigned to them." He then toured another half dozen villages, conferring with village captains representing some four hundred Indians. Because he was unsure whether they were living on lands actually reserved for them, he requested permission to do a survey. Coming together at Colton on April 13, the commission split again, with Moore, Smiley, and Lewis continuing on to San Francisco to interview Southern Pacific Railroad officials regarding the exchange of railroad lands within the Morongo Reservation. On May 5 Painter informed Noble that his current task was to check out the references of certain surveyors, which required a trip to Oceanside, San Diego, and San Jacinto. Once the interviews were completed, Painter selected two men "whose ability, integrity, and industry" were satisfactory. Edward L. Dorn of Escondido would go to the desert while R. M. Vail would accompany him to San Jacinto.[28]

### The Lone Commissioner

The commissioners were no longer young men. Moore was in his late forties, Painter in his late fifties, and Smiley a decade older. One was afflicted by lumbago, presumably Smiley, while the other two had contracted *la grippe* (influenza), with Painter writing about two serious attacks. Furthermore, the field work was arduous, taking them over long, winding roads through mountainous countryside to isolated villages without adequate accommodations. Questions continually arose that forced them to engage in a flurry of letters to Noble and Morgan. Only eight weeks into their work, Smiley and Moore decided to return home—Moore's departure hastened by an illness in his family and Smiley's because of commitments at Lake Mohonk.

In an April 1 letter to Noble, Smiley wrote that he had accepted his appointment before actually reading the legislation, initially understanding that "its scope extended only to the settlement of the Banning Indian Reservation." He was now aware that he could not "give *continuous* work till the close of the labors of the Commission." He intended to leave California around the first of May, returning at the end of October. Moore, who wanted to return to Michigan at the end of April, requested a permanent release, but Smiley wrote Noble that both he and Painter believed that the success of their work depended upon Moore's presence. Describing him as a "man of quick perceptions, and sound judgment" who had already "gained a pretty thorough knowledge of the situation," Painter and Smiley would need the benefit of his sound judgment before writing the final report. Smiley believed that the work could be "carried on most economically and satisfactorily" by Painter, aided by a surveyor and Lewis, whom he described as a most competent and valuable assistant. It was agreed that in the autumn the three would meet in California and "arrive at an intelligent judgment based on a full knowledge of details." Painter had reasoned that if all three remained during the summer, the funding would be exhausted.[29]

Smiley and Moore were granted their leaves until early November; the work to be continued by Painter and Lewis, who had finally received his official appointment as commission clerk.[30] Although the younger man more than pulled his own weight, Painter, as the only formal member of the commission, bore the brunt of the stress and responsibility. Headquartered at the Hotel Glenwood in Riverside, on April 20 he wrote that Moore had left that day, with Smiley leaving soon. He himself would leave the following day for San Jacinto. "I have a long, hard pull before me," he noted. Earlier in the month he had informed Welsh that it would be up to him and Lewis to continue to gather all the facts, push the surveys, "and have things in shape for the intelligent action" when Smiley and Moore returned to complete the report. It was fortunate "that one of our Association was put on the Commission as a permanent quantity, otherwise we do not know into what shape matters may drift." Although he dreaded the long summer's work and absence from home, they had come so far, "and having now a good prospect of securing in some degree the objectives for which we have sought, it would seem foolish and childish to give it up before it is finished." Painter was also fearful he would lose financially. He had dropped his official IRA work on February 20, although he continued to write Welsh from the field on various issues. Now earning only half his usual IRA salary, he had already experienced great expense during his two episodes of *la grippe.*[31]

Painter spent a week in the Los Angeles land office, making notes of the surveys. "This preliminary work has been tedious," he wrote Noble, "but I feel that I am now getting it well in hand." He already had a map and field notes of former surveys to give to Vail, whom he was meeting on May 6 at San Jacinto. To Morgan he wrote that he expected to spend a week with the surveyor so he could fully learn the character of the land and what sections could be traded with the railroad. He intended to remove as many of the "odd sections and fractional sections so as to avoid a deal" with them. According to his published IRA report, negotiations with the Southern Pacific was made more complicated because the land granted the railroad by the government was mortgaged and held under a deed of trust, "the terms of which prohibited the road from parting with them except for cash." And the commission had no cash. Furthermore, settlers had moved onto this railroad land, making improvements and acquiring valuable water rights.[32]

Although intent on his commission work, Painter did not ignore his uncompleted IRA business. In mid-May he informed Welsh that he had received the extracts from the *Durango Herald* relating to the Ute issue and believed that "the Chief danger lies in the proposed visit by Dawes to the Country." He explained, "If he [Dawes] goes out under Teller's lead, chaperoned by the Durango people, he may say he has found good reasons for the removal." Dawes was preparing to show he had been deceived by those who opposed it. A month later Painter assured Welsh that the association's two leaflets against Ute removal sufficiently brought the discussion up to date. The only solution was to allot Ute lands in Colorado and then force the Interior Department to fulfill prior treaties, build schools, and issue farm equipment.[33]

During Painter's absence, the IRA had continued its campaign against Ute removal. The *Herald* was not the only paper critical of its position. The *Colorado Sun* described the association as having "a fixed, unconquerable, vindictive, vicious determination to keep the Utes in this State," claiming it was "a strangely misnamed society" that had never even built a church or a school for the Indians, only interfered in Indian affairs "in an officious, meddlesome, hurtful and seemingly malicious way," and had too much influence with the current administration. The IRA reprinted the article as an example of "a fair illustration of the kind of argument employed to justify the Ute Removal."[34]

Painter had sent the second surveyor, Edward Dorn, to the desert near Indio, and by early June he was having difficulty establishing the boundary lines because the corners established during the previous survey had been removed. Painter was forced to assist in a lengthy search in the foothills before they discovered one of the original corners. Those stakes were "in a marvelous state of preservation considering the fact that they were placed some 35 years ago," noted Painter dryly. Furthermore, they were redwood, which had not been imported into Southern California until recently. Obviously, Painter concluded, the original surveyor who had platted out the town site "had followed his own imagination or the will of the employer, and put his lines and corners to suit the needs of the town site," especially in reference to the railroad hotel and the station house. They also learned that the town site of Indio had been built largely on a section previously set aside for the Indians, and therefore they were not living on lands reserved for them. And they refused to move. "These difficulties have made tedious and expensive the surveys I have been compelled to make," Painter wrote Noble. The Indians were not the only ones alarmed about the possibility of moving. White residents who had built homes and businesses on the reservation were also concerned. "It will be a great boon not alone to the Indians but to the Whites when these questions are finally settled," Painter wrote Welsh. Not looking forward to his upcoming week in the desert, Painter expected great discomfort and hardship. Several weeks previously the temperatures there had stood at 100 degrees, and the hot weather had not started yet.[35]

Fortunately, Vail's seventeen-day-long survey at San Jacinto had gone smoothly, and he was now off to the Cahuilla Reservation. During their work, Painter and Vail had found Mariano Leon and his family living in a small canyon off the Soboba Reservation. Since they had been there for years, Painter ordered a supplementary survey, explaining to Noble that their home and their labor must be secured. In all his surveys, primarily because of the desert terrain, Painter was taking steps to have all available water secured for Indian use, a task made difficult because water filings had to be made following immediate use. Because it would take time for the Indians to come into possession of their new reservation lands, white settlers in the meantime could easily file.[36]

Painter's use of surveys was questioned by officials. On May 11 he wrote Secretary Noble, asking "that certain Reservations be allotted at once, and the surveys be made out of funds appropriated for such work." On June 9 Morgan accused him of exceeding "the scope of [his] authority in the matter of surveys." Ever the diplomat, Painter explained that since the Indians had "reached the limit of possible progress under a tribal arrangement of land tenure," the next step was allotment. It was unwise to select land without knowledge of exact boundaries or whether it was government or railroad land. The Southern Pacific had been awarded alternate sections along the track line, much of which was still not surveyed. However, even surveyed lands posed a problem because wood thieves changed corners, requiring new surveys. Painter concluded his letter with the suggestion that the reservations of Rincon, Pechanga, and La Jolla be allotted immediately, "independently of the question" of extending the commission's ten-thousand-dollar fund. Five days later he again repeated the need to allot these reservations, stressing that "the limit of progress has been about reached under a tribal tenure of land." He had been prompted to do so by an inquiry from Agent Rust, who was building a new school house at La Jolla and needed to know exactly where the Indians were to be located.[37]

Painter's request for allotment slowly moved through the chain of command. Not until October did Acting Interior Secretary George Chandler forward Assistant Attorney General George H. Shields's opinion on the matter to Commissioner Morgan, who believed that allotments could not be made until the commissioners had completed their task and the reservations were patented. Earlier in July, Shields had advised the interior secretary that he saw no legal reason why patents could not be issued before the commission completed its duties. Chandler concurred. However, not until 1893 would Rincon become the first Mission Indian reservation allotted, divided into fifty-one parcels.[38]

In early July Painter informed Noble that the desert surveys were completed. The forty-five days required to do so had "been attended with great hardships to all engaged," with temperatures soaring to 110 degrees in the shade, little water, and extreme difficulties in procuring supplies. To get to Twenty-Nine Palms, they had to travel on horseback for nearly fifty miles, although they found "a small, but old Indian settlement—good water and a sufficiency of good land." At Torres they found a thrifty Indian village of some seventy people with fifty head of stock, running water, and "some very good houses, fruit trees and alfalfa fields—gardens and grain fields." Painter noted that although the amount of land was insufficient to meet the requirements of the Dawes Act, or even the needs of these people, there was enough neighboring land to give them. At the Cabezon Reservation, they found no Indians and no water. The son of old chief Cabezon and some of his followers had been living on another section, watered by inferior wells. Painter described the area as worthless.[39]

For six weeks Painter had supervised the two surveyors, traveling back and forth between San Jacinto, Indio, and the Government Land Office in Los Angeles to check on field notes and older surveys. He meticulously described each Indian group encountered: their numbers; names of their headmen; their employment, whether ranch work or shoveling coal for the railroad; the condition of their lands, whether it included sufficient water; legal actions to be taken, including requests that Lewis bring suit to cancel specific land filings by white settlers; suggestions for exchanges or additions; and recommendations reserving certain sections for Indian use. He also requested that specific sections containing some Indian homes be withdrawn from the public domain and set aside for Indian use when the villagers did not want to remove to a reservation. Painter had systematically set aside a total of 16,680 acres for the 320 to 370 desert Indians, "who have never received any attention from the government." Although this was primarily desert land, he hoped that with water, some areas might be arable. At present there were no filings on any of this land, and little of it was around springs, which might tempt white men to drive in cattle. Painter requested that Noble reserve these sections for Indian use. Bragging a bit to Welsh, Painter wrote in a July 1 letter that "there shall be little need for our work here when I get through, unless it be to look after the allotments when they come to be made."[40]

On August 10 Painter informed Commissioner Morgan that for twenty-two consecutive days he had travelled some five hundred miles by wagon and horseback, ninety-five of those over mountainous Indian trails. At one point the fifty-eight year old commissioner had been forced to sleep on the ground wrapped in a blanket for seven straight nights, taking his meals with various Indians "or, worse, in the houses of white frontiersmen." His first day of rest was a Sunday, and it "was not broken by attendance upon church service: a more thoroughly wearied man never loafed through the quiet of a Sabbath on the beach," noted the cleric turned reformer. During this arduous trip, he had visited nineteen small reservations and villages and three families living on public land overlooking Santa Ysabel. After a quick trip to San Diego, he informed Morgan he was off again to visit another small group of Indians, accessible only by trail, and then on to Rincon, Pauma, Pala, and Pechanga, returning to the agency at Colton.[41]

For three weeks in September and October, Painter traveled—to Santa Barbara, Santa Ynez, San Luis Obispo, and San Francisco—looking up old records along the way. "If this work had been done several years since these poor Indians would have been made secure in the possession of some of the very best land in the state," he wrote Welsh. Painter also explained that when he received Smiley's letter stating he could not return to California until the first of December, he vigorously protested, as would Martha when she saw Smiley at the October Lake Mohonk Conference. Because a new Congress would be formed in December with the election of a speaker and the selection of various committees, Painter asked Welsh to inform Smiley that he had to return to California earlier. "I want to be through with this work, and within easy reach of Washington when Congress meets in Dec.," he wrote. Painter's indignation and Welsh's intervention succeeded in forcing both Smiley and Moore to return by the first week of November. Smiley's diary account reflects a busy month, with return visits to nearby reservations, conferences with Indian leaders and various attorneys representing claimants, interspersed with consulting sessions with Lewis and Ward.[42]

The commission's work was of great interest to the WNIA, which had invested time and money in missionary, educational, and medical work among these Indians. The September issue of *The Indian's Friend* described Painter as "hard at work under the burning midsummer sun," looking after the surveys and negotiations concerning Indian lands. He is "winning favor and help from some whose interest, it was feared, would not aid them." The article concluded that "all classes of citizens will rejoice to see the long-vexed Indian question" end, and to "see all races prospering together in our bountiful land."[43]

Painter had hoped to be home for Thanksgiving, but they were still hard at work in mid-month. "We have found many very embarrassing complications in this work" but hoped to "see daylight ahead," he informed Welsh. "It will be a great thing for us in our work to have these poor Indians settled, and I hope practically off our hands." Eight days later, after explaining that the commission had spent a full day at Capitán Grande dealing with Charles Hensley and his lawyer, he requested permission from Commissioner Morgan to go home before traveling to Washington. He had, after all, been away from his family since January 1, while Smiley and Moore had been given a leave of absence.[44]

### A Promise Fulfilled

On December 4 Smiley informed General Whittlesey, BIC secretary, that the commission had completed their report and would be forwarding it to Noble that evening. The most difficult and important part of their work had been adjusting the claims of the Southern Pacific Railroad and private claims on the Morongo Reservation. It was imperative that Noble attend to this part of the report at once, he cautioned. A settlement had to be made before the first of January, otherwise the arrangement could fall through because Charles Barker, attorney for all claimants for damages for eviction, held their power of attorney only till that date. There were one hundred or so Indians living primarily in the village of Potrero at the mouth of a five-mile-long canyon, their existence threatened by the handful of whites who had settled on railroad land in the canyon and already filed on water rights. It was essential to defend their claims.

In early December Painter informed Morgan that the commission was "closing up their report." Requesting him to regard this letter as personal, Painter asked him to call this complicated arrangement at Morongo to the attention of Secretary Noble and "give it such push that if it fail[ed] of approval it shall not be for lack of consideration." He again emphasized that if this arrangement was not approved by the first of the year, there was danger of it failing apart and the commission's "work . . . lost, so far as that case is concerned."[45]

Painter, Smiley, and Moore believed that their efforts would lead to "a reasonably comfortable and adequate home for every Mission Indian who care[d] to avail himself of the provisions made for them on these reservations." They had not only set apart reservations but land parcels within confirmed grants and advised a number of Indians to take up homesteads. To properly locate some of these homesteads, they had ordered surveys and requested that Frank Lewis "take the proper steps to secure the lands they desire in this manner." This process, the commissioners believed, was better than establishing numerous small reservations. They had also tried to protect Indian rights on private grants, surveying Indian holdings on Warner Ranch, Santa Ysabel Ranch, and San Felipe, but they had been unable to arrange a firm settlement with ranch owners. Instead they recommended that Lewis defend Indian rights if any action was taken to remove them. The commissioners praised his efficient service, describing him as a friend of the Indian. "We have seen much of him and regard the legal interests of the Indians safe in his hands as he possesses integrity as well as ability."[46]

On December 7, 1891, Lewis, as the commission's clerk, sent the lengthy final report to Commissioner Morgan, calling his attention to the Morongo Reservation and the two offers that accompanied the report: one from Barker and the other from the Southern Pacific Railroad. "To avoid all difficulty" he "respectfully urg[ed] that the latter be approved" and "the matter closed up before January 1, 1892." He described the commission as having finally "brought about a very favorable settlement of the disputes that have so long hung over this reservation." Their report listed twenty-six separate reservations, embracing some 136,000 acres, as homes for between 3,100 and 3,200 Mission Indians. At least thirteen were new reservations, home to some six hundred fifty people. President Benjamin Harrison approved the commission's report on December 29, 1891.[47]

The original twenty executive order reservations had embraced nearly 270,000 acres. In the give-and-take atmosphere of the commission's work, the commissioners returned land to the public domain—73,915 from the 88,475-acre Morongo Reservation, largely because of controversial alternate sections of railroad lands, and 56,390 acres of perceived worthless desert land from the 60,870 acres belonging to Agua Caliente. In his critique of the commission's work, Larry Burgess cautions modern readers that "mountains and deserts were viewed as obstacles to be overcome and tamed, not as areas for recreation and permanent living." Desert land at that time was therefore viewed as useless. What Painter and his fellow commissioners, all volunteers near retirement age, had accomplished was the protection, albeit small, of acreage and reservations that today are still extant. And their enormous task was accomplished under budget.[48]

On December 15 Painter wrote Welsh that he felt he had fully redeemed his promise to Helen Hunt Jackson to protect the Mission Indians. He was home now, recovering from surgery for an abscess he had discovered on his back ten days before leaving California. The day before, Smiley had telegraphed him from Redlands, urging him to go to Washington "to prevent the success of certain schemes with reference to the Reservation at Banning." Painter was barely over his surgical treatment and not up to going, he informed Welsh, besides which Martha "interposed an absolute veto." Instead he had written both Commissioner Morgan and General Whittlesey about the matter.[49] To Morgan, Painter transcribed the text of Smiley's telegram, explaining that apparently someone was attempting to press a claim on part of the land at Morongo. "I cannot overstate the importance of this arrangement to the Indians on this Reservation," he noted, "if it fails they will be in a deplorable condition: if it be ratified they are most happily and abundantly provided for." This matter required "immediate and *conclusive* attention."[50]

Painter was forced to remain at home, stuffing a rag into his abscess "to keep it from external healing before it has ceased to discharge." Frustrated about not being in Washington, he was particularly anxious about the Morongo arrangement, explaining to Welsh that Commissioner Morgan was away, and Acting Commissioner Belt did "not seem to grasp the situation," even though Painter had written him to explain the matter on December 24. General Whittlesey was taking care of the matter. His son, Charles, was home, and both Charles and Martha were quite unwilling for him to go to

Washington. "I hope it may not be necessary," he noted, "and yet am healing myself ready to start at a moment's notice."[51]

Belt finally responded on December 26, 1891, and from the tone of his letter it appears he had misunderstood the situation. Patiently Painter explained that early in the spring the commission had made an arrangement with Barker, which was "dependent upon an arrangement with" Southern Pacific for an exchange of land—an arrangement the commissioners were unable to inform the Indian Office of until the end of November. Painter was fearful that some of Barker's clients would make trouble. To clarify the situation, Painter informed Belt that "the necessity for action has not been 'forced upon your office' by any action, or want of action on the part of this Commission; but was a condition in the power of Attorney conferred upon Barker long precedent to the creation of this commission, which it had no power to modify." Painter saw no cause for delay since the commission had submitted the request for this exchange in March, and it had been approved. The only reason for delay might be that the Indian Office intended to send out an appraiser to compare values and report on the "equities of the exchange" it had made. That would not only endanger the arrangement but would "give opportunity to make trouble, and it was this we are anxious to avoid," Painter concluded.[52]

Painter need not have worried. At the end of December, President Harrison approved the commission's report, subject to congressional acceptance of land purchases and exchanges with private parties. On December 30 Secretary Noble informed Morgan of the presidential action and his receipt of a communication from Assistant Attorney General Shields, who saw no objection to approving reservations free from outside claims. Shields suggested, however, that Morgan prepare a draft of a bill to be submitted to Congress, giving the interior secretary authority to purchase or exchange recommended lands. Morgan's letter and the draft bill, written on January 13, 1892, were submitted to Noble, who in turn sent them to Harrison. On January 25 the president forwarded the letters to Congress.[53] In the span of a month's time, the report of the California Mission Indian Commission had been forwarded to Congress with a presidential recommendation for the earliest possible action.

Months later, on March 23, 1892, Painter informed Welsh that the Senate had passed the bill the previous morning, ratifying the agreement made at

Morongo. He had feared it might be necessary to bring some pressure to bear upon the House. The first week of April, Painter submitted his final expense account, totaling $411.85. A week later he received a letter from Lewis that two land suits had been settled, one at Soboba and the other at Pauma, and that he was continuing with the San Felipe case.[54] By the end of 1892 Painter was able to inform Welsh that the commission had settled many of the difficulties facing the Indians; however, there were additional cases that needed to be addressed in the courts, especially "those on old grants against whom suits of ejectment have been bought, or may yet be bought."[55] Surveys for lands they had reserved would continue until 1910, with trust patents issued along the way.

Had Painter's only service been his work on the Mission Indian Commission, he would still have held an elevated position among Indian reformers. Referred to as the Smiley Commission, it more appropriately should be known as the Painter Commission. The following year, no such extensive travels would be required of him; he would work mostly in Washington, defending Indian education, holding off the Ute removal, and taking on new tasks, such as Oneida allotments and enrollment of the Stockbridge Indians.

▼ ▼ ▼

# CHAPTER 8

# DEFENDING INDIAN EDUCATION AND STOCKBRIDGE ENROLLMENT, 1892–1893

On January 7, 1892, Painter described the work of the California Mission Indian Commission before the annual BIC meeting, announcing that the commission members had completed their work in a year and returned almost $1,200 to the Treasury. Although the commission was criticized for reducing the acreage of the executive order reservations, he assured his audience that the Indians were in possession of "lands adequate to their needs, enough for their support," and their situation was better than he had supposed possible. Most of the restored land was utterly worthless, in a country where the temperature reached between 130 and 140 degrees in the shade. He was most gratified that he could do something for them after his promise to Helen Hunt Jackson. Although he missed part of the meeting while conferring with Secretary Noble, he wrote to Welsh that what he attended was "of unusual interest."[1]

Painter's lengthy 1892 report for the IRA reflected another busy year. The association's work, he explained, could not be measured solely by the number of bills it got through Congress; also to be considered were its efforts in "smothering bad measures, so that no report is ever heard from them." This latter success was of "vastly more importance than the enactment of a law." As examples, he included the continued blockage of the Southern Ute removal bill and his success in refuting the "old charges of 'extravagance, waste, and failure of Indian education'" brought up by new members of the House Indian Committee. Diligently and solemnly he had gathered new evidence to prove that current monies were sufficient to educate only one-third of Indian children. Appropriations were now stabilized, and threatened schools were left untouched, although additional monies had not been provided.[2]

Senator Dawes was again blocking IRA efforts to protect educational funding. If he "is really serious in anything except a threatened attack upon Indian education he deserves a more serious reprimand," Painter wrote Welsh on January 1, 1892. Apparently Welsh and the senator had argued, for Painter praised him for poking Dawes "under the ribs so vigorously." Two weeks later Painter wrote that the most pressing item was still the proposed cut in education, and he was waiting for Morgan to prepare materials for him. Over the last six or seven years appropriations for education had been increasing; therefore Painter believed the IRA had a good fighting chance of holding them at the present figure, even with a large Democratic majority. He described Indiana Senator William S. Holman, leader of the Democrats, as "very fair and liberal in regard to Indian matters," although he later came to regret that opinion. Several months later Painter informed Welsh that although quite a number of committee members had come over to their side, he recommended that active measures be taken to gain public support during the current spring and summer to ensure against congressional members blocking the appropriations. "We have made the discovery several times that they are amenable to public sentiment."[3]

Taking the hint, Welsh wrote an open letter for the February issue of the *Southern Workman*, sending Painter a copy. Welsh warned that congressional "assailants of Indian education" would initially assault Eastern schools, such as Hampton, Carlisle, and Lincoln Institute, with a show of a "specious friend-ship" for Western schools. If these attacks were successful, however, Western schools would share the same fate. Because a positive public sentiment had succeeded in increasing appropriations for Indian schools from $20,000 in 1877 to $2,291,650 in the current year, Welsh concluded that "we therefore appeal to the serious and patriotic people of this country for judgment in this grave emergency."[4]

To reinforce Welsh's open letter, on March 1, 1892, the IRA published Painter's twenty-two page pamphlet, *Extravagance, Waste and Failure of Indian Education*, in which he argued that appropriations could hardly be extravagant when only one-third of the Indian children were educated. If some schools were inefficient, it was because superintendents were hired who met "the demands of Congressmen in the payment of political debts" not because of their credentials. Painter printed eleven positive letters by agents, missionaries, army officers, and a post trader, excerpted from the annual report of the superintendent of Indian education, to refute an earlier claim by an unidentified senator that Hampton and Carlisle students from the Sioux reservation returned home to become expert horse thieves. These testimonials reflected the continued "civilized" dress of the returned students and their hard work and marriages. Reform was needed, Painter agreed, with better school locations and the removal of education hiring from the spoils system. He concluded that the solution to the current problem was "unquestionably to be found in the education, literary and industrial of the Indian children, under moral and Christian influences."[5] On March 2 Painter informed Welsh that the Indian appropriation bill had passed the previous day with only petty amounts of reduction but enough to cause the ire of the "penny wise and pound foolish" current House of Representatives.[6]

## The Ute Bill Again

The crisis of Indian education passed, Painter faced Ute removal head-on at the end of March, when Colorado Senator Edward O. Wolcott publicly criticized him. Wolcott accused Painter and the IRA not only of making false statements but of "lobbying in an unholy cause," with Painter supposedly working on behalf of the Pittsburgh Cattle Company. Welsh, responding in a public letter, described Painter as possessing "sound judgment, integrity," and "unimpeachable" courage and serving in a role no different from that of Wolcott, who was a paid agent for the people of Colorado. "Whatever disgrace attaches to him [Painter] for receiving pay for legitimate work rendered attaches likewise to you," retorted Welsh. The day before Painter had informed Welsh that Wolcott had introduced a resolution instructing the president to cease allotting Southern Ute lands in Colorado until after Congress acted. Venting the "ill feeling of Colorado," Wolcott had credited Painter and the IRA with defeating their removal efforts. In the Senate, Dawes uncharacteristically complimented Painter, standing up to Wolcott "very manfully, dealing with the facts much more intelligently than I had anticipated, showing that he [had] firmly grasped them," Painter wrote. Although Wolcott's resolution passed, Painter concluded that it was of little importance unless the current Congress took some action on the Ute bill. On April 1 Painter wrote that when Dawes was through with his tongue-lashing, Wolcott "must have felt that he had writ himself down in characters of unusual size, 'an ass.'"[7]

In mid-April, Painter informed Welsh that he had started preparing a statement for the press with the idea of writing an open letter to Wolcott, but more important things had demanded his attention and he had set it aside. In his formal report, he wrote that "with a full knowledge of the evil character of the Ute Bill," the House Committee on Indian Affairs had reported on it favorably, six to four.[8] On April 19 he informed Welsh he had been asked to write the minority report to strengthen their fight in the House at large. Two days later he turned in not only the report but a bill to accompany it. Then in early August Painter assured Welsh that the Ute bill would not come up during the current session, and he was undisturbed by a "newspaper rumor that Wolcott was trying to whip up the Senate."[9]

Also in mid-April, having misplaced his "memoranda of letter writing," Painter tried to reconstruct his IRA work since the beginning of the year: He had written some three hundred letters, many of which were preceded by a visit to the Interior Department for additional information, and he had given three public addresses, in Philadelphia, Washington, and at Hampton. He had prepared two pamphlets, one on Indian education and the second on Southern Ute removal, and attended three hearings before the House Committee on Indian Affairs, one on Ute removal and two on education. He had prepared two bills, one for relief of the Stockbridge and Munsee Indians, and a second ratifying arrangements made by the Mission Indian Commission. In addition he had escorted various Indian delegations, including those from Santee Sioux, Chippewa, Menominee, and Stockbridge tribes, to the department to either recommend a bill, protest allotments, or secure annuity payments in cash. He also conducted numerous interviews and collected testimony against an agent who had used coercion to secure signatures on contracts.[10]

### Oneida Allotments

By month's end, Painter reported a lull in Indian matters, both in Congress and in the Interior Department, providing him time to right a wrong with regard to Oneida allotments in Wisconsin, due, he believed, to the work of a drunken allotting agent. On April 2, 1892, he had written Cornelius Doxtater, a prominent Oneida Indian who had been a member of Company F of the Fourteenth Regiment Wisconsin Infantry Volunteers during the Civil War. Doxtater had been to Washington to complain that certain allotments had not been done properly. At some point, presumably, he visited Painter, who explained that to support the claim the Oneidas had to prove the following: that some parties were not entitled to allotments; that some who were entitled had not received them; that the same land had been allotted more than once; that unjust discrimination had been practiced; and that some Oneida lands remained unallotted. To respond to each of Painter's points, on April 11 the Oneidas held a formal council in the Duck Creek Council House on their Wisconsin reservation.[11]

In early May, another lull in congressional Indian matters allowed Painter to travel to Virginia to visit his family for ten days, especially to see his eldest brother, who had health issues. Upon his return he informed Welsh that an earlier cough was now gone, but he was still suffering with a severe attack of rheumatism in his left arm. At the end of the month, in a personal and newsy letter, he informed Welsh that his wedding anniversary was coming up on June 2 and for years he had disappointed his wife, leaving her to celebrate alone. His son was coming home for a two-week vacation before his final exams. "I have been but three weeks in my home since the 6th of January, one year ago," he noted, and he was hoping to go home either that day or the following.[12]

Also in early May, Painter informed Welsh that he had received a letter from J. M. Lee, a captain in the Ninth Infantry who had served for a year as acting agent at the Cheyenne and Arapaho Agency in Darlington,[13] and John. H. Seger, informing him that these two tribes had been fraudulently assessed legal fees of $67,500 from monies paid them for their interest on their Cherokee Outlet lands. Lee named as the perpetrators former agents John D. Miles, D. B. Dyer, and G. D. Williams and attorneys Samuel J. Crawford of Topeka, Kansas, and Matthew G. Reynolds of St. Louis, Missouri. One of these men—the letter did not say which—had been Secretary Noble's former law partner. On June 17, 1892, Painter informed Welsh he would go at once to Chicago to confer with Lee and if necessary go to the Indian Territory to investigate. At the end of the month, he reported on a series of interviews

with both Captain Lee and General Nelson Miles and had returned from
Chicago with substantial documentary evidence. On July 1 he reported he had
a long talk with the chief of the Indian Division in the Interior Department
on the matter and hoped to see Secretary Noble the next day. By mid-month
he had arranged to have a resolution introduced in the Senate instructing
Commissioner Morgan to appoint a committee to investigate the case.[14]

Months later, during his fall investigation, Painter would meet in Kansas
City with John Miles and Crawford to learn their explanation for the first
contract, signed on May 23, 1889, at Oklahoma City, Indian Territory, and
what services they had rendered for their fee. When he inquired the reason
for the second contract, he was told that Noble had refused to approve the
first contract because the fee was too high. However, in comparing the two,
Painter discovered the second one, signed on August 20, 1889, at Arkansas
City, Kansas Territory, was actually more favorable to the attorneys. To remove
any suspicion of impropriety, Secretary Noble in his 1892 annual report would
include a seven-page vindication of his actions.[15]

Painter fully corroborated Lee's facts and conclusions during his own
investigation. Willing to stake his reputation and commission upon his
findings, Lee had described the contracts as "tainted with misrepresentation, fraud, and bribery," representing only a minority of the Indians. Their
signatures had been gained "through misrepresentation and deceit," and
they "never knowingly authorized" any attorneys to receive a fee. Lee also
shared portions of a letter written by a Mr. McMeekin, an Oklahoma City
attorney, whom he described as "an honorable gentleman whose veracity
is beyond question." McMeekin had written that in early spring of 1889, he
and a fellow attorney, a Mr. Bentley, had visited the Cheyenne and Arapaho at Darlington regarding negotiations for sale of surplus lands. Former
agent Dyer intervened, held his own council with the Indians, and conferred
with the current agent, who accused McMeekin of stirring up trouble and
ordered him to leave. Forwarded to the Interior Department, the contract
was approved, despite Bentley's protest that it was fraudulent. Lee claimed it
had been signed by Indians who were not recognized as chiefs, and that no
general council had been held. He concluded "that this whole business, in its
final outcome, was a fraud." Months earlier, the two tribes had sent petitions
to their agent to be forwarded to Congress. Lee, musing that they must have

been pigeonholed, was willing to submit to the IRA "specific charges and stand or fall by the result."[16]

As late as August Painter was still uncertain about his fall itinerary. He might return to the Sac and Fox Reservation on the Murphy case, which was not fully settled, and he had promised the Wisconsin Oneidas to do more on the matter of their faulty allotments. Also Dawes had requested that he look into the Colville, Puyallup, and Shoshoni issues and thought it best to comply, although it would take considerable time. He also wanted to learn more about the Winnebagoes, and finally he had promised the Indians on Long Island he would look into their case.[17]

## Lake Mohonk

In mid-October, accompanied by Martha, Painter returned to the genial atmosphere of Lake Mohonk, having missed the previous two meetings because of conflicting obligations. This conference reunited Smiley and Painter with Judge Joseph Moore, who had served with them on the Mission Indian Commission.[18] During the fourth session, the evening of Thursday, October 13, Painter presented his paper on threats to Indian interests, beginning with the Dawes Severalty Act, now five years old. He described its failures as "unfortunate"; its "spirit and intent of the law," at times totally violated. He reiterated that this legislation was "not the end we seek," only "a much needed means to that end." He stressed that the proposed removal of the clause protecting allotted lands from taxation at the end of the twenty-five-year period was virtual property confiscation. The government should either continue to pay the tax or it should be paid out of surplus lands.[19]

Painter had initially viewed the "land-grabber" as the worst assailant of Indian interests. Now he viewed claimants and their lawyers, who demanded depredation compensation for Indian-inflicted damages, as a more serious threat to Indian trust funds. Indians were not even notified when a claim was filed. Soon there would be little money left to tempt a lawyer, chided Painter. More than $26 million worth of depredation claims had already been filed with the U.S. Court of Claims,[20] to be paid out of the offending tribe's funds. When funds were depleted, claims were assessed against annuities.[21] Months earlier he had written, "I think it a cruel injustice that these Indians should thus be allowed to be brought into court as wards of the Government, their

Mountain House at Lake Mohonk, taken from the Skytop Path, 1893.
*Mohonk Mountain House Archives, New Paltz, New York.*

funds placed in peril, and they be compelled to employ attorneys for their defense."[22] Another danger was fraudulent contracts, such as that of the Cheyenne and Arapaho. With such largess available, shyster lawyers would have a field day either suing Indians or defending them from suits. "This kind of service gives encouragement to extravagant dreams," he concluded. Painter intended to convince Congress to rescind the Cheyenne and Arapaho fees; in this endeavor, unlike his success in saving the annuities of the Sisseton Wahpeton scouts, he would fail.[23]

On October 14, 1892, attendees of the Mohonk Conference issued a one-page flyer, hand signed by a committee of five, soliciting funds to continue their efforts on behalf of the Mission Indians. Presenting a brief history of their work, beginning with their 1886 appointment and five-thousand-dollar contributions from LMC members, they described the saving of Soboba, the legal work of Shirley Ward and Frank Lewis, and the passage of the 1891 Mission Indian legislation and its commission. Now, four years later, because it was unthinkable to relinquish the Indians' defense, the committee was earnestly soliciting money, requesting twenty-five hundred dollars for Lewis to continue his work.[24]

## Tour of Indian Territory

Leaving the solicitation of money in the capable hands of the Mohonk committee, Painter set out for the Indian Territory. Although the investigation into the background of the fraudulent Cheyenne and Arapaho contracts was his primary goal, he also intended to visit reservation schools and look into the current success of the allotment process. This trip had been planned for months, but unfortunately he had been too busy to break free until now. He would not return home until late November.

Painter arrived in Darlington, Indian Territory, on October 25 after conferring with General Miles in Chicago and arranging for Captain Lee's cooperation in the contracts case. From Chicago, traveling with army officers from Forts Reno and Sill, his journey had been "one of some discomfort, and much delay." He was still debating whether to go to Anadarko or to the Seger Colony. "There are a number of things here that seem quite queer," he wrote Welsh, and he had to feel his way "carefully and come by accident upon the facts for which I cannot directly seek." He had conferred with some military officers and found the relations of the army to the matters he was investigating to be creating some jealousy on the part of the Indian department. "My connection with these officers will have to be guarded," he informed Welsh.[25] Unfortunately, Painter never again referred to this issue.

In early November Painter drove over two hundred miles by wagon; he visited the Seger Colony, traversed Wichita, Caddo, and Delaware lands, and traveled to Fort Sill to investigate conditions on the Kiowa, Comanche, and Arapaho Reservation, visiting various schools along the way. "I have been paying special attention to the effects of allotments as made here, prematurely and with undue, I had almost said criminal, haste," he informed Welsh. "I am satisfied that the great dangers now threating the Indians is in the hasty allotment of land, the slovenly way in which it is being done, for the most part." He noted cases where allottees had died, their claim cancelled by the Indian Office without notification to relatives, with whites immediately filing on lands that the surviving family members believed they had inherited.

In his formal report, published the following March, he emphasized that the wise provisions of the Dawes Act had been violated. The process was going poorly; scarcely a day passed without some "case of injustice, or wrong, or mistake, fruitful of ill feeling and trouble." Lands should only be allotted to agricultural Indians, "who were so far advanced in civilization that land in severalty was necessary for their further progress," and the process should not be rushed to satisfy white settlers but should take at least four years.[26]

Painter found that conditions had worsened since his first trip to the territory in 1885. The hopeful beginnings of house building and farming that he witnessed earlier in the vicinity of the Cheyenne and Arapaho agency had deteriorated until "the last vestige, almost, of house, tepee, and farm had disappeared." For some inscrutable reason, the government had set aside a six-mile-square area near the agency, pushing the Indians "off their fair beginnings back upon the unbroken prairie to take root once more." As a result, they were "in a frame of mind entirely unfavorable to any immediate progress." Although Painter did find an improvement in some schools, especially the Cheyenne school, he described the twenty-year-old Kiowa school as "still the incomplete, inconvenient death-trap it had always been—no bathrooms, no suitable laundry, no suitable accommodations for teachers." He was most disturbed with the mission schools, especially the Mennonite school, which in 1887 he had described as the "one hopeful feature of the work among the Indians at the Agency." During this visit its student body was markedly reduced due to government regulations preventing the school from competing for students—a crushing policy for all Indian mission schools. Months later, he would address this topic before the annual January BIC meeting.[27]

Five years earlier, while visiting the Wichitas and Caddos, Painter had seen extensive fenced corn fields and cattle herds. This trip he described the Indians as having barely a single load of corn. Now everywhere he looked he found "evidences of demoralization and retrogression." He placed much of the blame on Interior Secretary Noble, whom he claimed had "no interest in the Indian as a man and possible citizen." Hagen, in his history of the IRA, writes that Noble "was not disposed to try to humor eastern do-gooders." Not only had Welsh been unsuccessful in establishing a good working relationship with Noble, but it was two years into Noble's administration before he even made Painter's acquaintance. On the other hand, Painter thought well of Noble's Indian commissioner, Thomas Jefferson Morgan, describing him months later as on the whole a good commissioner. Although Morgan had laid a broad foundation for school work, Painter still criticized him for not building on it, leaving the work for his successor.[28]

One day Painter witnessed a pathetic issue of beef, one steer per twenty-five men. Factoring in hides, horns, and bones, there was little available meat to begin with. After complaining that many steers were small and thin, he was informed that if the beef was rejected, the Indians would go hungry until new steers were purchased. Even with this beef issuance, the *Brooklyn Daily Eagle* reported that since the summer the government had cut rations by half because the Indians were "expected to aid in their own support by cultivating their lands." The *Eagle* quoted Painter as describing the hungry Cheyennes and Arapahos as cross and restless, "sure to put on war paint unless the government gives them food," in the belief that they were being "swindled by unscrupulous white men in the sale of their lands and their feeling toward the government [as] one of intense hatred."[29]

Before beginning his report on the two Cheyenne and Arapaho contracts the following March, Painter searched through government records and the text of both agreements, one signed in 1889, the second the following August. The tribes had originally claimed some 30 million acres between the North Platte and Arkansas Rivers, extending from the Rocky Mountains to the middle of Nebraska and Kansas. In an 1865 treaty, they had exchanged this land for a reduced reservation of 1.6 million acres in the Cherokee Outlet, to which the government held no title. The following year the Cherokee negotiated a treaty giving the government the right to settle certain friendly Indians on their lands west of the Arkansas River. In 1867 the two tribes negotiated another treaty exchanging their prior lands for some 5 million acres in the recently acquired Cherokee Outlet, but they never moved there. Instead, the government set aside an executive order reservation further south, in Wichita country on the North Canadian River, where they lived for the next twenty years. In 1890 they ceded all claims to both the 1867 reservation and the executive order reservation, receiving allotments of 160 acres on the latter. They were paid $1.5 million for the sale of surplus lands on their home reservation; the first payment of $250,000 had been paid in full. The second payment was short $67,500; Noble claimed the missing money had been paid to attorneys under an approved contract. Painter responded that this fee was not "paid with the full knowledge and consent of these Indians."[30]

Painter had explained in mid-December that he was preparing for an anticipated "big fight in this C & A case," assembling a large amount of material and trying to fully master it. He was still revising his report as late as the following February, informing Welsh on the twentieth that he had added two footnotes to the appendix. A week later he asked Welsh to insert a new paragraph. Despite Painter's investigation, extensive research, and lengthy report and Captain Lee's support, Congress refused to set aside the fraudulent fee. Hagan described this as "part of an emerging pattern of contracts between hustling attorneys and apprehensive tribes" that Painter viewed as "an unbounded vista of assault . . . upon the funds of various bands of Indians."[31]

The diversity of Painter's usual work was again reflected in an undated report, written from memory, listing thirty-two tasks he had completed, some only partially successful, others in which he failed. They included attending two hearings on the Stockbridge bill, during which a favorable report was agreed upon; assisting a delegation of White Earth Chippewas in their allotment agreement; unsuccessfully protesting illegal Oneida allotments; testifying before the Court of Claims for the Sisseton; successfully having the Ute bill placed last on the list to be considered; investigating the status of the Mescalero Apache Agency; delivering four addresses on Indian affairs; and writing a paper for the Mohonk Conference. He also tried but failed to save the Cherokee school in North Carolina; worked on behalf of the Menominees for sale of their pine timber; and traveled to Pittsfield, Massachusetts, to confer with Senator Dawes.[32]

## Cleveland Returns

The November 1892 presidential election returned Grover Cleveland to the White House. He took office on March 4, 1893. Had Painter not been on his investigative tour, he informed Welsh, he would have voted for him. Presumably Welsh agreed, for after four years of Harrison's presidency, he recalled that during his first term Cleveland had been "genuinely interested in the welfare of the Indians." A few months into his new term, a newspaper account reported that Cleveland had lectured a senator for appointing his son as clerk of the committee he was chairing, a practice Painter described as arrogant and threatening. Painter was concerned that Cleveland's action would bring the new president some grief, for many legislators were "deeply committed to the theory that to the Congressman belong all the spoils and plums of his district, as part of his means to secure his own re-election."[33]

Cleveland's re-election was a comfort to Painter, who visited the White House often as well as corresponding directly to the president to suggest certain agent appointments and recommending what in his "carefully formed judgment [he] declared the good of the service urgently demands." During his second term, Cleveland appointed army officers as agents, twenty-seven out of a total of fifty-seven. Painter and the IRA fought hard to keep those competent military agents in office, conferring when necessary with the president. As Hagan writes, between those letters from people attempting to hold on to their jobs and others seeking employment, the IRA at times appeared as an employment agency.[34]

On January 12, 1893, the annual meeting of missionary representatives and the BIC was called to order at the Riggs House by chairman Darwin R. James, a former member of the House of Representatives from New York. In his introductory remarks, James noted that it was crucial to explain to the public and the incoming administration that the Indians had friends "who [were] not afraid to give expression to their feelings upon all matters which concern" their welfare. He then opened the floor to the heads of the various missionary boards to describe their year's work. When finishing his address, Rev. A. B. Shelley of the Mennonite Church requested that Painter take the podium. Painter, familiar with the Mennonite school in the Indian Territory, described it as the bright spot in his Indian work during his first visit. He had, however, found it virtually empty during his most recent trip because government schools were required to be filled first—a policy Painter found both ineffective and interfering with church work. He later wrote that the government was not simply against contract schools but against mission schools in general, even when fully funded by the churches, an action he described as "both premature and hurtful.[35]

During his address, Painter discussed the current status of the Dawes legislation, reiterating that allotments should be made to Indians "who are so far advanced that when the intercourse laws are removed by which they have been guarded they will still be safe." Undue haste left them at the mercy of both the whiskey seller and a lower class of settlers. The ability of the allotting agent was also critical, he argued, describing the Cheyenne and Arapaho agent as a saloon-keeper "who had furnished the whisky to give stimulus to the patriots in the preceding election."[36]

Two days later, Painter informed Welsh that he had been pleased with the meeting, finding it "fully up to those of the past, if not somewhat in advance." Politics as usual were afoot as various constituent groups, including the BIC, had organized committees to urge Cleveland to appoint an Indian commissioner sympathetic to their views. Members of the Boston Indian Citizenship Committee had already met with the president. "So Grover is likely to be made acquainted with the wishes of the sentimentalists," concluded Painter. His use of the president's first name revealed their professional relationship. Although no doubt pleased to again have Cleveland to work with, Painter was still dealing with the long-festering Ute removal, explaining to Welsh that Commissioner Morgan had given Rev. Thomas Childs "a pretty severe cudgeling," accusing him of writing to the people of Durango asking them "to interfere and prevent the putting of Ute children into the school at Fort Lewis, because if they allowed it, it would have a tendency to fasten the Utes in southern Colorado." Months later, Painter accused the Southern Ute agent, Charles A. Bartholomew, of representing the citizens of Durango and southwestern Colorado to ensure there were no more Indians living in the state. Bartholomew had also informed Painter he was cooperating with the effort "to keep the Indians disturbed" and supported the effort to prevent Indian children from attending school at Fort Lewis. In the meantime, residents of Durango were moving onto the proposed Ute Reservation in Southern Utah, and a rich placer deposit had been discovered on the lower San Juan River, prompting Painter, tongue in cheek, to write that he doubted public pressure would call for Ute removal to that land.[37]

His BIC obligation over, Painter returned to monitoring congressional actions. On February 8, 1893, he alerted Welsh to a report that the current Indian appropriation bill cut support for schools by $275,565. The very next day, Welsh quoted from Painter's letter in a printed two-page notice urging IRA members and parties interested in "a wise solution of the Indian problem" to report facts to show that Indian education had met "with reasonable and solid success." The funding for Indian education was being threatened at a time when a sound economic policy dictated a moderate increase. Welsh recommended that all who received his alert write their congressmen and local newspapers. The bill also had provided for the sale of lands allotted to the Puyallups, setting aside only a forty-acre homestead for each allottee protected for only ten years, instead of the twenty-five as provided in the Dawes Act. Painter responded that "Tacoma is persistent in her determination to oust these Indians and secure the last acres of their land," recommending that Welsh "best call for a howl along the lines with reference to these matters."[38]

However, Painter almost immediately modified his stance on the Puyallup issue, describing their land across the bay from Tacoma as quite valuable and most profitable for market gardening. Forty acres of such land so near the city was ample, he concluded, and he had decided not to have the restriction removed. He had recently learned that various Indians had already made contracts for leasing their lands—contracts that would in a short time become deeds of conveyances. All that was needed was legislation ratifying these leases. "This little game was blocked," he noted, and now the Indians will be allowed to sell all but their forty acres.[39]

On February 22 the Indian appropriation bill was brought before the House, and New York Representative Hosea Rockwell attacked Commissioner Morgan's extravagant school building, "which I have all along said would be to us some time a source of trouble," Painter reminded Welsh.[40] Rockwell also criticized the practice at Hampton and Carlisle of bringing in children from different climates, which introduced diseases, but this opinion, Painter noted, had been expressed many times and proven false. Six days later he wrote that the bill had been "put through yesterday afternoon without further debate or question," with one-half accepted as reported by the committee. He described the several days of discussion as largely frivolous. The letters and support for Indian education generated by Welsh's alert had proven successful. In mid-March Painter reported that the Senate had increased school appropriations, although not as much as the previous year.[41]

### Stockbridge Defense

By mid-February Painter was in the midst of a fight on behalf of the Stockbridge Indians of Wisconsin. In 1875, 138 Stockbridge Indians (known as the Citizens Party) had been persuaded to sever tribal relations in return for per capita payments and citizenship rights under the provisions of the 1871 "Act for the relief of the Stockbridge and Munsee tribe of Indians." The remainder of the tribe (the Indian Party), numbering 118, had chosen not to do so. By 1874 the Stockbridge agent, Thomas N. Chase, reported that most of the Citizens Party's business was being conducted by congressmen and a special commission, who had visited the tribe three times that year. "I have not been able to shut my eyes to what have seemed to me great wrongs practiced upon a portion of this tribe," he wrote, "but have felt that it would be useless to raise my voice in their behalf." Almost immediately members of the Citizens Party regretted their decision and for the next two decades worked toward re-admission, opposed by Wisconsin lumbering interests. During the 1880s and 1890s, two competing proposals had been presented: one by Wisconsin Senator Philetus Sawyer, a Republican, to sell all remaining tribal lands and terminate the tribe; the other, by Senator William Vilas, a Democrat and formerly the interior secretary, to leave the tribe intact and restore the Citizen Party members as wrongfully expelled.[42] For the next four successive congresses, Painter worked to move this latter legislation forward.

This was not the first time that Painter had defended these Indians. Learning in 1886 that Wisconsin lumbermen were attempting to influence Congress to remove some of them from their reservation, he had successfully gotten the order suspended.[43] However, Painter's lobbying effort on behalf of the enrollment of the terminated members proved time consuming and frustrating. He endured unfriendly committee meetings, drafted numerous bills, and complained repeatedly to Welsh about Senator Dawes's lack of support and his at times very odd behavior, including an unnecessary sensitivity to the wishes of Senator Francis Brown Stockbridge, a Michigan Republican engaged in the lumber business and a henchman of Senator Sawyer.[44]

On March 1, 1889, Painter had described Dawes's role in the earlier Stockbridge bill as dishonest and disreputable. Now four years later, in mid-February 1893, he described the senator as fleeing the Senate chamber to avoid voting on the bill. Painter had also learned from a congressional report on the Stockbridge matter that all of the current trouble grew out of the scheming of Senator Sawyer and a certain Mr. McCord. If published, it would "put them in a very bad light," he concluded. He had also learned that Sawyer had tried earlier and unsuccessfully to cheat the Menominee Indians. In a February 20 letter, Painter described Sawyer's supporter Senator Stockbridge as exceedingly tricky, capable of putting "any obstacle in the way that he can, without openly antagonizing the bill."[45]

Five days later Painter informed Welsh: "I think I got the cinch on Mr. Sawyer very effectually." He had notified the lawyer who was working the case with Sawyer that if the senator tried to play a game of delay, his "connection with the whole matter should be thoroughly exposed before the Senate." His "henchman," Senator Stockbridge, had relayed the same information to Sawyer, noted Painter.[46]

On March 1 Painter, accompanied by General Whittlesey, made two visits to the White House. On the first visit, after learning that the Stockbridge bill had been sent over to the Interior Department for an opinion, they hurried over to find the assistant secretary opening it. Painter had just finished his explanation of the bill when Sawyer entered the room, addressing the secretary in such a hushed voice that Painter was unable to hear. Whatever Sawyer said did not deter the secretary from signing the bill, and Painter and Whittlesey followed it back to the White House to meet with President Harrison, who explained that he had been told the bill contained the same provisions that had prompted his veto two years earlier. After Painter and Whittlesey explained that this was a different bill, Harrison requested their opinions and objections in writing. Whittlesey delivered their brief the next day. Painter, convinced that Sawyer had tried to sway the president to veto it, concluded: "It will be a great disappoint[ment] if he does veto it, but I shall not be greatly surprised."[47]

In a hastily scribbled note on March 1, Painter explained to Welsh that he had been out of the office all day, "chasing a Bill through the Departments, and to the White House to get it signed"—a reference to the Stockbridge bill. He only hoped he had "countermined old Sawyer." In his formal published report he announced that on March 3, 1893, the legislation had finally been enacted.[48] However, Harrison's signature meant that Painter's work was only just begun. In August he reminded Welsh that to ensure its passage, the IRA had chosen not to amend the bill to request an appropriation to meet the expense of the actual enrollment. Instead Painter and Whittlesey had agreed that if the Interior Department asked them to undertake the task,

either or both would do so, free of expense. Wisconsin Congressman Thomas
Lynch, a member of the House Committee on Indian Affairs, suggested to
General Armstrong that Painter be appointed for the task. With both men
in agreement, they urged Interior Secretary Hoke Smith to appoint him as
a special agent to the Stockbridge Indians, with travel and living expenses
paid by the department. In late August Painter visited Indian Commissioner
Daniel M. Browning to inform him that, at the request of the IRA's Executive
Committee, he would enroll the Indians.[49]

Painter's trip to Wisconsin was delayed until the fall because of a prior
commitment to visit the Florida Seminoles and the Apaches at Mount Vernon
Barracks. Therefore he did not arrive at Keshena, at the Green Bay Agency
on the Stockbridge Reservation, until September 20, 1893. Three days later
he wrote that he had "an ugly job ahead," complicated by questions growing
out of the legislation that led to the Indians' termination. "It requires all
the native and acquired sweetness of my calm temper to serve as a sort of
Soothing Syrup, all my firmness, which my wife calls stubbornness, to hold
the parties to mere facts," he wrote Welsh. At times the bitter hostilities
between the Indian Party and the Citizens Party reached a boiling point.
While on the reservation, he also took the time to learn more about the logging issues among the Menominees, something he had dealt with earlier. He
was convinced that the former agent had served outside parties but that the
present agent, Thomas Savage, previously the agency farmer, was serving all
the Indians well. At one point General Whittlesey joined him, and together
they wrote letters to the Interior Department, urging that no new land be
opened to logging until all cut timber was cleared away. On November 4
Painter was invited to explain everything he had learned about Menominee
logging to Secretary Smith. To ensure that he was well prepared for the
meeting, Painter brought along the logging report that he and Whittlesey
had written. Painter had the commissioner sign off on a letter endorsing their
views and requesting that action be taken.[50]

Instructed to enroll those entitled under the treaty of 1856, Painter enrolled
all descendants of those, including women, who had left the tribe. Both
sides watched carefully, hopeful that their "quarrels might at last be settled."
Enrollment came to a happy conclusion, concluded Painter, "with manifest
relief to all concerned" except for the family that had been chiefly responsible

for these difficulties, about whom he gave no further details. He had enrolled 411 Stockbridge Indians, about the same number that were living in 1733 when authorities in colonial Massachusetts originally set aside the town of Stockbridge for them. However, not until June 1894 was Painter able to inform Welsh that his Stockbridge rolls had been approved.[51]

The Munsees, a division of the Delaware Indians, were also entitled to enrollment, having been included with the Stockbridges in the 1856 treaty. Because they lived on the Onondaga, Cattaraugus and Allegheny Reservations in New York, Painter now had an opportunity to visit there. At Onondaga and Cattaraugus he was delightfully surprised to find well-tended farms and homes, with a majority of the residents adhering to the Christian Party, which favored citizenship and private ownership of property, instead of pagan beliefs and communal property traditions.[52] He estimated that the amount of land available would provide an average farm of about eighty-three acres to a family of five. However, white residents were eagerly leasing land from those Painter described as following pagan ways. Taking the opportunity to visit reservation schools, Painter found to his dismay that the educational system on the Onondaga Reservation provided for only slightly more than one-third of the 118 children. Schools were poorly equipped and teachers unimpressive, prompting Painter to announce that it was time for the reformers to give their earnest attention to the condition of these people. He submitted his final report on the enrollment process on January 29, 1894.[53]

This work had been accomplished despite a "very anxious frame of mind," as Martha had been diagnosed with a mild case of typhoid fever. Although their son Charles was home from school, Painter had hired a trained nurse, and reports were positive. Meanwhile, Painter worked day and night "to the utmost limit" of his ability to complete the job, taking a few days to verify his notes and eliminate all possible mistakes. At least he would have ample material for a talk at the upcoming Mohonk Conference.

Then, on his way to the Onondaga and Allegheny Reservations, he received a telegram to come home. Although the crisis had passed and Martha's temperature was abating by the time he wrote Welsh about it in October, she was still too sick for him to leave. His presence at Lake Mohonk was out of the question. As soon as her health improved, he assured Welsh, he would return to the Allegheny and Onondaga Reservations to complete his work. Painter did take time off to attend to IRA business in Washington. In a November 4 letter he assured Welsh that his wife was progressing rapidly and that the arrangements he and Charles had made for her recovery were so complete and satisfactory that he was no longer anxious. Writing from the Cattaraugus Reservation three weeks later, he reported that he had just completed a week at the Onondaga Reservation and was heading for the Allegheny Reservation on Monday. From there he could be reached at the Arlington Hotel in Buffalo, where he planned to write his reports. He had hoped to make a quick trip to the Tonawanda and Tuscarora Reservations, but the weather had turned severe, with roads that were simply horrible. Invited to speak in Buffalo on November 26, he had not finished working in time to do so. The following day, from the Hotel Keating in Salamanca, New York, he explained he had left the letter he had written from Cattaraugus on the table in his hotel room and hoped that it would eventually reach Welsh; it did.[54]

Writing from Buffalo on December 1, Painter informed Welsh that the agent for the Stockbridge Indians was holding their annuity money, and the Indians were anxiously awaiting his rolls, which were to be used to make their payments. One of them had even written Painter "pitifully of their need of the money now in the hands of the Agent." Because there had already been a long delay because of Martha's illness, Painter thought it best not to wait any longer. He would go home first before heading for Washington to take care of a few matters and then set out for the Stockbridge Reservation. However, he was still in Washington on December 13, conferring with Browning, explaining to him how to save "his school work from being crippled." Painter also spent two days with members of the Indian Committee, learning their opinions of the appropriations bill and conferring with individual congressmen.[55]

In a lengthy letter written on Christmas day, Painter sent Welsh best wishes for the upcoming new year and detailed all the various tasks he had just completed before coming home. As usual they were many, including visits to House committees, to Commissioner Browning on a possible removal of the industrial teacher at Otoe, and to Secretary Smith on various issues. He still had many letters to write and had only partially completed his report on the New York Indians, but he had at least sent Mathew Sniffen a list of his seven public addresses.[56]

Since his return from California, Painter had been busy with ongoing efforts such as holding off Ute removal and defending educational appropriations before Congress, an annual issue. Although he had successfully enrolled the Stockbridge Indians, he had failed to set aside the illegal fees against the Cheyenne and Arapaho contracts and to find a permanent home for the Apache prisoners. His next challenge would be working on behalf of the Florida Seminoles.

▼ ▼ ▼

# CHAPTER 9

# THE APACHE PRISONERS AND THE FLORIDA SEMINOLES, 1893–1894

On March 17, 1893, Painter and General Whittlesey discussed the situation of the Apaches at Mount Vernon Barracks and whether or not an investigative tour should be undertaken to find them a permanent home. If so, Painter also wanted to visit the Florida Seminoles, "about whom we know nothing," he wrote to Welsh, except for an ambiguous mention in Secretary John W. Noble's 1892 report of a school among them "which does not exist, and yet exerts a beneficial influence." For Welsh's benefit, Painter included a paragraph on the school from the report. His curiosity piqued, Painter visited the Indian Office, where he learned that the so-called progress in Florida was the construction of an elaborate and expensive sawmill with sufficient lumber to build a school—all of which had recently been consumed in a fire. Two years earlier in Banning, California, Painter had met up with Amelia Stone Quinton, who at the time had just returned from Florida. She, too, had reported on "the beneficial influence of this school," which her association, the WNIA, was sponsoring. Since Whittlesey was also interested in the Seminoles, Welsh agreed that a visit was appropriate. Therefore, Painter requested money from Welsh—his train ticket to the nearest point, Fort Myers, would be thirty-five dollars, aside from a sleeper. The return trip would be more. Although Martha was still unwell and he was dreading the heat in Florida, Painter left Washington on March 28 aboard a train for Punta Gorda in Southern Florida. From there he endured a full day's boat ride south to Fort Myers, and another long hard ride by carriage to the school site. Complaining that the trip had taken four days longer than anticipated, he reported that the delay had forced him to postpone his visit to the Eastern Cherokees in North Carolina. He would not return to Washington until April 17.[1]

## Seminoles and Apaches

Painter's destination was the Allen Place—a small compound composed of various structures on four hundred acres purchased by the WNIA for a Seminole industrial school. The association's membership had first been introduced to the Florida Seminoles in November 1889 by Miss J. L. Axtell, a Chicago resident long involved with philanthropic work with her parents. A few Seminoles still lived in Florida, she noted, and "a God of retributive justices waits for us to make restitution to them." That fall the WNIA began investigating a land purchase and organizing workers and equipment. Quinton, whose policy was to visit all potential WNIA mission sites, arrived at Fort Myers on March 16, 1891. Accompanied by a small group, she visited distant Seminole camps, inspected and purchased a four-hundred-acre plot near Lake Trafford—land that Painter later described as being some twenty to thirty miles from the nearest Indians. To aid in this missionary work, Quinton organized a WNIA auxiliary in Fort Myers.[2]

The WNIA mission launched that June with the arrival of missionaries Dr. Jacob E. Brecht and his wife, Clara. In addition to doctoring the sick, the Brechts opened a temporary tent school, and Clara Brecht opened a store, where the Seminoles could sell their skins and purchase goods more cheaply than in the town forty miles distant. Work was disappointingly slow, however, largely because the Seminoles who lived in scattered camps did not visit the missionary site regularly. Instead, on occasion the Brechts visited them, buying their skins, inviting them to dine, playing with the children, dispersing seeds, and purchasing various items from them.[3]

When Painter arrived at the WNIA mission nearly two years later, he found Dr. Brecht busy rebuilding the mill preparatory to sawing lumber for the school—this was the status of the school that Noble had said was in full operation. Although the Brechts had made trips to nearby Seminole camps and were gaining some confidence among the Indians, Painter expressed doubt that the sawmill and the missionaries could offer "sufficient attractions to draw [them] permanently from the recesses of the Everglades" to the mission site, into a successful civilization program. Painter stressed the need for a more immediate effort than a useless sawmill and a nonexistent school miles from their camps. He did, however, describe the Indians as enjoying physical comforts that were far better than those of the majority of poor whites and blacks. While the Seminoles fished and grew sweet potatoes, pumpkins, melons, and corn, their hogs feasted on an abundance of palmetto berries and acorns.[4]

"There is nothing to report except that there is nothing done, or being done that has any relation to their advancement," Painter wrote Welsh. He was embarrassed to utter such negative facts in the face of Quinton's glowing reports. The project, undertaken on her recommendation by the government, was "*utterly* absurd."[5] Painter's next letter was even more critical: "I will simply say at this time there is *no school* good or bad for the Seminoles." He explained that Quinton had sold eighty of the four hundred acres to the government to build the school. At great expense and with much difficulty, the government had brought in the original sawmill, which had burned in October 1892 and was now only partially rebuilt, along with several cheap cottages for the mill hands. There also was a house, stable, and several small and cheap houses in which Clara Brecht was teaching the children of government employees. The Seminoles had originally been informed that this was a private enterprise. But with government involvement, and given the Seminoles' feelings about the government, Painter doubted whether they could "ever be induced to come to this place, and certain it is they will never be coerced into bringing their children to the school." He was convinced that any inspector "would advise the Secretary that it was an utter folly, and waste of money." Although he thought the school useless, Painter was personally reluctant to criticize "the effort made of these good ladies."[6]

Leaving Florida, Painter headed for Mount Vernon Barracks, Alabama, to visit the Chiricahua Apache prisoners. Part of his reason for going was the recent murder of two Apache soldiers by white soldiers—an incident that brought to mind "again very urgently this whole question of the enlistment of Indians as soldiers"—a practice that Painter believed was very bad. He also questioned the future these Apaches had, despite Lieutenant William W. Wotherspoon's glowing accounts of their progress during his last two appearances at the Mohonk Conference.[7]

Painter had high praise for Wotherspoon's accomplishments. The miserable huts he had seen during his first visit four years earlier had been replaced by comfortable frame houses, built by the Indians and surrounded by well-attended grounds. Eighty children were taught by Margaret and Sophie Shepard at a school sponsored by the Massachusetts Indian Association, a WNIA auxiliary. "And no better school work have I seen among Indians," he noted. However, Wotherspoon had "reached the limit of what can be done for the adults, under present circumstances," and he agreed with Painter that it would be best to settle them permanently in North Carolina.[8]

Returning to Washington on April 17, Painter wrote Welsh the following day that with a great sense of relief he had received news of Cleveland's appointment of an Indian commissioner. Painter had been fearful he would be "held responsible for the administration of Indian affairs during the next four years." His wife had written him jubilantly when she saw the appointment notice in the newspaper. "She was quite unwilling that I [should] take the place," he informed Welsh. "It was also a comfort to me that I was never spoken of in the papers, so far as I know, as a candidate," he noted. Returning home, Painter found that Martha had returned to her sick bed, this time with tonsillitis. Fortunately, Charles had been home on his Easter vacation during part of his father's absence.[9]

The suggestion that Painter might be appointed commissioner had been seriously promoted by the Boston Indian Citizenship Committee. The previous January, Painter had been invited by committee members to a luncheon to discuss his ongoing work, and the conversation turned to Morgan's replacement. Joshua Davis had remarked that Prof. James Thayer identified "Painter [as] the man before all whom we ought to press for this position." Those attending the busy luncheon—Thayer, Davis, Henry Houghton, Frank Wood, and Samuel B. Capen—all agreed. When asked about his relationship with President Cleveland, Painter responded that it was "of the pleasantest character." Asked if he would accept the position if offered, he responded in the negative, considering it to be "the hardest, most thankless, and fullest of all that is unpleasant under the government." Moreover, since he had been "in the position of critic so long," he could ill afford to put himself "in position to invite criticism." But by the end of the meeting his friends' cordial and earnest efforts had won him over. He found their praise "a great surprise, and wholly unsought." He told Welsh "if my friends feel thus about it, of course, I shall consent: if it is thought best to attempt it of course I [should] not like to fail." At year's end, the Boston Committee was still pressing him to consider, and he informed Welsh that he had thought a great deal about the prospect but was still "very uncertain."[10]

In early 1893, Welsh had an hour-long interview with President Cleveland, who made several inquiries about Painter. In a letter to IRA executive board member Phillip Garrett, Welsh noted that the president had remarked on the "important information and advice that Mr. Painter had given him during his previous term on Indian matters" and then inquired whether Painter "had any prejudices or was at all a partisan." Welsh had assured him that he did not and was not. At the same time, he assured Garrett that he had been careful not to press for Painter's appointment because the IRA did not want to lose him.[11]

The decision was taken out of Painter's hands. Cleveland, ignoring all the reformers' suggestions, finally selected Daniel M. Browning. An Illinois politician more interested in an appointment as land commissioner, Browning knew nothing of Indian affairs. He took office on April 18, 1893. His predecessor, Thomas Jefferson Morgan, had resigned effective March 4, 1893, to accept the position of corresponding secretary of the American Baptist Home Mission Society. On April 19 Painter called on the new commissioner. "Favorably impressed," he described Browning as "a manly man, approachable, and simple in his manners," and "when he gets hold of matters will make a good Comm., or I am off in my judgment." By mid-May, Painter wrote that Browning had "expressed himself as fully committed to the educational and reform policy we have advocated." Although Browning was initially ignorant of Indian affairs, his boss, Interior Secretary Hoke Smith, a Georgia politician, proved a quick study, with advice and counsel from the IRA. The leaders of the association formed a more pleasant relationship with Smith than they had with his predecessor, Secretary Noble.[12]

In mid-May Painter informed Welsh that General Armstrong had died. It had not been unexpected because he had heart trouble. "To limited human view, his death seems a great blunder on the part of a great Administrator of mundane affairs," he wrote, "but I have learned that no one man is essential to any work." Armstrong had played an important role in Painter's professional life, recommending him as a lobbyist for the AMA and the IRA early on and then serving as his advisor and confidant. Painter expressed great fondness for the general, finding him always a tonic and an inspiration. Although he would miss him greatly, he had confidence that Armstrong's work would not suffer. "Twenty five years of his life has been more than one hundred of nineteen other men," he concluded.[13]

Once home from Florida and Mount Vernon, Painter busied himself with his usual letter writing and with interviews with the Indian commissioner and other department officials, calling their attention to issues the IRA wanted addressed. On one day he had spent more than an hour with the president, discussing policies and looking over a list of Indian agents to be removed. In an early June letter to Welsh, he described this interview as "highly satisfactory," learning later that his follow-up letter to the president with his "views fully in regard to a number of things" had been read during a cabinet meeting, and that his advice had been of great help. At this time Painter was juggling numerous issues on behalf of the IRA (he listed from memory twenty-two), dealing with at least sixteen different tribes.[14]

Painter was now home-based for a time, and in addition to his usual tasks he took on more speaking engagements. By early August he had made several addresses before groups interested in the work of the IRA. Over the year he would give seven major speeches, often before large audiences. He spoke in Kingston, New York, before a WNIA auxiliary in early August, noting that the national association had done a lot for the Cahuilla Mission in California. He also addressed the Congregational Club of Berkshire County, a large audience of leading Congregationalists, both ministers and laymen. An earlier talk at New Britain, Connecticut, had yielded fifty dollars for the IRA coffers. He was also invited to the South Berkshire Association of Congregational Ministers and hoped it would open the door for him to speak before more churches in their association. He also mentioned an upcoming talk at Lee, Massachusetts, on August 9.[15]

## The Board of Indian Commissioners

Painter's work in the fall of 1893 enrolling the Stockbridge Indians and visiting the New York reservations had been stressful because of Martha's poor health, which forced him to do much of his work by correspondence. In a mid-October letter he informed Welsh that she had been confined to her bed for a month with a case of typhoid fever. He was caring for her with the help of a trained nurse. Unable to find anyone to do housework, he complained that he was "almost unable to get even laundry work." In an October 25 letter, he noted that Martha still was unable to "sit up a single moment as yet."[16] He was, however, able to attend the annual BIC conference with missionary board representatives. Usually held in January, this one was in mid-December. Merrill Gates, board president, presided, acknowledging the importance of missionary societies in Indian work and reminding those present that although the government had become "fairly committed to a policy of education somewhat adequate to the need of the Indian," philanthropists and Christian workers must continue their efforts to awaken public opinion to hold Congress to their obligation. He followed with a brief history of the BIC and its "avowed intention of calling upon the religious societies and denominations to advise with the government steadily in regard to the policy to be pursued." He then called for the year's reports.[17]

During his presentation, Painter explained that although the Apache prisoners had a good school and Wotherspoon was doing all he could, these Indians had no future. "The friends of the Indian ought to take up this matter, and give the administration no peace until a permanent home is found for them." He followed with a brief discussion of his enrollment work among the Stockbridge Indians and subsequent visit to the New York reservations, finding the Cattaraugus Reservation the most impressive. When he had addressed a church sociable at the neat and commodious Presbyterian Church there, he needed no interpreter. The women invited him to visit their sewing society and the Iroquois temperance society. The dinner he was served was comparable to any he would get visiting a farmhouse near Great Barrington. The down side was that whiskey sellers were continually entering the reservation, despite Painter's complaints to the agent. In a late December letter to Welsh, Painter noted that it was essential to local whites to "uphold the pagan power, because it is through this party they gain such concessions in regard to land." He concluded that "some kind of protection must be given the Christian minority."[18]

The BIC meeting over and the holidays passed, Painter welcomed the coming new year. On January 9, 1894, he informed Welsh, "I think you will suffer me if I show a little foolish pride." His son Charles had been appointed to the Children's Hospital in Boston, winning the position against four-year men.[19] Then twenty days later, President Grover Cleveland appointed Painter to the prestigious Board of Indian Commissioners. This new position, he informed Welsh, would provide him with "authority for making inquiries which heretofore I have made on the strength and size of cheek, and my rights as an American citizen."[20]

Painter used this new authority wisely. His IRA report for 1894 was the longest ever—forty-three pages—and reflected only some of his accomplishments, including holding off Ute removal again.[21] One positive note was the success of the Civil Service reform that he and Welsh had pushed. Painter reported a great improvement in classified personnel, although there were still major problems, with unclassified positions, such as agents, inspectors, allotting agents, and industrial teachers appointed by the president and not subject to the Civil Service Commission. These latter positions he described as "unstopped holes in the service," large enough for political influence "to still filter in to do infinite damage."[22] As usual, his investigative tours were frequent but short—a trip to South Dakota to deal with the Flandreau Indians, suffering because of a drought, a visit to the Mexican Kickapoos of Oklahoma and the Shawnees and Pottawatomies, all with allotment difficulties, and a return to the Cheyenne and Arapaho Agency. Along the way he continued his practice of visiting Indian schools. He also had to deal with the ongoing claims of the Murphy clan on the Sac and Fox Reservation[23] and allotment issues among Mission Indians of Southern California.

### The Mission Indians

From his first visit to their villages in 1885, Painter had developed an intense interest in the Mission Indians' welfare. On April 26, 1893, he had written President Cleveland that he feared he had "been unfortunate in the selection" of their agent. In fact, Painter believed the Mission Agency should be abolished altogether, describing the Indians as "injured and not helped" by it. Supplies necessary for the aged and helpless could easily be issued from the several schools if the supervisor of education were entrusted with this duty and aided by a good clerk.[24] Ironically, five months later Painter would praise the same agent, Francisco Estudillo; he was "very much delighted" with the agent's lengthy letter to the Indian Office and believed that his opinion of the recommendations of his predecessor (Horatio Nelson Rust) had been spot on. Estudillo had condemned those that should have been condemned "and threw great emphasis upon the importance of others." Based on this businesslike manner and what he had learned of the new agent, Painter declared "that he will make the best agent those Indians have had."[25]

Concerned about the Mission Indians and secure enough in his relationship with Cleveland to complain, Painter criticized Secretary Noble's "sentimental appointment" of Kate Foote as allotment agent for the Rincon Reservation. He described her as "utterly incompetent for this work." However, relevant records reveal that Foote, a WNIA member, appeared to be diligent, holding frequent meetings with the Indians and viewing the work of the surveyors daily.[26]

Painter next complained about allotting agent John F. Carerre of Spokane, appointed by Noble at the request of Republican Representative John L. Wilson from Washington and in Painter's opinion "both incompetent and unfit." Painter's disgust may have been due to the fact that he had his own candidate for the position—Edward Dorn, a graduate of Ann Arbor, Michigan, "a splendid man, a competent land and water surveyor" whom Painter had employed as a surveyor for the Mission Indian Commission. When he completed his surveying for Painter, Dorn had been called way on other duties before he could plot and map the surveys—a task not completed until early 1892.[27] At present, he was employed by the current allotting agents in California. The California Mission Indian Commission had put forward his name, but he was not appointed as his views were not "in political accord with the administration." Painter placed his name before the president again in 1893.[28]

On January 22, 1894, Painter wrote Welsh that after a long wait the previous Saturday and an hour wait that very morning he had finally been able to see Secretary Smith in an attempt to hold off Special Agent Harry W. Patton, the allotment agent for the Mission Indians, from removing Dorn as surveyor.[29] Four days later Painter was still "very much disturbed," accusing Patton of trying to remove Dorn, a Republican, and replacing him with Cave Couts Jr., a Democrat. A search of Land Office records revealed that Couts was unfit to hold the position, and his appointment was delayed until Democratic California Senator Stephen White[30] had stepped in, visited the Land Office, argued on Couts's behalf, and vouched for him. Dorn was removed and Couts appointed, prompting Painter to describe the incident as "a most important step in the direction of making allotments with reference to white interest." White, Painter reminded Welsh, had been counsel for former governor John Gately Downey and the Bank of San Francisco, plaintiffs in the Warner Ranch case, who had succeeded in ejecting the Indians from the ranches' five villages. Painter was also still "swearing mad" about Foote's appointment, believing that had she not been appointed, Dorn might have been. "Sentimentalism is as bad, if not worse, than pure cussedness in Indian affairs," he concluded.[31]

On February 2 Painter described a "very satisfactory interview" with Cleveland. The president requested that he write a clear statement of his objections to Dorn's dismissal and Couts's appointment. Painter also suggested that Patton be removed. However, by late February Painter had also become exasperated with Cleveland and Secretary Smith; no action had been taken to remove Patton. "I feel very strongly that we ought to look into the manner in which these allotments are being made," he informed Welsh, and "discover, if we can, the ulterior purpose of Senator White, and allotting agent Patton, in bouncing Dorn and getting such a man as Coutts [*sic*] in his place."[32]

### Indian Depredation Claims

On February 2 Painter also broached the problem of Indian depredation claims being paid from Indian funds held in trust, an issue he had addressed at the October 1892 Mohonk Conference. Wanting to know the proper time for the IRA to appoint a special attorney to defend Indian interests, Painter visited Assistant Attorney General Charles B. Howry, who explained that "as long as the cases are to be defended by the Attorney-General, the interest of the Indians and the United States are such that one defense will answer for both." Only when the government actually made the Indians pay a rendered judgment would it be advisable to appoint a special attorney.[33]

Temporarily satisfied that there was no need to employ a new attorney, Painter took the issue to the public in a letter to Quinton, who earlier had questioned him about the probable impact of actions brought by claimants against Indians.[34] This letter, printed in the February issue of *The Indian's Friend*, prompted a mild rebuke from longtime friend and member of the IRA executive board Charles Pancoast. Painter, who did not believe he deserved the rebuke, told Pancoast so. Painter had explained that the government always punished Indians responsible for depredations committed during war. While these wars were seldom "if ever inaugurated by the Indians," they always resulted in the government recouping finances by forcing punitive cessions upon the Indians, thereby acquiring vast amounts of land. Since August 1 actions brought against various tribes had amounted to $40 million dollars, while the total amount of Indian-held funds in the last report was only $33 million. If this law continued to operate, "a large part, if not all of these funds,—certainly all that are not protected by some treaty stipulation, will disappear," complained Painter. He explained that recently legislation had been introduced before Congress repealing the law allowing these claims, the Indian Depredation Act of 1891, and Commissioner Browning had written a strong letter to Interior Secretary Smith recommending its passage. "The efforts of the friends of the Indians should be directed to this end," Painter concluded, "or to secure the payment of such claims from the United States Treasury."[35]

## Old Issues

The ongoing Ute removal bill also continued to require Painter's constant attention. On February 15, he informed Welsh that he had attended three hearings before the House Committee on Indian Affairs and would be attending another the following day. Four days later he described Rev. Thomas Childs, who had the floor on Saturday before the Indian Committee, placing "himself in a very bad position with respect to 'truth and veracity.'" Painter's questions relevant to whether Childs's Ute Commission had taken sufficient time to make a reliable report was leading to a confrontation until committee members informed Childs that such "controversy would have no place in the report they had to make." This was only one of "several instances of glaring departures from what was true," Painter remarked. He also noted that his recent appointment to the BIC made it possible for him to now accompany General Whittlesey to Chicago for the opening of livestock bids since part of the board's responsibility was to be present at the purchase of Indian goods. However, Commissioner Browning protested Painter's departure with the Ute fight still at hand, leading Painter to assume that Browning was opposed to their removal and had "some appreciation of the work of the Association." Four days later Painter wrote that with the Ute bill stalled, those interested in the Indians' removal were contemplating an agreement with the New Mexico congressional delegate to remove them there. In mid-April, when the Ute bill was reported to the full committee, it was again voted down.[36]

Another long-term concern was finding a permanent home for the Chiricahua Apaches. In 1889 Painter and John Bourke had visited various sites, including the Eastern Cherokee Reservation in North Carolina, which both men agreed would be satisfactory. On February 23 Painter wrote Welsh that he had conferred about the issue with John P. Clum, a former Apache agent, and that he had recently received a letter from Bourke. "It would seem as if there was a movement in the minds of men in different parts of the country as to the necessity of dealing with this question," concluded Painter. He knew of no better solution than to urge the purchase of the North Carolina land. A week later, while visiting the office of Adjutant General George D. Ruggles in regard to another issue, he brought up the Apache prisoners. Ruggles sent him on to the office of the assistant secretary of war to confer with a Captain Davis, who shared with him Wotherspoon's report on his latest investigative visit to North Carolina; the lieutenant had disliked the site. It was too rugged and had narrow valleys, with too many Cherokee and white occupants. Disappointed, Painter pointed out that this visit had been made in the winter when the country was at its worst. Davis agreed, and offered to accompany Painter in the spring, inviting Wotherspoon to join them.[37]

In early April Painter informed Welsh that Whittlesey and he were ready to return with Davis to North Carolina. However, when he arrived at the War Department to make the arrangement, he learned that Davis was off on another inspection tour. Painter decided it was not prudent to leave Washington at the time, and Whittlesey went on his own.[38] Later, in October 1894, without advance notification, the War Department moved the Apaches to Fort Sill in Indian Territory. This move, Painter reported, was "a very great surprise to many, especially as it seems to have been promoted by certain army officers who protested against it a few years ago." He continued, "It is to be regretted that no preparation was made for their reception at Fort Sill;

that they were dumped unprotected upon this land so near the beginning of winter." Painter would visit the Apaches at Fort Sill during his fall trip to the Indian Territory. On that bleak raw day, he found many of them living in brush and cloth teepees, fondly remembering the comfortable homes they had occupied at Mount Vernon. During a spring visit to Mount Vernon three years earlier, Quinton had described these two-room houses as made of planks, with good floors, open fireplaces and arranged around a large open plaza. Painter only hoped that this plunge back to "teepee life" would not be demoralizing.[39]

It was fortunate that Painter had remained in Washington that spring, monitoring congressional hearings. He was kept extremely busy in April and May 1894. On April 17 he informed Welsh that the subcommittee for the House Appropriations Committee had proposed to abolish the Office of the Superintendent for Indian Schools, along with three of its inspectors. "I have little fear that Congress will ratify such a price of stupidity but a fight is called for," he concluded. Two days later, he informed Welsh he had met committee members "and let them have a broad side in their proposal to abolish the office of Superintendent." At month's end he reported that the House Appropriations Committee proposed cutting funding drastically, crippling the Indian service, cutting agents' salaries, and withholding the annual five thousand dollars for traveling expenses for members of the BIC. Painter described this latter move as absurd. Board members were men "whose services the government could not purchase at any price, but which are freely given." Federal law required that the Indian commissioner make all purchases of Indian supplies subject to the inspection of the BIC. When funding had been cut several years earlier, General Whittlesey had personally maintained the office, and some members paid their own expenses. The following year funding was returned and everyone was reimbursed. However, this time Whittlesey refused to use his own money. Painter warned that the office might close, thus returning purchasing to the former condition of "partnerships between agents, traders, and contractors." This was a recipe for undelivered supplies, blank vouchers filled in with fraudulent sums, annuity goods either going to agents or employees or being sold to locals—"all the abuses which were so general that honesty and morality in the service were exceptional," concluded Painter.[40]

Painter called these draconian cuts "Holmanism,—microscopic guardship of the spigot," a reference to Indiana Congressman William S. Holman, former chair of the Appropriations Committee, who was legendary for his frugality. In April Painter had learned that the Appropriations Committee had grown quite exasperated with Holman, who kept flying out of his seat, tramping up and down, describing his visit years ago to a reservation, and making it impossible for them to get any work done on the bill. In early May Painter had met with several congressmen, including Holman, who had assured him that conditions had changed since the BIC had been created in 1869 and that there was no danger of fraudulent contracts given that considerable inspections of supplies were already in place. This did not allay Painter's fears, however. Painter was also dismayed that the Appropriations Committee never consulted President Cleveland or, apparently, Commissioner Browning, who had informed Painter that he wanted the BIC to remain, not simply to secure better supplies "but because of the confidence it gives to bidders." Painter expressed hope that all would be made right in the Senate. He would supply Welsh with names of congressmen the IRA could call upon for support.[41]

In mid-May Painter informed Welsh that the Indian Appropriation Bill as reported in the House by the Committee on Indian Affairs was $1.2 million less than in the current year, not only "cutting to the quick in the school work" but also providing no compensation for the BIC. In fact the bill had proposed to abolish the board altogether. In mid-July Painter reported to Welsh that the Senate Committee had amended the House bill, and although it was not all they wanted, it was improved. Education funding had been increased, and the BIC had been saved, enabling him to write in his final IRA report that when passed, the bill was "shorn of some of its most objectionable features." Nevertheless, it "still "impose[d] vexatious limitations where there should have been generous expansion."[42] In his letters to Welsh, Painter had provided sufficient evidence to enable the IRA to take action. Therefore in its annual report, the association attributed the four-thousand-dollar appropriation for the BIC and less drastic reductions in the remainder of the provisions to "the protests called forth by the appeals issued to our members and friends, and the general public," as well as the cooperation of the press.[43]

In early April, Browning invited Painter to accompany him to Chicago and New York to be present when bids were opened for Indian supplies. The commissioner's objection about Painter being absent from Washington was no longer valid now that the Ute bill had again failed. Painter planned a quick trip to the Indian Territory afterward, in regard to the Kickapoo issue. The second week of May, he left for Chicago, from there informing Welsh on the twenty-second that they had purchased 41 million pounds of beef at $2.75 per hundredweight. The BIC had saved so much money on Indian supplies that one hundred thousand dollars could be added back to educational work. His work on the bids was interrupted by a lengthy visit to the dentist for an abscess that for the past several years had been troubling him, forcing him to take a later train to New York than Commissioner Browning.[44]

With the bidding for Indian supplies in Chicago and New York completed and the appropriation bill passed, Painter informed Welsh in late July that he was taking time off and heading for the Connecticut seaside with Martha, who was still unwell. On August 8 he wrote that they had returned refreshed by their "sniffs of salt air," but the heat and dryness at home had since taken away all they had gained. Scheduled to leave in two days for St. Paul, Minnesota, to represent the BIC at the Institute for Teachers in the Indian Service Conference from August 13 to the 18, he feared he would miss his brother's homecoming from China. The St. Paul meeting was the last in a series held under the supervision of Dr. W. N. Hailmann, superintendent of Indian Schools. One hundred and forty teachers, superintendents, and matrons attended, paying their own way. Painter observed a "manifest improvement" of the teaching force since schools had been placed under Civil Service reform regulations. Explaining that reservation schools perpetuated the tribal idea while off-reservation schools gave students a taste for comforts and decencies, he pondered which method was the best.[45]

## Investigative Tours

Following his appearance in St. Paul, Painter visited the Tuscarora and Tonawanda Reservations in Western New York to finish work he had started the previous year. The IRA's Executive Committee had decided it was time to investigate the Indians' present condition and urge Congress to take appropriate action to relieve the more progressive tribal members. The previous winter the Christian Party on the Onondaga, Cattaraugus, and Allegheny

Reservations had petitioned for citizenship. Based on what he saw, Painter was convinced that this was in their best interest.[46]

From there he paid a visit to the Winnebago and Omaha Reservations in Nebraska, writing Welsh on October 5 how painful it was for him to "report the deplorable conditions in which these Indians are at present." When he visited them four or five years earlier, Alice Cunningham Fletcher was allotting the Winnebago Reservation, having already allotted the Omaha Reservation. "Their best land had been given them, and they were entering upon their new life as segregated farmers and citizens with a degree of intelligent enthusiasm most encouraging," he glowingly wrote at the time. Most lived in comfortable homes and were breaking their land and cultivating their crops. However, during this visit, with the exception of those who had been farming prior to allotments, he found few engaged in agriculture. Without submitting a contract to the Interior Department as required, the Flournoy Live Stock and Real Estate Company had leased forty-seven thousand acres from the Indians at mere pennies per acre, subletting the same at a fair rental and pocketing the difference. Acting Agent William H. Beck, a captain of the Tenth Cavalry, had tried to eject the lessees but was then served with a restraining order by a U.S. District Court judge. Painter explained to Welsh that the case was on appeal and everyone was anxiously awaiting the decision. In the end, the company continued to make leases without a contract.[47]

The situation at the Omaha Reservation was little better. He passed through ten to fifteen miles of pasture, corn fields, and vast meadows, all but a few acres leased to white farmers. Although the Omahas had gotten more for their land than the Winnebagoes had, this only made the opportunity for debauchery greater. Many had left their homes, constructed with financing by the Connecticut branch of the WNIA, and had moved into "teepees along river bluffs," living "degraded and demoralized lives." Saloon keepers, afraid to sell liquor directly, reached them through middle men. Painter explained that all Indians were irreparably injured by this leasing program and were directly or indirectly "put back a score of years in their civilization." He concluded, "[T]here has never been a time when the situation has been so full of danger to the Indian with reference to his land as now."[48]

Painter's attendance at Lake Mohonk in October provided him with a much larger audience than merely Welsh and the IRA. On Thursday, October 11, 1894, he described to the attendees what he had recently witnessed on the Omaha and Winnebago Reservations. "We need to awake to the danger which now threatens these children of our care; for children most of them are as yet, so far as ability to cope with the white man for land is concerned," he warned.[49]

## Mexican Kickapoos

His obligations at the Mohonk Conference completed, Painter set out on his next investigative tour, following up on a request made the previous winter by a delegation of Mexican Kickapoo Indians protesting their allotment process. On November 10 and 11, he interviewed a number of their leaders at their village and in the mission school. These Kickapoos were under the jurisdiction of the Sac and Fox Agency, in Oklahoma, as were the Sac and Fox, the Iowas, the Absentee Shawnees, and the Citizen Band of the Pottawatomies. The Kickapoo Reservation, which included the Quaker-run Kickapoo Mission, was some forty-five miles southwest of the Sac and Fox Agency. Their ancestors had moved to Texas and, following the Texas war of independence, had been driven into Mexico, where they remained until they were forced to return to the Indian Territory in 1873. During their visit to Washington, the head of the delegation, Pa-pa-shekit, had informed Painter that commissioners who wanted them to divide their lands had visited their reservation; after three days of council, a vote had been taken with only two dissenters against allotment. Although the commissioners never returned, sometime later a man named Hill persuaded seven tribal members to go to Oklahoma City, where they met up with the original commissioners.[50] There it was agreed that a delegation would go to Washington to sign a paper. No money changed hands. Then one day someone came to allot their lands. Painter later learned that the Indian delegation, which had visited Secretary Noble's office several times, had unknowingly signed an agreement selling part of their land and allotting the rest.[51]

Painter consulted the commissioner's report, which confirmed that councils had been held with reference to this sale and allotment. After a thorough investigation and an examination of the un-notarized document, Painter concluded that the entire transaction bore such "palpable marks of fraud" that it was difficult for him to understand how the commissioner or interior secretary could be so deceived. Since no rolls had been taken, it was impossible to know whether names on any signed papers were Kickapoo. Contending that they never sold the land, some 226 out of 284 refused their allotments and left their houses and farms to move into a makeshift camp.[52]

As he drove across the Kickapoo Reservation, Painter saw only abandoned buildings, desolate orchards, and ruined fields, with a large group of Indians living in "bark huts and tepees—the nearest approach to wild Indians that can be found." Whites had already taken over the land, perching like vultures ready to descend. On the positive side, Painter favorably described the Kickapoo Mission and school, run by devoted Quaker women supervised by Elizabeth Test, a government field matron. According to Painter, these missionaries felt strongly that the Indians' treatment "had alienated and made them averse from civilized pursuits."[53]

At the request of the BIC, Painter also visited the Shawnees and Pottawatomies in November to explain to them their authorization to sell recently allotted lands in excess of eighty acres. By this time, most of the Indians had leased their allotments, and unscrupulous whites were using "all means to rob them of their lands." A group of educated tribal members had formed a committee whose approval was required for future leasing arrangements. Painter was impressed with their noble work, which provided a protective wall. He hoped to encourage and support them in their continued fight, describing their efforts as an illustration "that education is the solution of our so-called Indian problem."[54]

Painter found "repair, thrift and tidiness" at the Cheyenne and Arapaho Agency, whereas before he had found only "decadence and dilapidation." Loafers, both Indian and white, had largely disappeared. Waxing poetic, Painter described his feeling as "a tonic ozone of energy impregnate[ing] the air which for years has been loaded with a suffocating miasma of indolence." The government schools were overflowing, and the mission school was "once more full of promise." He praised the acting Indian agent, Captain A. E. Woodson of the Fifth Cavalry, commenting that the "wisdom of selecting army officers for the position of Indian agent" was definitely justified at this reservation. He visited nine schools during this tour.[55]

Painter arrived at the Kiowa and Comanche Reservation at Anadarko, Oklahoma, on November 19, 1894, the same day that Frank D. Baldwin, captain in the Fifth Infantry, assumed his duty as acting agent. Baldwin's appointment "was regarded by army officers who are friends of the Indians as being a wise one." While there Painter witnessed a beef issue, which he described as "more than *fair!*" The future of these two tribes, Painter noted, depended upon the action taken "with reference to the approval or non-approval of the recent agreement made with them by the Cherokee Commissioners." Painter believed with certainty that these Indians had been "defrauded outrageously in this agreement."[56]

The Cherokee Commission, appointed in July 1889, was composed of Lucius Fairchild, former Wisconsin governor; John F. Hartranft, former Pennsylvania governor; and Judge Alfred M. Wilson of Arkansas. The commission was authorized to negotiate with the Cherokees and all other tribes that claimed or owned land west of ninety-sixty degrees longitude in the Indian Territory for the cession of their land to the public domain. The commissioners had begun with the Indians living in the Cherokee Outlet and continued negotiating with the rest of the territory's tribal inhabitants. Based on his own observations, Painter was convinced that the commission—inspired and supported by Secretary Noble, who was overly ambitious in opening up as much Indian land as possible to white settlement—had "put back the cause of Indian civilization in that Territory more than fifty years." He described the history of this commission's dealings with the Kickapoos, Cheyennes and Arapahoes, and Kiowas and Comanches as bringing "the blush of shame to the cheek of the honest citizen." He accused them of using "trickery, coercion, threats, and cunning" as they over-reached and defrauded "these dependent and trusting wards of the Nation."[57]

His investigative tour concluded, Painter was one of the nearly one hundred IRA members who gathered at the Holy Trinity Parish House on December 6, 1894, to listen to the twelfth annual report and addresses by prominent speakers. Painter himself spoke to several issues, beginning with crop failures that set up potential starvation among western tribes unless Congress provided speedy relief. He also addressed the misuse of leasing Indian lands, giving the example of a five-year lease of 250 acres "of the finest land to be found anywhere" for the cost of a barbed-wire fence and a house and barn worth thirty-five dollars. The *Philadelphia Inquirer* reporter described him as speaking "in tears and tones of shame and indignation at the outrageous conduct of the Cherokee Commission towards the Kickapoos."[58]

On December 18 Painter sent Welsh his report, which he described as "my manuscript *volume*." He suggested that because of its length, it might be more economical to print it as part of the IRA annual report instead of as a separate pamphlet. Welsh followed his suggestion. Painter in the meantime was off to the War Department to protest against the withdrawal of the cavalry from Forts Sill and Reno. He planned on spending the holidays in his old home in Pulaski City, Virginia, in order to visit with his brother, who had recently returned from China. "We are to have one more, and doubtless our last family reunion," he informed Welsh. He planned to be back at Congress promptly after the recess.[59]

Because his return train was late getting to Lynchburg, Painter was stranded there overnight and did not reach Washington until January 2, two days before the House of Representatives opened after the holiday recess. His stenographer had failed to come to work, and he made little progress in getting his correspondence answered. A large number of Indian agents from the Dakotas and Minnesota were gathered in the capital to attend a general conference called by Secretary Smith to decide the "best and most urgent things to be done" for the Sioux and Chippewas. To Painter's delight, the Ute bill still had not become law; it had passed the House the previous spring as he was headed for Chicago and New York, and he therefore had assumed it would pass the Senate. He then met two Colorado members who "expressed the idea that I must be very happy because I had defeated them so utterly," he informed Welsh. He concluded with a health update. He had taken a severe cold the other day, and noting his "think machinery [was] much out of running order," he feared he would have trouble with both his left ear and an eye tooth, both of which had given him trouble in the past.[60] Six days later he was dead.

Washington physician Dr. William H. Seaman informed Welsh that Painter had died on the evening of Sunday, January 13, after a few hours of illness. General Eliphalet Whittlesey, who had spent much of Saturday with Painter, wrote Welsh that his death was a "great shock." Francis E. Leupp, a Civil Service reformer who would succeed Painter, informed Welsh that Painter had stopped by his office at 5:00 that afternoon for a long talk. Theodore Roosevelt, who had worked with Painter on Civil Service reform, lamented his death, suggesting Leupp as a possible replacement.[61]

Painter's final year for the IRA had been characteristically busy, as reflected by his forty-three page report. He had revisited old and ongoing issues, such as a permanent home for the Chiricahua Apaches, preventing the Ute removal, and an interest in the Mission Indians, while taking on new issues, such as the Florida Seminoles and the Mexican Kickapoos. He had engaged in a number of small investigative tours and, as usual, had attended and participated in the annual BIC and Lake Mohonk Conferences. His sudden death left the Indian reform movement without a key player in Washington.

▼ ▼ ▼

# CONCLUSION

On January 13, 1895, Charles Cornelius Coffin Painter died of a heart attack. Six days later in a special meeting, the Indian Rights Association Executive Committee described his Indian reform work as "as valuable as [it] was inconspicuous." He "possessed qualities of rare usefulness; he united with the highest purpose and the truest ideals sound judgment, keen perception, accurate knowledge of men, unbending purpose, and unfaltering courage." His advice was sought by legislators, his aid was welcomed by the executive branch, and his reservation journeys "were the means of bringing to public attention both the needs of the Indians and the practical methods by which those needs were to be considered and relieved." He met his personal and domestic duties fully along with "those wider obligations of American citizenship."[1] A year later his loss was described as "irreparable," "deeper rather than diminish[ing]"; his service as faithful and able; his character as "sterling," with a "fearless spirit [that] made him a champion of Indian rights all over the country."[2]

The Board of Indian Commissioners, during its January 15, 1895, meeting, unanimously adopted a tribute that described Painter as "peculiarly fitted for his position, having great vigor and energy in discovering and exposing abuses in the Indian service, zeal in the defense of the Indians' just rights, and perseverance in urging upon the Government and Congress important measures in their interest." His long experience made "him one of the best informed men in this country on the Indian question," someone who was frequently consulted by the president and Congress."[3] The following day, during the board's annual conference with representatives of missionary societies, Board President Merrill Gates informed members that on Sunday morning Painter had not been quite well and that by the close of day "he had passed on into the larger life." Gates expressed a special sadness because the various threads of different lines of Indian work that Painter had so skillfully worked were now severed. "No one has yet been able to gather up all the lines of effort which he held when he so suddenly fell in his place at his work," he lamented. At the conclusion of the proceedings, during personal remarks, Rev. Lyman Abbott, head of Brooklyn's Plymouth Congregational Church, described Painter as being the "eyes for our Indian friends and Indian workers," seeing complicated issues "with that kind of clearness which belongs to the wholly disinterested nature." John Eaton, former U.S. Commissioner of Education, had welcomed Painter as a frequent visitor to his office. He stated, "It was delightful for me to see the fidelity of the man, and the wisdom and courage of the man. How many times was he assailed, but. . . . he stood firmly for the Indian according to the best wisdom of the time. Rarely have I seen a man so wise, so patient, so faithful, so unerring."[4]

General Eliphalet Whittlesey, BIC secretary, who for years had sat by Painter's side in the same office, described him as both advisor and helper, watching him grow into "a man of experience in the work." He was an "earnest, faithful worker, loving the cause in which he was engaged, and in which he has done such good service," and Whittlesey concluded it would be difficult for the IRA to find a "man adequate to fill his place." And Dr. A. I. Church, a pastor who had served in Stafford Springs, Connecticut, at the same time as Painter, described him as a "capable man, a faithful, and efficient pastor" who took "a poor society, without shelter or home, and at the risk of his own health and by his personal exertions left a new, beautiful church, and a united and strong society."[5] Church was referring to the Stafford Springs Congregational Church; when the town reservoir broke, it had been swept away, along with most of the business portion of the borough, and Painter almost single-handedly had built a new church. The current congregation in his memory unanimously adopted the following: "We feel that in his death the church universal has lost a faithful worker, one true to the great principles taught by Christ, and our prayer is that we may imitate his life of uprightness, righteousness and Christian philanthrophy [sic]." The Sunday after his death, they held a memorial service in his honor.[6]

Painter's hometown newspaper described him as an "uncommonly good judge of human character," able to deal successfully with Congress and its various committees. On a more personal note, he was viewed as possessing a "strong and abiding confidence in human friendship," with a special "interest in young people."[7] Both the WNIA and Hampton Institute published tributes. *The Indian's Friend* described him as bringing to his Indian work "great natural ability and practical wisdom" and showing "faithful preparation, courage, fidelity and devotion," while Hampton's *The Southern Workman* described his loss as "incalculable." He was patient and persistent, possessed of a "shrewdness and exactness with a breadth of nature and of view; he was unpartisan, a man honest and fearless, and also a man of fairness, judgment and tact."[8]

The Lake Mohonk Conference tribute came in the fall of 1895. Painter's loss was deeply felt. Rev. Lyman Abbott described his fellow cleric as representing "the opinions of philanthropic and Christian coworkers in the cause of the Indians" before Congress, fulfilling "his always difficult and often thankless task with keen vigilance, tireless energy, good judgment, and unfailing tact." His influence was responsible for the "generally cordial co-operation between government and voluntary agencies."[9]

Collectively these tributes reveal the true essence of the Congregational minister turned Indian reformer who for a decade served as a voice of reason within the late-nineteenth-century Indian reform movement. His work left a lasting impact on the government's relations with Indians on reservations across the country, and it deserves to be recognized today.

▼ ▼ ▼

# NOTES

The following abbreviations are employed in source notes:

AMA       American Missionary Association
ASQ       Amelia Stone Quinton
BIC       Board of Indian Commissioners
CIA       Commissioner of Indian Affairs
CCP       Charles C. Painter
Ex. Com.  Executive Committee
GPO       Government Printing Office
HHJ       Helen Hunt Jackson
HW        Herbert Welsh
IRA       Indian Rights Association
LMC       Lake Mohonk Conference
LR        Letters Received
NA        National Archives & Records Administration
SCA       Samuel Chapman Armstrong
SI        Secretary of the Interior
WNIA      Women's National Indian Association

## Preface

1. Valerie Sherer Mathes, "The California Mission Indian Commission, 1891: The Legacy of Helen Hunt Jackson," *California History* 72, no. 4 (Winter 1993–94): 339–59.

## Introduction

1. "The Tribute of a Friend: In Memoriam," *Berkshire Courier*, January 24, 1895, 3.
2. William T. Hagan, *The Indian Rights Association: The Herbert Welsh Years, 1882–1904* (Tucson: University of Arizona Press, 1985; hereafter *The IRA*), 23; "The Late Rev. Charles C. Painter," *Springfield Sunday Republican*, January 20, 1895, 3 (quoting the *New York Evening Post*).

3. Francis Paul Prucha, S.J., *The Great Father: The United States Government and the American Indians* (Lincoln: University of Nebraska, 1984), 1:479–533.

4. "The Two Indian Policies," *American Missionary*, April 1878, 102.

5. These representatives were unpaid philanthropists and humanitarians nominated by major Protestant denominations, authorized to exercise joint control with the Interior Department in the purchase and inspection of food, disbursement of funds, negotiation of treaties, and organization of inspection tours.

6. "The Indian Commissioners," reprinted from the *New York Tribune* in the *American Missionary*, March 1878 (New York: AMA), 80.

7. The AMA also sent missionaries to Chinese immigrants in California; to the white population in the mountainous region of the South, establishing Berea College in Kentucky; and to Africa, Jamaica, and other foreign locations.

8. Prucha, *The Great Father*, 2:695.

9. By 1877 Congregational agents were in place at the Red Lake Agency in Minnesota, the Green Bay Agency and the Lake Superior Agency in Wisconsin, Fort Berthold Agency and the Sisseton Agency in Dakota Territory, and the S'Kokomish Agency in Washington Territory. See "The Indians," *Thirty-First Annual Report of the American Missionary Association* (hereafter *AMA*) (New York: AMA, 1877), 92–99. However, by 1881, the AMA oversaw only the Fort Berthold, Sisseton, and S'kokomish agencies; see "The Indians," *Thirty-Fifth Annual Report of the AMA* (New York: AMA, 1881), 103–105.

   See also "The Indians," *History of the American Missionary Association with Illustrative Facts and Anecdotes* (New York: AMA, 1891), 67–78; Augustus Field Beard, "Mission among the North American Indians," *A Crusade of Brotherhood: A History of the American Missionary Association* (Boston: Pilgrim Press, 1909), 65–93.

10. For a list of agencies and agents, see "Among the Indians," *American Missionary*, February 1878, 48.

11. "The Indians: Report of the Committee," *American Missionary*, December 1879, 394. The Boston Indian Citizenship Committee also promised these same goals, which would be later adopted by the other reform organizations as well. See "Final Recommendations," *The Indian Question: Report of the Committee Appointed by Hon. John D. Long* (Boston: Frank Wood, Book and Job Printer, 1880), 25–26.

12. See "Our Indian Work," *American Missionary*, October 1883, 291; "Report of Committee on Indian Missions," *American Missionary*, December 1883, 370. With the exception of its Indian missions, the board's work was located in foreign lands, while the AMA's work, with the exception of their West African mission, was within the United States. This transfer of the board's Indian missions to the AMA unified the AMA's work.

13. See *The Bi-centennial Celebration of the Founding of the First Baptist Church of the City of Philadelphia* (Philadelphia: American Baptist Publication Society, 1899), 391; *The Women's Baptist Home Mission Society 1877 to 1882* (Chicago: R. R. Donnelley, 1883), 7. See also Helen M. Wanken, "Woman's Sphere and Indian Reform: The Women's National Indian Association, 1879–1901" (Ph.D. diss., Marquette University, 1981);

Valerie Sherer Mathes, *Divinely Guided: The California Work of the Women's National Indian Association* (Lubbock: Texas Tech University Press, 2012); *The Women's National Indian Association: A History*, ed. Valerie Sherer Mathes (Albuquerque: University of New Mexico Press, 2015).

14. Amelia Stone Quinton (hereafter ASQ), "Care of the Indian," *Woman's Work in America*, ed. Annie Nathan Meyer (New York: Henry Holt, 1891), 377; WNIA, "A Historical Sketch," *The Indian's Friend*, October 1896, 2; Valerie Sherer Mathes, "Mary Lucinda Bonney and Amelia Stone Quinton, Founders of the Women's National Indian Association," *American Baptist Quarterly* 28:4 (Winter 2009), 421–40.

15. ASQ, "Care of the Indian," 379. Quinton was an organizer in Brooklyn for the Woman's Christian Temperance Union, while Bonney was an educator and founder of the Chestnut Street Female Seminary. Solvent because of her school, in 1878 Bonney had also won a judgment valued at $5,675 ($130,000 today) against the Fort Scott Illuminating Gas Company. See *Fort Scott Weekly Monitor*, May 23, 1878.

16. "Memorial Letter, Accompanying the Indian Petition of 1881," in ASQ, "Care of the Indian," 380.

17. U.S. Congress, House, "Observance of Indian Treaty Stipulations," 46th Cong., 2nd sess., February 20, 1880, *Congressional Record*, vol. 10, part 2, 1044; ASQ, "Care of the Indian," 378. See also Jeffrey Burton, *Indian Territory and the United States, 1866–1906: Courts, Government, and the Movement for Oklahoma Statehood* (Norman: University of Oklahoma Press, 1995.

18. U.S. Congress, Senate, "Senator Dawes Presents Petition," 46th Cong., 3rd sess., January 27, 1881, *Congressional Record*, 953–54; ASQ, "Care of the Indian," 379–80.

19. Proceedings on the Occasion of the Presentation of the Petition of the Women's National Indian Association, by Hon. H. L. Dawes, February 21, 1882 (Washington, D.C.: 1882), 1–12; U.S. Congress, Senate, "Rights of Indians," 47th Cong., lst sess., February 21, 1882, *Congressional Record*, vol. 13, part 2, 1327. See also ASQ, "Care of the Indian," 382.

20. ASQ, "Care of the Indian," 383.

21. Valerie Sherer Mathes, "Boston, the Boston Indian Citizenship Committee, and the Poncas," *Massachusetts Historical Review* 14 (2012), 119–48. The committee went through several name changes—"Ponca Indian Committee," "Committee of Five," and "Boston Committee on Indian Reforms and the Ponca Wrongs"; see "Mr. Schurz and the Poncas," *New York Times*, January 10, 1881, 5. The earliest use of "Boston Indian Citizenship Committee" was in T. H. Tibbles, *The Ponca Chiefs: An Indian's Attempt to Appeal from the Tomahawk to the Courts* (Boston: J. S. Lockwood, 1887), after 146.

22. Tibbles, *Buckskin & Blanket Days* (Lincoln: University of Nebraska Press, 1957), 199. See also Valerie Sherer Mathes and Richard Lowitt, *The Standing Bear Controversy: Prelude to Indian Reform* (Urbana: University of Illinois Press, 2003); Thomas Henry Tibbles, *The Ponca Chiefs: An Account of the Trial of Standing Bear* (Lincoln: University of Nebraska Press, 1972).

23. The first committee members were Benjamin Webb Williams, Boston Lecture Bureau; Rev. Hale; Rev. William Bradley, pastor of the Heath Street Mission; Baxter Perry

Smith, philanthropist and historian; and Charles R. Ladd, former state legislator and current state auditor. See "The Poor Poncas; Suffering of Friendly Indians under Our Laws," *Boston Daily Advertiser*, July 31, 1879, 1.

24. New members were Frederick O. Prince, Boston mayor; Thomas Talbot, recently retired governor; Edward Isaiah Thomas, state legislator and philanthropist; Henry Oscar Houghton, publisher; Frank Wood, printer; John S. Lockwood, book seller and state assistant adjutant general; Joshua W. Davis, financier; Levi Clifford Wade, speaker of the Massachusetts lower house; Rev. Samuel Kirkland Lothrop, former pastor of the Church in Brattle Square; Henry Mason, owner of Mason & Hamlin Organ Company; and Samuel B. Capen, banker. See "The Ponca Indian Committee," August 11, 1879, 1, and "Local Miscellany," August 12, 1879, 4—both in the *Boston Daily Advertiser*.

25. Valerie Sherer Mathes, *Helen Hunt Jackson and Her Indian Reform Legacy* (Austin: University of Texas Press, 1990), 21–37.

26. *The Indian Question: Report of the Committee Appointed by Hon. John D. Long*, 25–26, and "The Secretary of the Interior and the Indian Question," *Advertiser*, February 3, 1880, 2.

27. Henry S. Pancoast, *Impressions of the Sioux Tribes in 1882, with Some First Principles in the Indian Question* (Philadelphia: Franklin Printing House, 1883); Herbert Welsh (hereafter HW), *Four Weeks among Some of the Sioux Tribes of Dakota and Nebraska, Together with a Brief Consideration of the Indian Problem* (Germantown, Philadelphia: Horace F. McCann, 1882).

28. Hagan, *The IRA*, 11–19; "The Object of the Association," *Fourth Annual Report of the Executive Committee* (hereafter *Ex. Com.*) *of the IRA for the Year Ending December 14, 1886* (Philadelphia: Office of the IRA, 1887), 3–4.

29. Hagan, *The IRA*, 25. In 1888 the IRA had twenty-eight branches, over half "moribund" (48). By 1885 the WNIA, in contrast, had fifty-six branches in twenty-seven states; see ASQ, "Care of the Indian," 385.

30. IRA of Cambridge, *Secretary's Records, March 1885*, Cambridge Public Library, Cambridge, Massachusetts, 2; "Cambridge and the Indians," *Cambridge Tribune*, December 24, 1887, 2.

The youngest child of Congressman Stephen Longfellow and his wife Zilpah Wadsworth Longfellow, Samuel attended Harvard Divinity School. Brother to Henry Wadsworth, he was a clergyman, an abolitionist, a pacifist, and a supporter of women's rights.

31. Hagan, *The IRA*, 23, 256. Sniffen's association with the organization began in 1884. He was Welsh's assistant until 1909, and he later became the IRA's executive secretary and was eventually on the board of directors, serving until 1942—an association of fifty-eight years.

32. Hagan, *The IRA*, 257.

33. Larry E. Burgess, "The Lake Mohonk Conferences on the Indian, 1883–1916" (Ph.D. diss., Claremont University, 1972).

34. Burgess, "The Lake Mohonk Conferences," 70–71.

35. Burgess, "The Lake Mohonk Conferences," quotes on 20, 22.

36. Davis, vice president and chairman of the Boston Indian Citizenship Committee, was a corporate member of the American Board of Commissioners for Foreign Missions and a director of the Congregational Sunday School and Publishing Society. See "Mr. Davis Dead," March 26, 1909, and "Mrs. Joshua W. Davis," April 2, 1909, in the *Newton Graphic.*

37. *First Annual Report of the Ex. Com. of the IRA for the Year Ending December, 1883* (Philadelphia: Office of the IRA, 1884), 5–6.

## Chapter 1. From Preacher to Indian Reformer

1. "A Steamer in Flames: The Granite State Burned to the Water's Edge," May 19, 1883, and "The Granite State Disaster," May 27, 1883, both in the *New York Times.* Painter's May 19 letter to Armstrong is found in Samuel C. Armstrong (hereafter SCA) Papers, Hampton University Archives, Hampton, Virginia.

2. On Painter's freshman year, see *Catalogue of the Officers and Students of Williams College for the Academic Year 1854–55* (Williamstown, Mass.: 1854), 15; and for his senior year, see *Catalogue of the Officers and Students and Register of Societies in Williams College, for the Academic Year 1857–58* (Williamstown, Mass.: The Sophomore Class, 1857), 55. See also *The Williams Obituary Record* (Williamstown, Mass.: Society of Alumni, 1895), 272–73; *The Delta Upsilon Quinquennial Catalogue* (Delta Upsilon Fraternity, 1884), 171; *The Delta Upsilon Decennial Catalogue* (Published by the Fraternity, 1902), 139; *First Congregational Church: Great Barrington, Mass. Parish Bulletin, 1895* (Great Barrington, Mass.: Edward V. Foote, 1895), 13.

3. *Historical Catalogue of the Theological Institute of Connecticut* (Hartford: Case, Lockwood & Brainard, 1881), 92. Founded in 1833 by Congregational ministers and located at East Windsor Hill, the institute was moved to Hartford in 1865 and is now known as the Hartford Theological Seminary. *The Williams Obituary Record* (273) and Rev. Mallary ("The Tribute of a Friend," *Berkshire Courier,* January 24, 1895) claim that Painter studied in Connecticut. However, the *First Congregational Church* (13) and "Death of Rev. C. C. Painter" (*Berkshire Courier,* January 17, 1895, 1) have him attending Andover Theological Seminary, founded in 1807 in Massachusetts.

4. For Painter's pastorates, see *Historical Catalogue of the Theological Institute of Connecticut,* 92; *The Delta Upsilon Decennial Catalogue,* 139; *First Congregational Church,* 13; *The Williams Obituary Record,* 273–74; *The Congregational Year-Book, 1896* (Boston: Congregational Sunday School and Publishing Society, 1896), 31; Bernard Drew, *Great Barrington Great Town Great History* (Great Barrington, Mass.: Great Barrington Historical Society, 1999), 70–71.

5. "Churches and Ministers," *New York Times,* December 29, 1878, 10. See also "New Appointments: Fisk University" (*American Missionary,* February 1879, 48), where Painter's home is listed as Stafford Springs, Connecticut.

Beth M. Howse, Special Collections Librarian at the John Hope and Aurelia E. Franklin Library at Fisk University, found no reference to Painter in Fisk records (personal e-mail dated March 26, 2009). Sources disagree as to his service: *The Delta*

*Upsilon Decennial Catalogue* (139) has him there as late as 1883; while *The Congregational Year-Book* (31) lists him only to 1880. It appears he was still soliciting money for Fisk as late as 1882; see "Mr. Teller's Ocean Grove Letter: A Letter from Professor Painter, of Fisk University," *Cherokee Advocate*, October 6, 1882, 1. Hamilton Child, in *Part Second: Business Directory of Berkshire County, Mass, 1884–85* (Syracuse: Printed at the Journal Office, 1885, 99), lists him as a professor at Fisk and secretary of the National Educational Committee, living in Great Barrington on Castle Street.

6. Clinton B. Fisk, a distinguished Civil War general, served as president of the BIC from 1881 until his death in 1890.

7. "New Appointments," *American Missionary*, January 1879, 48; "Educating the Negro," *Berkshire Courier*, January 7, 1880.

8. *Thirty-Third Annual Report of the AMA* (New York: AMA, 1879), 42; "American Missionary Association," *American Missionary*, May 1880, 129; *Thirty-Fourth Annual Report of the AMA* (New York: AMA, 1880), 40; *Thirty-Fifth Annual Report of the AMA* (New York: AMA, 1881), 51, *Thirty-Sixth Annual Report of the AMA* (New York: AMA, 1882), 52; *Thirty-Seventh Annual Report of the AMA* (New York: AMA, 1883), 10.

9. Hagan, *The IRA*, 21. Strieby, an 1842 graduate of Oberlin College, attended Oberlin Seminary and after ordination served for eleven years as pastor of the church at Mt. Vernon, Ohio. He moved to Syracuse, New York, where he organized the Plymouth Congregational Church, serving as pastor and preacher until becoming corresponding secretary for the AMA. He died on March 16, 1899. See "Rev. Michael E. Strieby, D.D.," *American Missionary*, April 1899, 1.

10. Charles would become an orthopedic surgeon; he attended Johns Hopkins University and received his medical degree in 1895 from Harvard. At the time of his father's death, he was working at Massachusetts General Hospital, later becoming dean at Tufts Medical College. During World War I he served at Chelsea Naval Hospital. He authored several books, including *Diseases of the Bones and Joints*. His father's older brother, Isaac Anderson Temple Painter, was also a doctor. See "Stricken with Heart Disease," *New York Times*, January 14, 1895; Drew, *Great Barrington Great Town*, 486; "Dr. C. F. Painter, Orthopedist, Dies," *Berkshire Courier*, January 23, 1947, 1.

11. Hamilton Child, *Part First: Gazetteer of Berkshire County, Mass., 1725–1885* (Syracuse: Printed at the Journal Office, January 1885), 150. See also Charles J. Taylor, *History of Great Barrington (Berkshire County) Massachusetts*. Great Barrington: Clark W. Bryan, 1882.

12. "American Missionary Association," *American Missionary*, May 1880, 129.

13. C. C. Painter (hereafter CCP), "The Negro for His Place," *American Missionary*, June 1881, 165–67, quotes on 167.

14. CCP, "Fisk University," *American Missionary*, July 1881, 203–5, quotes on 204.

15. For background on Carlisle, see *Carlisle Indian Industrial School: Indigenous Histories, Memories, and Reclamations*, Jacqueline Fear-Segal and Susan D. Rose, eds. (Lincoln: University of Nebraska Press, 2016); Jacqueline Fear-Segal, "The Man on the Bandstand at Carlisle Indian Industrial School," *Boarding School Blues: Revisiting American*

*Indian Educational Experiences,* ed. with introduction by Clifford E. Trafzer, Jean A. Keller, and Lorene Sisquoc (Lincoln: University of Nebraska Press, 2006), 99–122 and 13–15; Richard Henry Pratt, *Battlefield & Classroom: Four Decades with the American Indian, 1867–1904. An Autobiography,* ed. Robert M. Utley (Norman: University of Oklahoma Press, 2003); David Wallace Adams, *Education for Extinction: American Indians and the Boarding School Experience, 1875–1928* (Lawrence: University Press of Kansas, 1995), numerous pages.

16. Amory H. Bradford, "The Indians. Report of the Committee," *American Missionary,* November 1880, 364–65.

17. Financial difficulties resulted in the school's 1885 removal to Salem, Oregon. Renamed Chemawa Indian School, it continues in operation today.

18. Price represented Iowa in Congress in 1863 and was an early supporter of Indian reform. He served as commissioner of Indian Affairs from 1881 to 1885, promoting land allotment in severalty and establishing policies that curtailed Indian religious customs. See Floyd A. O'Neil, "Hiram Price 1881–85," in *The Commissioners of Indian Affairs, 1824–1977,* ed. Robert M. Kvasnicka and Herman J. Viola (Lincoln: University of Nebraska Press, 1979), 173–79.

19. Hiram Price, October 10, 1882, *Annual Report of the Commissioner of Indian Affairs* (hereafter *CIA) to the Secretary of the Interior* (hereafter *SI) for the Year 1882* (Washington, D.C.: Government Printing Office [hereafter GPO]), 1882), xxxii, xxxvi, xxxvii, xxxix–xlii.

20. CCP, "Governmental Aid to Common Schools: What Congress May Do and What Needs to Be Done," *American Missionary,* April 1882, 101–2.

21. "Dr. Strieby," *The Southern Workman and Hampton School Record,* April 1899, 124–25; "Obituary," *Chicago Tribune,* March 18, 1899.

22. Born in Connecticut, Whittlesey was a graduate of Yale and its divinity school. He served as a Congregational minister, taught at Bowdoin College and later at Howard University, and was a member of General Oliver O. Howard's staff during the Civil War. He was an assistant commissioner and adjutant of the Freedmen's Bureau, as well as an assistant and later secretary of the BIC from 1875 to 1899. See "Eliphalet Whittlesey," *Men of Mark in America: Ideals of American Life Told in Biographies of Eminent Living Americans,* ed. Merrill Edwards Gates (Washington, D.C.: Men of Mark, 1906), 2:394–96.

23. CCP to Strieby, January 14, 1882, AMA Archives, Amistad Research Center, Tulane University.

24. "Charles C. Painter," *Berkshire Courier,* January 17, 1895, 4. When he was home, Painter fulfilled various church obligations; see, for example, "Great Barrington First Congregational Church," *Berkshire Courier,* September 26, 1883.

25. Born in New York State, Teller moved to Colorado in 1861 and engaged in railroad and real estate concerns before his election to the Senate. He served as interior secretary from 1882 to 1885 before returning to the Senate until 1909. See Elmer Ellis, *Henry Moore Teller: Defender of the West* (Cadwell, Idaho: Caxton Printers, 1941).

26. "Journal of the Twelfth Annual Conference with Representatives of Missionary Boards," *Fourteenth Annual Report of the Board of Indian Commissioners* [hereafter *BIC*], *for the Year 1882* (Washington, D.C.: GPO, 1883), 57.

27. Porter, who had Creek ancestry on his mother's side, grew up in an affluent bilingual and bicultural family. A member of the Confederate First Creek Regiment during the Civil War, he later served as superintendent of Creek schools. Beginning in 1872 he made annual trips to Washington as a tribal spokesman. He also served as an informant on Creek culture for Smithsonian Institution ethnographers. See Michael D. Green, "Porter Pleasant," *Encyclopedia of North American Indians*, ed. Frederick E. Hoxie (Boston: Houghton Mifflin Company, 1996), 502–4.

28. CCP to Strieby, January 25, 1882, AMA Archives. Kirkwood, born in Maryland, practiced law in Ohio before moving to Iowa, where he served in the state senate and as governor twice before being elected to the U.S. Senate. He served as interior secretary from 1881 to 1882.

29. CCP to Strieby, April 4, May 17, and June 19, 1882, AMA Archives. See also CCP, "Education by Congressional Aid," *Southern Workman*, March 1882, 28; CCP, letter to the editor, *Southern Workman*, March 18, 1882, 52.

30. Eells had in fact been appointed on June 1, 1871, and would serve as agent until 1894. His brother, Myron, the AMA-appointed missionary at the S'Kokomish Agency, moved permanently to the reservation in 1874, remaining there the rest of his life, documenting the culture and writing articles and books. The Eells brothers were the sons of Rev. Cushing Eells, an early Congregational missionary to Oregon and later to neighboring Washington and founder of Whitman College. See George P. Castile, "Edwin Eells, U.S. Indian Agent, 1871–1895," *Pacific Northwest Quarterly* 72, no. 2 (April 1981), 61–68.

31. CCP to Strieby, June 23, 1882, AMA Archives.

32. CCP to Strieby, July 21 and July 31, 1882, AMA Archives. In a letter dated October 5, 1882, Painter noted he was meeting with a number of "monied" men, "calling their attention again to our need at Fisk."

33. Rev. J. C. Hartzell, comp. and ed., "Editor's Note," *Christian Educators in Council: Sixty Addresses by American Educators with Historical Notes upon the National Education Assembly Held at Ocean Grove, N.J. August 9–12, 1883* (New York: Phillips & Hunt, 1884), 6; for daily schedule, see "Historical Notes, *Christian Educators in Council*, 233–34. Both the Ocean Grove facility and the National Holiness Association were founded by William B. Osborn, and the facility at Ocean Grove, chartered in 1869 under the Ocean Grove Camp Meeting Association of the Methodist Episcopal Church, grew into a functional resort, enjoyed by the public, major conventions, and several presidents. See Morris S. Daniels, *The Story of Ocean Grove: Related in the Year of Its Golden Jubilee* (New York: Methodist Book Concern, 1919). For the National Educational Assembly, see 250.

34. "National Aid for National Education," *American Missionary*, October 1882, 292–94, 294 for Teller's letter.

35. See Hartzell, *Christian Educators in Council*, "Historical Notes," 234 for Blair's address and 233 for quote.

36. Hartzell, *Christian Educators in Council*: for Painter's letter, see "Historical Notes," 234–35; for the text of the memorial, see "Memorial of the National Education Assembly," 235.

37. CCP to Strieby, August 15, 1882, AMA Archives.

38. CCP to Strieby, December 19, 1882, AMA Archives.

39. CCP to SCA, February 27, 1883, SCA Papers.

40. CCP to SCA, March 8, 1883, SCA Papers. Presumably, the bill did not pass, for Painter did not mention it again.

41. Fletcher lived among the Omaha Indians in Nebraska for a year. An advocate for land allotment in severalty, she served as the allotting agent for the Omahas, the Winnebagoes, and the Nez Perces. She and LaFlesche, whom she treated as an adopted son, collaborated on *The Omaha Tribe* (1911). From 1903 to 1929 LaFlesche worked for the Bureau of American Ethnology and authored *A Dictionary of the Osage Language*. See Joan Mark, *A Stranger in Her Native Land: Alice Fletcher and the American Indians* (Lincoln: University of Nebraska Press, 1988).

42. CCP to SCA, March 8, 1883, SCA Papers. Harriet was the first president of WNIA's Washington auxiliary, and following her death in 1886, her sister assumed the position. For more, see "Kate Foote Coe," *A Century of Meriden, Part II* (Meriden, Conn.: Journal Publishing, 1906), 320–22; Sarah Whitmer Foster and John T. Foster Jr., "Historical Notes and Documents: "Harriet Ward Foote Hawley: Civil War Journalist," *Florida Historical Quarterly* 83, no. 4 (Spring 2005), 448–67; and Maria Huntington, *Harriet Ward Foote Hawley* (BiblioLife, 1923 reproduction).

43. CCP to SCA, March 19, 1883, SCA Papers.

44. Hagan, *The IRA*, 21, 23.

45. It is unclear how long the committee continued after 1884.

46. C. Joseph Genetin-Pilawa, "Thomas Bland's Moment, 1875–1886," in *Crooked Paths to Allotment: The Fight over Federal Indian Policy after the Civil War* (Chapel Hill: University of North Carolina Press, 2012), 125.

47. HW to SCA, May 1, 1883, SCA Papers; Hagan, *The IRA*, 21.

48. CCP to SCA, May 14, 19, and 25, 1883, SCA Papers; Hagen, *The IRA*, 26. For funding, see Davis to HW, May 15, 1883, *The IRA Records*, collection 1523, box 1, folder 4, Historical Society of Pennsylvania, Philadelphia, Pennsylvania (hereafter *IRA Records*).

49. In a May 19 letter to Armstrong, Painter described his escape. For his itinerary, see May 25 and 29, 1883—all in SCA Papers.

50. For the delegation, see "Our Indian Work," 291–92, and Rev. Addison P. Foster, "A Visit to the Dakota Mission," 292–94, both in *American Missionary*, October 1883.

51. In a letter to Teller (n.d., probably late 1882, AMA Archives), Painter introduced himself as the AMA secretary and recommended Thomas L. Riggs for the position of inspector of Indian schools, describing him as possessing a "sterling character" and "eminently" qualified for the position based on years spent as an Indian educator.

He thanked Teller for his work on behalf of "Indian Education, Indian Treaties & the management of the whole problem."

52. Foster, "A Visit to the Dakota Mission," 292–94, quote on 293. For a detailed report, see Rev. William Hayes Ward, "The Report of a Visit to the Dakota Mission," *Thirty-Seventh Annual Report of the AMA*, 11–18. Ward mentioned Painter's presence only briefly.

53. See "Visit to Dakota—Report of Commissioners Smiley and Whittlesey, July 20, 1883," *Fifteenth Annual Report of the BIC, for the Year 1883* (Washington, D.C.: GPO, 1884), 33–35; HW, *Report of a Visit to the Great Sioux Reserve, Dakota, Made during the Months of May and June, 1883, in behalf of the IRA, by Order of the Ex. Com.* (Philadelphia: Office of the IRA, 1883); Ward, "The Report of a Visit to the Dakota Mission," 16–18.

54. "Report of Commissioners Smiley and Whittlesey," quote on 34. See also "Address of Mr. A. K. Smiley," *Proceedings of the Twelfth Annual Meeting of the Lake Mohonk Conference* [hereafter *LMC*] *of Friends of the Indian, 1894* (LMC, 1894), 38; HW, *Report of a Visit to the Great Sioux Reserve*, 17; Burgess, "The Lake Mohonk Conference on the Indian," 1–3. For background on the Great Sioux Reservation, see Francis Paul Prucha, *American Indian Policy in Crisis: Christian Reformers and the Indian, 1865–1900* (Norman: University of Oklahoma Press, 1976), 169–87; Prucha, *The Great Father*, 2:632–40; and Hagan, *The IRA*, 38–46.

55. HW, *Report of a Visit to the Great Sioux Reserve*, 17. For Hare's statement and signatures, see "In Regard to the Pending Sioux Treaty," *Fifteenth Annual Report of the BIC, 1883*, 34–35.

56. "Address of Mr. A. K. Smiley," 38.

57. For Painter's comment on Edmunds's legislation, see CCP to SCA, March 2, 1883, SCA Papers: "The Sioux treaty knocked in the Senate. What may be done in the Conference Com. is yet to be seen." See also Hagan, *The IRA*, 39–40.

58. HW, "Christianity in Its Relations to Indian Civilization," *Christian Educators in Council*, 99–102, quote on 100.

59. CCP to SCA, August 8, 1883, SCA Papers; "Report of Prof. C. C. Painter," *Christian Educators in Council*, 85–88.

60. ASQ, "Woman's Work in Solving the Indian Problem," *Christian Educators in Council*, 102–5.

61. "Dedicating a Church," *New York Times*, September 21, 1883, 5.

62. "The Fourth Mohonk Conference," *Lend a Hand: A Record of Progress and Journal of Organized Charity* (November 1886), ed. Edward E. Hale, D.D. (Boston: Published by Lend a Hand), 672.

63. ASQ, *The Mohonk Indian Conference* (Leaflets of the WNIA, 1885), 1.

64. Prucha, *American Indian Policy in Crisis*, 176; "Address of the LMC," *Fifteenth Annual Report of the BIC, 1883*, 39–40.

## Chapter 2. First Investigative Tour

1. "Journal of the Thirteenth Annual Conference with Representatives of Missionary Boards, January 22, 1884," in *Fifteenth Annual Report of the BIC, 1883*, 60.

2. "Journal of the Thirteenth Annual Conference," 62 and 68.

3. "Journal of the Thirteenth Annual Conference," 62.

4. In "Indian Legislation: Some Hopeful Gains Made by the Forty-Eighth Congress," (*American Missionary*, October, 1884, 291–93, quote on 293), Painter reported that the Forty-Eighth Congress had appropriated twenty-five thousand dollars for the employment of "practical farmers" for the Indians, calling it "a long step in the right direction."

5. "Journal of the Thirteenth Annual Conference," 63 for Bland quote, 66 for Painter quote; Prucha, *American Indian Policy in Crisis*, 227–28 for quote, 227–64 for a discussion of allotment.

6. "Journal of the Thirteenth Annual Conference," 68 for final resolutions, 64 for second resolution discussion.

7. "Journal of the Thirteenth Annual Conference," 66–67 for discussions, 68 for resolutions. Painter continually promoted the idea of a centralized administration, with the commissioner possessing powers equal to those of the commissioners of education and agriculture.

8. "Journal of the Thirteenth Annual Conference," 68–69, last quote on 66. For IRA support of the Coke bill, see "The Division of Land in Severalty," *Second Annual Report of the Ex. Com. of the IRA, 1884* (Philadelphia: Office of the IRA, 1885), 15–16.

9. CCP to SCA, April 18, 1884, SCA Papers.

10. CCP to HW, May 27, 1884, *IRA Papers, 1864–1973*, series 1-A, incoming correspondence, 1864–1968, microfilm edition (hereafter *IRA Papers*), reel 1. In a letter to Armstrong (CCP to SCA, July 2, 1884, SCA Papers), Painter noted his salary as $2,500.

11. On May 26, 1886, Welsh asked Painter if he would consent to continue at $2,200 per year (*IRA Papers*, reel 68); in a letter of May 27, 1886, Painter stated his salary was actually $2,300 (*IRA Papers*, reel 1). On May 29, Welsh responded that if that was Painter's understanding, then he agreed (*IRA Papers*, reel 68).

12. For duties, see "Methods of Work," *Second Annual Report of the Ex. Com. of the IRA, 1884* (Philadelphia: Office of the IRA, 1885), 7–8.

13. On May 26, 1886, Welsh wrote to Painter: "I fully appreciate the difficulties of your position, and the value of your work" (*IRA Papers*, reel 68).

14. For example, see William Dougherty's letter to Painter (June 15, 1888, *IRA Records*, col. 1523, box 6, folder 2), asking him to support the Hupa Indians' petition for a wagon road and to aid in the passage of a bill for that purpose.

15. "Methods of Work," *Second Annual Report*, 7–8; Hagan, *The IRA*, quote on 23; see also 21. A March 1893 pamphlet, *Brief Statement of the Nature and Purpose of the Indian Rights Association with a Summary of Its Work for the Year 1892* (*IRA Papers*, reel 102, B6), described Painter's position as bringing the influence of the IRA "to bear upon the Executive in the management of Indian affairs." Officials were "often glad to avail themselves" of his reliable information.

16. "The Indian Rights Association: What It Is," *Lend a Hand*, January 1886, 57.

17. CCP, *The Indian Rights Association, Its Aims, Methods, and Work* (Philadelphia: IRA, 1890), *IRA Papers*, reel 102, A123.

18. CCP to SCA, May 14, 1884, SCA Papers; "Indian Appropriation Bill: Adoption of the Alaska Amendment," *Chicago Tribune*, May 13, 1884, 1. See also CCP, "National Aid to Common School," *American Missionary*, September 1884, 261–63.

19. CCP to SCA, May 14, 1884, SCA Papers. Representing the Executive Board of the WNIA, Quinton wrote Senator Dawes expressing pleasure that the Senate had increased the funding and thanked him for preparing "the Bill relating to the sale & division of Sioux lands." See ASQ to Dawes, May 16, 1884, box 25, Henry Laurens Dawes Papers, Library of Congress, Washington, D.C.

20. CCP to SCA, May 19 and 20, June 8, and July 9, 1884, SCA Papers.

21. "The Mohonk Conference," account from the columns of the *Hartford Courant*, reprinted in *Sixteenth Annual Report of the BIC, for the Year 1884* (Washington, D.C.: GPO, 1885), 46 for quote.

22. Rev. Addison P. Foster, "The Indian Conference at Lake Mohonk," *American Missionary*, November 1884, 323; see also "Some of the Members," *Second Annual Address to the Public of the LMC* (Philadelphia: Printed by the Order of the Executive Committee of the IRA, 1884), 23.

23. For quote, see "Proper Execution of the Laws. Starving Indians of Montana," *Second Annual Report of the Ex. Com. of the IRA, 1884*, 18.

24. Young to Price, August 11, 1882, reprinted in *Annual Report of the CIA to the SI for the Year 1882* (Washington, D.C.: GPO, 1882), 98–100.

25. Young to Price, August 6, 1883, reprinted in *Annual Report of the CIA to the SI for the Year 1883* (Washington, D.C.: GPO, 1883), 98

26. Helen B. West, Information Leaflet No. 7, "The Starvation Winter of the Piegan Indians, 1883–84," U.S. Department of the Interior, Bureau of Indian Affairs, *Museum of the Plains Indians*, Browning, Montana, n.d.; Helen B. West, "Starvation Winter of the Blackfeet," *Montana: The Magazine of Western History* 9, no. 1 (Winter 1959), 2–19, quote on 12.

27. Allen to Price, August 14, 1884, reprinted in *Annual Report of the CIA to the SI for the Year 1884* (Washington, D.C.: GPO, 1884), quotes on 106, 107, and 108.

28. CCP to SCA, July 2, 1884, SCA Papers.

29. "Indians Dying from Starvation," June 25, 1884; "Starving Indians in Montana," June 30, 1884; "Piegan Indians Starving," August 9, 1884, 4; "The Starving Piegan Indians," August 30, 1884, 5, all in the *New York Times*.

30. "Why the Piegans Are Starved: Estimates Too Small and the Appropriations Cut Down," *New York Times*, August 31, 1884, 9.

31. For Crosby's telegram to Teller, see "The Starving Piegan Indians," September 1, 1884, 1; for Price's response, see "Food for the Piegan Indians," September 3, 1884, 2—both in the *New York Times*.

32. "The Outlook," *Christian Union* 30, no. 13 (September 25, 1884), 291.

33. Helen Hunt Jackson (hereafter HHJ) to Henry C. Bowen, October 15, 1884 (7080-b), HHJ Collection, Clifton Waller Barrett Library. Alderman Library, University of Virginia, Charlottesville, Virginia. Reprinted in *The Indian Reform Letters of Helen*

*Hunt Jackson, 1879–1885*, ed. Valerie Sherer Mathes (Norman: University of Oklahoma Press, 1998), 331–32 for letter; 332–33 for poem.

34. "Indian Rights. Work of the Associated Friends of the Red Man," *Philadelphia Inquirer*, October 11, 1884.

35. "Reducing Indian Reservations," *Fort Benton River Press*, October 29, 1884.

36. "Proper Execution of the Laws, Starving Indians of Montana," *Second Annual Report of the Ex. Com. of the IRA, 1884*, 19.

37. See CCP, "Our Indian Policy as Related to the Civilization of the Indian," in "Proceedings of the Mohonk Lake Conference," *Eighteenth Annual Report of the BIC, for the Year 1886* (Washington, D.C.: GPO, 1887), 69 for wagons, 68 for reference to Indian policy as a machine. In "An Indian Circumlocution Office," Painter described how he was forced to rush between numerous offices and officials, transporting the necessary documents, in order to get the appropriations; see *Proceedings of the Third Annual Meeting of the LMC* (Philadelphia: Sherman & Co., Printers, 1886), 13–14. For more details, see CCP, "An Indian Circumlocution Office," *Lend a Hand*, February 1886, 86–88.

38. Rhoads was president of Bryn Mawr College; see Henry Hartshorne, "Memoir of James E. Rhoads," *Proceedings of the American Philosophical Society* 34, no. 149 (December 1895), 354–57.

39. CCP to Rhoads, October 28, 1884, *IRA Papers*, reel 1, reprinted in *The Action of Congress in Regard to the Piegan Indians of Montana, IRA Papers*, A 31, reel 102, 2–4, which includes letters by Painter, Welsh, public letters, and a petition. A portion appears in "The Starving Red Men," *Philadelphia Inquirer*, December 4, 1884.

40. CCP to Rhoads, October 28, 1884, *IRA Papers*, reel 1.

41. CCP to Rhoads, October 28, 1884.

42. CCP to Rhoads, October 28, 1884.

43. Hiram Price, October 15, 1884, *Annual Report of the CIA to the SI for the Year 1884*, iv–v.

44. "Indians Who Earn Their Living," *New York Times*, December 14, 1884, 3; see also "The Starving Red Men," *Philadelphia Inquirer*, December 4, 1884; and Hagan, *The IRA*, 32–33, 38–39.

45. "Proper Execution of the Laws. Starving Indians of Montana," *Second Annual Report of the Ex. Com. of the IRA, 1884*, 19.

46. "The Starving Red Men," *Philadelphia Inquirer*, December 4, 1884.

47. Letter by HW, December 13, 1884, reprinted in *The Action of Congress in Regard to the Piegan Indians of Montana*, 5.

48. "Proper Execution of the Laws. Starving Indians of Montana," *Second Annual Report of the Ex. Com. of the IRA, 1884*, 18–22, suggestions and quote on 22. This December 12 meeting is mentioned in "Our Red Wards. Delegation from the Indian Rights Association," December 13, 1884, and in "Starving Indians: An Appeal on Behalf of the Destitute Montana Tribes," January 6, 1885, both in the *Philadelphia Inquirer*. See also "Starvation: Congressional Plan of Settling the Indian Question," *Times-Picayune*, January 11, 1885.

49. Letter by HW, December 13, 1884, reprinted in *The Action of Congress in Regard to the Piegan Indians of Montana*, 5–8, quotes on 5, 6, 7.

50. CCP to HW, December 18, 1882, reprinted in *The Action of Congress in Regard to the Piegan Indians of Montana*, 9–10, and in "Starving Indians: An Appeal on Behalf of the Destitute Montana Tribes"; see also "Proper Execution of the Laws. Starving Indians of Montana," *Second Annual Report of the Ex. Com. of the IRA, 1884*, 20.

51. "Responsibility for Starvation among the Piegans; An Open Letter to Mr. Ellis from Prof. Painter," December 24, 1884, reprinted in *The Action of Congress in Regard to the Piegan Indians of Montana*, 10–13; "Petition, December 27, 1884," reprinted in *The Action of Congress*, 14–16. For reference to Painter's open letter, see "What Congress Is Doing," *Lancaster Daily Intelligencer*, January 22, 1885.

52. WNIA, "The President's Address," 11; see also "The Starving Piegans," *Fourth Annual Report of the WNIA* (Philadelphia: November 1884), 44–45.

53. For telegram, see *The Action of Congress in Regard to the Piegan Indians of Montana*, 18; for appropriation, see "Notes on Current Indian Legislation," *Lend a Hand*, February 1886, 119, and "Food for the Starving Piegans, *New York Tribune*, January 7, 1885. See also "Relief of Destitute Indians," *Congressional Record: Containing the Proceedings and Debates of the Forty-Eighth Congress, Second Session*, vol. 16, part 1 (Washington: GPO, 1885), 483–85.

54. Hagan, *The IRA*, 39.

55. "At Washington. Rockwell Makes Ellis Squirm. C. C. Painter's Charges Sustained," *Springfield Republican*, January 23, 1885; see also "What Congress Is Doing," *Lancaster Daily Intelligencer*, January 22, 1885.

56. CCP to Rockwell, January 30, 1885, *IRA Papers*, reel 1.

57. "Journal of the Fourteenth Annual Conference with Representatives of Missionary Boards and Indian Rights Associations," *Sixteenth Annual Report of the BIC, 1884*, 61.

58. Allen to Price, August 15, 1885, *Annual Report of the CIA to the SI, 1885* (Washington, D.C.: GPO, 1885), 117.

59. Hagan, *The IRA*, 45, 47, 50–51, 50 for quote.

60. "Journal of the Fourteenth Annual Conference with Representatives of Missionary Boards and Indian Rights Associations," *Sixteenth Annual Report of the BIC, 1884*, 54, 56.

61. "Journal of the Fourteenth Annual Conference," 64, 58.

62. Hagan, *The IRA*, 52–55; "The Revocation of the Presidential Order," *Third Annual Report of the Ex. Com. of the IRA for the Year Ending December 14, 1885* (Philadelphia: Office of the IRA, 1886), 12–13; "Rescinding the Order of Ex-President Arthur to Open the Crow Creek Reservation to White Settlement," *Lend a Hand*, February 1886, 120. For Teller's defense, see "Notes on Current Indian Legislation," *Lend a Hand* 1, no. 4 (April 1886), 236.

63. CCP to HW, May 19, 1885, *IRA Papers*, reel 1. In a letter to Painter after visiting Crow Creek (October 31, 1887, *IRA Papers*, reel 68), Welsh asked if anything could be done for those settlers who had taken claims in good faith. In response (November 1, 1887, reel 2), Painter agreed to call this issue to the attention of Commissioner Atkins.

64. CCP to HW, May 9, 1887, *IRA Papers*, reel 1. For more on Atkins's tenure, see Gregory C. Thompson, "John D. C. Akins, 1885–88," in Kvasnicka and Viola, eds., *The Commissioners of Indian Affairs*, 181–88.

### Chapter 3. First Visit to Mission Indian Villages

1. CCP, *A Visit to the Mission Indians of Southern California and Other Western Tribes* (Philadelphia: Office of the IRA, 1886), 11–12. Jackson had a number of IRA and WNIA pamphlets in her collection and was therefore well aware of the reform work being done by both associations. For a list, see HHJ Papers, MS 0020, part 1, box 15, Tutt Library, Colorado College, Colorado Springs, Colorado.

2. Although Indians who lived in mission complexes were designated as "Mission Indians," this term was also applied to many Southern California natives who had adopted the Spanish language and Catholic beliefs and practiced agriculture and adobe construction.

3. Larisa K. Miller, "The Secret Treaties with California's Indians," *Prologue* (Fall–Winter 2013), 38–45; Samuel M. Brosius to Matthew K. Sniffen, October 3, 1904, *IRA Papers*, reel 17. Brosius had located copies of these treaties in the Indian Office.

4. For original submission, see U.S. Congress, Senate, "Message from the President of the United States," S. Ex. Doc. 49, 48th Cong., 1st Sess., 1884, 1–7; the Jackson/Kinney report followed, 7–37. See also Mathes, *Helen Hunt Jackson*, 55–75. Seeking relief from asthma, Kinney moved to Southern California and in 1880 built his ranch, Kinneloa, in Altadena. He later founded the cities of Ocean Park and Venice.

5. HHJ to ASQ, April 2, 1884, MA 4571, Pierpont Morgan Library, New York, New York, reprinted in Mathes, ed., *The Indian Reform Letters of HHJ*, 319.

6. ASQ, *Suggestions to Friends of the Women's National Indian Association* (WNIA: Philadelphia, 1884), 3; and IRA, *The Case of the Mission Indians in Southern California, and the Action of the Indian Rights Association in Supporting the Defence [sic] of Their Legal Rights* (Philadelphia: Office of the IRA, 1886), 3.

7. See Valerie Sherer Mathes and Phil Brigandi, *A Call for Reform: The Southern California Indian Writings of Helen Hunt Jackson* (Norman: University of Oklahoma Press, 2015), 113–48 and 161–83.

8. CCP, *A Visit to the Mission Indians*, 4–5. For a review of Painter's pamphlet, see *Lend a Hand*, August 1886, 494. Originally established in Tahlequah in 1880 by the Baptists, the school was later moved to Muskogee on land donated by the Creek Indians. In 1910 it was renamed Bacone College after missionary Almon C. Bacone.

9. CCP, *A Visit to the Mission Indians*, 8–10.

10. CCP, *A Visit to the Mission Indians*, 11 (see also 11–18); "Journeys Made to the Indian Country within the Year, Three, as Follows: Journey of Prof. C. C. Painter, June, July, and August, to the Indian Territory, California, and Nevada," *Third Annual Report of the Ex. Com. of the IRA, 1885*, 10; Hagan, *The IRA*, 68–70.

11. HHJ to the Coronels, June 27, 1885, Anthony F. Coronel Collection, Seaver Center for Western History Research, Los Angeles County Museum of Natural History, Los

Angeles, California, reprinted in Mathes, ed., *The Indian Reform Letters of HHJ*, 349. Born in Mexico, Coronel moved to Los Angeles with his family. He taught school, served as territorial deputy, street commissioner, justice of the peace, and inspector for the secularized missions. During the American period, he served as school superintendent, mayor of Los Angeles, and state treasurer.

12. CCP to Coronel, June 29, 1885, HHJ manuscripts, HM 38231, Henry H. Huntington Library, San Marino, California; see also CCP to Rust, June 29, 1885, Rust Papers, RU 462, box 8.

13. CCP to Coronel, June 29, 1885, HHJ manuscripts, HM 38231; Jane Apostol, "Horatio Nelson Rust: Abolitionist, Archaeologist, Indian Agent," *California History* 58, no. 4 (Winter 1979–80), 304–15; Valerie Sherer Mathes and Phil Brigandi, *Reservations, Removal, and Reform: The Mission Indian Agents of Southern California 1878–1903* (Norman: University of Oklahoma Press, 2018), 98–132. Born in New York, Markham was at the time a member of the House. From 1891 to 1895, he served as California's eighteenth governor. In 1881 Rust had moved to Pasadena, California, where he served with Abbot Kinney on the library board. Both Jackson and Kinney recommended him as Mission Indian agent. Appointed in 1889, his tenure was troubled.

14. Ubach to Rosecrans, September 4, 1885, included in Rosecrans to Commissioner John D. C. Atkins, September 10, 1885, Letters Received (hereafter LR) #21068–1885, record group 75, special case 31, Office of Indian Affairs, National Archives and Records Administration (hereafter RG 75, SC 31, OIA, NA). Rosecrans, a major general in the U.S. Army, represented California's First Congressional District in the House of Representatives from 1881 to 1885. Ubach, later a strong advocate for Indian rights, had come to San Diego from Spain in 1866 to take charge of the Catholic parish. See Edgar W. Hebert, "The Last of the Padres," *San Diego Historical Society Quarterly* 10, no. 2 (April 1964), 15–22.

15. CCP, *A Visit to the Mission Indians*, 12–14, 16–17 for specific villages, quote on 14.

16. *Proceedings of the Third Annual Meeting of the LMC*, 11.

17. For Painter's quotes, see *Proceedings of the Third Annual Meeting of the LMC*, 12–14; for final comment, see ASQ, *The Mohonk Indian Conference*, 4.

18. "Second Day-Morning Session," *Proceedings of the Third Annual Meeting of the LMC*, 29–31.

19. "Tribute to Helen Hunt Jackson," *Proceedings of the Third Annual Meeting of the LMC*, 69–70.

20. "The Southern California Indians," *Proceedings of the Third Annual Meeting of the LMC*, 73–76. In *A Visit to the Mission Indians of California* [(Philadelphia: IRA, 1887), 5], Painter described the land commission, created by Congress in 1857, before which all claimants under old Spanish and Mexican laws had to appear to establish their title.

21. HHJ, "Exhibit M. The Pachanga Indians," in "Report on the Condition and Needs of the Mission Indians of California, Made by Special Agents Helen Jackson and Abbot Kinney, to the CIA," *A Century of Dishonor: A Sketch of the United States Government's Dealings with Some of the Indian Tribes"* (Norman: University of Oklahoma

Press, 1995), 504–5. See also HHJ, "The Temecula Exiles," in Mathes and Brigandi, eds., *A Call for Reform*, 113–23.

22. HHJ, "Exhibit A. Brunson & Wells, Los Angeles, Ca., May 12, 1883," in *A Century of Dishonor*, 475–78. With a group of American land speculators, Byrne had purchased some seven hundred acres, which included the two-hundred-acre Soboba village.

23. See Brewster to Teller, June 26, 1883, LR #11698–1883, RG 75, SC 31, OIA, NA.

24. *San Diego Union*, December 13, 1883; "The Saboba Case," undated four-page summary, in Painter's handwriting in *IRA Papers*, reel 3; LMC, "The Southern California Indians," *Proceedings of the Third Annual Meeting of the LMC*, 74. In a letter to Coronel (June 29, 1885, HHJ manuscripts, HM 38231), Painter wrote that the friends of the Indians were disappointed with Wells's "professional conduct in the case of Byrnes" and hoped to get from him "definite & clear ideas as to what may be hoped for as the result of any future effort in the courts." Brunson & Wells were not entirely to blame. They had begun the transfer to the U.S. Supreme Court, which required a bond, but the paperwork had been mistakenly forwarded to the Indians. By the time funding was arranged with the help of Mary Sheriff, the Soboba schoolteacher, "a default had been taken against the Indians" for failure to appear. See Wells, Van Dyke & Lee (Successors to Brunson & Wells) to Hon. H. H. Markham, June 20, 1885 [enclosed with Markham to Interior Secretary Lamar, June 30, 1885], LR #15095–1885, RG 75, SC 31, OIA, NA.

25. "The Southern California Indians," *Proceedings of the Third Annual Meeting of the LMC*, 76.

26. For WNIA missionary work among these Indians, see Mathes, *Divinely Guided*, 177–261, and Mathes, "Helen Hunt Jackson, Amelia Stone Quinton, and the Mission Indians of California," *Southern California Quarterly* 96, no. 2 (Summer 2014), 172–205.

27. "Friends of the Red Men: The Indian Rights Association in Session at New-Haven," *New York Times*, November 20, 1885.

28. "To Help the Red Men: Speeches before the Indian Rights Convention at New-Haven," *New York Times*, November 21, 1885.

29. "The Indians' Welfare. Meeting of the Indian Rights Association," *Philadelphia Inquirer*, December 16, 1885. Lincoln Institute was founded in 1866 for the sons of Episcopalian soldiers who died during the Civil War; the institute later educated young Indians.

30. "The Indian Problem. How Professor Painter Thinks the Trouble Arises and How It Can Be Settled," *Philadelphia Times*, December 20, 1885.

31. CCP, "Report on Indian Work," *American Missionary*, December 1885, 348–49. By "tribal relations" Painter referred to the Indians' tribal allegiance and identity.

32. "Mr. Painter's Work," *Fourth Annual Report of the Ex. Com. of the IRA, 1886*, 15 and, for praise of Painter, 12.

33. "Mr. Painter's Work," *Fourth Annual Report of the Ex. Com. of the IRA, 1886*, 11–15 for his year's work.

34. For Ward's appointment, see Garland to Secretary Lamar, January 14, 1886, LR #1447–1886, RG 75, SC 31, OIA, NA; Shirley Ward to Garland, March 16, 1886, LR

#8672–1886, RG 75, SC 31, OIA, NA; and HW to Rust, January 26, 1886, Rust Papers, box 8. For the work before his appointment, see "Shirley C. Ward, Special Attorney for the Mission Indians," U.S. Congress, House of Representatives, 49th Congress, 2d Session, Ex. Doc. No. 161. For appropriation, see CCP to HW, February 5, 1887, *IRA Records*, coll. 1523, box 226, folder 2. Ward was born near Nashville, Tennessee, on June 30, 1861, and moved to Southern California with his family. A graduate of Hastings Law School, he was admitted to the California bar in 1885 and formed the partnership of Wicks & Ward in Los Angeles, specializing in water rights, corporate law, and Mexican land grants. See "Shirley C. Ward," *History of the Bench and Bar of California*, ed. J. C. Bates (San Francisco: Bench and Bar Publishing, 1912), 543–44; for obituary, see "Pioneer's Obsequies Today," *Los Angeles Times*, November 26, 1929.

35. Ward to HW, March 30, 1886, in IRA, *The Case of the Mission Indians*, 19.
36. CCP to HW, February 25, 1886, in IRA, *The Case of the Mission Indians*, 14–15; see also "Mr. Painter's Work," *Fourth Annual Report of the Ex. Com. of the IRA, 1886*, 12–13.
37. CCP, *A Visit to the Mission Indians*, 5.
38. CCP to HW, February 25, 1886, in IRA, *The Case of the Mission Indians*, 15–16 for all quotes. In a letter to Welsh (April 28, 1886, *IRA Papers*, reel 1), Quinton pledged to get WNIA members to write officials on behalf of an increase in Ward's salary. For Painter's pledge to compensate Ward, see "The Saboba Case," *IRA Papers*, reel 3. On February 24, 1888, Dawes informed Welsh that he was trying to get monies for Ward (*IRA Papers*, reel 3).
39. CCP to HW, January 8, 1886, *IRA Records*, box 226, folder 1. Painter noted he had planned to decline to serve if Bland was appointed; however, Bland was appointed, along with Painter and Gates. "I went to Fisk and told him the situation," he wrote Welsh. "He [Fisk] said he put him [Bland] in so that we [Painter and Gates] might control him, and wanted we should stick."
40. CCP to HW, January 8, 1886, *IRA Records*, box 226, folder 1. In a later letter to Welsh (January 10, 1887, *IRA Records*, box 226, folder 2), Painter again "disproved" a complaint made by Dawes, who had made "a great outcry against" a section of his severalty bill that he had apparently misread.
41. CCP to HW, January 22 and February 9, 1887, *IRA Records*, box 226, folder 2.
42. "Journal of the Fifteenth Annual Conference with Representatives of Missionary Boards," *Seventeenth Annual Report of the BIC, for the Year 1885* (Washington, D.C.: GPO, 1886), 124, 127.
43. Ward to HW, March 30, 1886, in IRA, *The Case of the Mission Indians*, 4 for Jackson quote; *Lend a Hand*, August 1886, 494. Two thousand copies of the pamphlet were printed.
44. CCP to HW, May 10 and 13, 1886; Ward to CCP, May 20, 1886, *IRA Papers*, reel 1.
45. Coronel to CCP, May 22, 1886, Manuscript Collection of Grant Jackson, 1828–1954, mss HM 38186, Huntington Library, San Marino, California.
46. "The Indian Training School," *New York Times*, May 13, 1886, 1. See CCP to HW, May 13 and 16, 1886, for funeral, and June 8 and 14, 1886, *IRA Papers*, reel 1 for Apache

students. On May 24, apologizing for not responding, Painter explained he had overworked his eyes, and his doctor had forced him to remain shut up in a darkened room for several days.

47. CCP, "The Supreme Court on Indian Citizenship," *Lend a Hand*, May 1886, 283–84. See also Stephen D. Bodayla, "'Can an Indian Vote?' Elk v. Wilkins, a Setback for Indian Citizenship," *Nebraska History* 67, no. 4 (Winter 1986), 372–80. Cooley served as chief justice of the Michigan Supreme Court from 1864 to 1885 and on the Interstate Commerce Commission beginning in 1887.

48. CCP to HW, July 17, August 31, and October 2, 1886, *IRA Papers*, reel 2.

49. CCP to HW, September 24 and October 6, 1886, *IRA Papers*, reel 2.

50. For the findings in *M. Byrne v. Antonio Alas, et al.*, see J. M. Dodge, San Diego County Clerk, to Leland Stanford, U.S. Senator, August 7, 1886, LR #6885–1886, RG 75, SC 31, OIA, NA. After the San Diego County Superior Court ruled against Soboba, Ward carried an appeal to the California State Supreme Court, arguing that under Mexican law, the villages had held a possessory right to their lands, and that by the Treaty of Guadalupe Hidalgo, the United States had pledged to honor all existing land rights in California. In early 1888, Ward won the case, and Welsh's bond money was returned. For initial loss, see Ward to A. H. Garland, U.S. Attorney General, July 10, 1886, *IRA Papers*, reel 2; for victory, see Ward to J. D. C. Atkins, February 21, 1888, LR #5713–1888, RG 75, SC 31, OIA, NA. In a letter to Painter (July 25, 1888, *IRA Papers*, reel 3), Ward explained he had filed a fifty-page brief to get the case back before the court.

51. For payment, see Ward to Henry Pancoast, October 9, 1886, *IRA Papers*, reel 2, and "The Mission Indians of California," "Proceedings of the Mohonk Lake Conference," in the *Eighteenth Annual Report of the BIC, 1886* (Washington, D.C.: GPO, 1887), 45–46, 82. For Painter's attendance, see "Friends of the Indians: Work of the Lake Mohonk Indian Conference," *New York Times*, October 14, 1886, 4, and "The Red Man's Friends: Opening of the Conference at Lake Mohonk," *Philadelphia Inquirer*, October 14, 1886, 1.

52. CCP to HW, July 22, 1886, for visit with the Attorney General, and August 31, 1886, *IRA Papers*, reel 2.

53. Francis Paul Prucha, "A 'Friend of the Indian' in Milwaukee: Mrs. O. J. Hiles and the Wisconsin Indian Association," *Historical Messenger of the Milwaukee County Historical Society* (Autumn 1973), 78–95; Mathes, *Helen Hunt Jackson*, 92, 95, 101–6; and Mathes, *Divinely Guided*, 183–89, 191, 194.

54. "The Mission Indians of California," "Proceedings of the Mohonk Lake Conference," in *Eighteenth Annual Report of the BIC, 1886*, 79–82 for Hiles's report and 83 for the committee; CCP, *A Visit to the Mission Indians*, 4 for his expanded duties. See also "To Protect the Indians: Steps Taken to Help the Indians of South California," *New York Times*, October 16, 1886, 5; "Wrongs of the Redskins," *New York Herald*, October 15, 1886, 5; "The Case of the Mission Indians," *Springfield Republican*, October 16, 1886, 5. Committee members were Philip C. Garrett of Philadelphia, Moses Pierce of Norwich, Connecticut, Joshua W. Davis of Boston, and Austin Abbot and Elliott F. Shepard, both of New York City. For their undated three-page pamphlet, "The Mission

Indians," presumably created for fund-raising purposes, see MS. 1, Special Collections, Milton S. Eisenhower Library, Johns Hopkins University, Baltimore, Maryland.

55. Elmer Wallace Holmes, *History of Riverside County* (Los Angeles: Historic Record Company, 1912), 575; "Indians Who Will Vote," *San Francisco Chronicle*, September 26, 1888, 6. Born in Wisconsin, Lewis attended law classes at the National University in Washington, D.C. After passing the bar in 1888, he moved to California. Painter's letters reflected conferences with Lewis, giving him "instructions for his guidance" and "full and detailed statement of all [he] knew and of cases to be looked after." See CCP to HW, February 15 and March 5, 1888, *IRA Papers*, reel 3. For appreciation of his work by the LMC, see Lewis to Davis, December 26, 1888, *IRA Papers*, reel 4. For application of the Dawes Severalty Act to the Mission Indians, see Lewis to Rust, August 26, 1889, Rust Papers, box 9.

56. CCP, "Our Indian Policy as Related to the Civilization of the Indian," in "Proceedings of the LMC," *Eighteenth Annual Report of the BIC, 1886*, 61–69. Reprinted in *Americanizing the American Indians: Writings by the "Friends of the Indian, 1880–1900*, ed. Francis Paul Prucha (Cambridge, Mass.: Harvard University Press, 1973), 66–73. See also "To Help the Indian: Important Resolutions Passed by the Conference," *New York Times*, October 15, 1886, 2.

57. CCP to HW, August 31 and September 24, 1886, *IRA Papers*, reel 2.

58. CCP, "Our Indian Policy," 62.

59. CCP, *Proceedings of the Third Annual Meeting of the LMC*, 29. See also "The Indian Conference," *Chicago Tribune*, October 15, 1886.

60. CCP, "Our Indian Policy," 62–64.

61. CCP, "Our Indian Policy," 64–66.

62. CCP, "Our Indian Policy," 66–68.

63. CCP, "Our Indian Policy," 68–69.

64. For all quotes, see CCP, "Our Indian Policy," 69; for a reference to his commission proposal, see CCP to HW, February 15, 1887, *IRA Papers*, reel 2.

65. "The Fourth Mohonk Conference," *Lend a Hand*, November 1886, 677.

66. CCP to HW, October 20, 1886, *IRA Papers*, reel 2; CCP, *A Visit to the Mission Indians*, 4–5, see 5 for quote, 17 for Ubach. See also Teresa Baksh McNeil, "St. Anthony's Indian School in San Diego, 1886–1907," *Journal of San Diego History* 34, no. 3 (Summer 1988), 186–200.

67. For a biographical sketch of Rocha, see John R. Johnson, "The Indians of Mission San Fernando," *Southern California Quarterly* 79, no. 3 (Fall 1997), 249–90. News accounts include "Rogerio Rocha's History: Old Timer Tells of the Cruel Ejectment," January 29, 1896, and "A Story of the Terrible Wrongs That Have Been Put upon Rogerio Rocha," February 2, 1896, both in the *Los Angeles Herald*. Several years later, while planning her trip to California, Quinton inquired of William Weinland, WNIA missionary among the Mission Indians, whether Rocha was still alive. If so, she had a donor willing to contribute toward buying or building him a home. She also wrote Agent Rust. See ASQ to Weinland, December 9, 1890, and January 7, 1891, Papers of William H. Weinland, box 7; ASQ to Rust, February 10, 1891, Rust Papers, box 9.

68. CCP, *A Visit to the Mission Indians*, 6–8.

69. For affidavits and sworn testimony on the San Fernando case, see CCP, *The Condition of Affairs in Indian Territory and California: A Report by Prof. C. C. Painter* (Philadelphia: Office of the IRA, 1888), 74–90, especially Rocha's affidavit on 87–88, first quote on 88. Also see CCP, *A Visit to the Mission Indians*, final quote on 8. An undated pamphlet (probably 1886) entitled "The Mission Indians," signed by the Mohonk Committee for the Legal Defense of the Mission Indians, also presented Rocha's plight and a short history of the Soboba case.

70. CCP, *A Visit to the Mission Indians*, 8–11, 14. In a letter to Welsh (March 28, 1887, *IRA Papers*, reel 2), Painter wrote that intruders on the Mission reservations had been given until September 1 to leave. On April 1, 1887 (reel 2), he told Welsh he had thanked Secretary Lamar for issuing the order to clear San Gorgonio and Capitán Grande.

The San Gorgonio Reservation, known as such at the time because it was in the San Gorgonio Pass, was later also known both as the Morongo Reservation and as the Potrero Reservation. As Painter himself explained: "A reservation near San Gorgonio, sometimes called the San Gorgonio Reservation, sometimes the Protrero [*sic*], but on the maps designated "Maronge" [*sic*], contains 88,475.32 acres." He himself used all three names. Hereafter "Morongo Reservation" will be used in this book.

71. CCP to HW, January 10 and January 22, 1887, *IRA Records*, box 226, folder 2.

72. This was possibly Henry D. Barrows.

73. CCP to HW, November 11, 1886, *IRA Papers*, reel 2.

74. CCP to HW, November 26 and December 3 and 15, 1886, *IRA Papers*, reel 2.

75. "Herbert Welsh in Sanders Theater," *Cambridge Chronicle*, December 11, 1886, 4.

## Chapter 4. The Dawes Act and a Return to the Indian Territory and California

1. CCP to HW, January 5, 1887, *IRA Papers*, reel 2.

2. CCP to Joshua Davis, July 12, 1887, *IRA Papers*, reel 2. See also "Reservation News: A Raid on the Capitan Grande Indians at San Diego," *Los Angeles Herald*, July 22, 1887.

3. BIC, "Journal of the Sixteenth Annual Conference with Representatives of Missionary Boards and Indian Rights Associations," *Eighteenth Annual Report of the BIC, 1886*, 94.

4. On February 9, 1887, Painter wrote Welsh that Bland's National Indian Defense Association "did all it could to prevent his [President Cleveland's] signing" (*IRA Records*, box 226, folder 2). See also "General Allotment Act," in Prucha, ed., *Documents of United States Indian Policy* (Lincoln: University of Nebraska Press, 1990), 171–74; and *Felix S. Cohen's Handbook of Federal Indian Law* (Albuquerque: University of New Mexico Press, 1971), 78, 207–36.

5. Prucha, *American Indian Policy in Crisis*, 228 for quote, 227–64 for background; Prucha, *The Great Father*, 2:659–861.

6. Prucha, *American Indian Policy in Crisis*, 257 for Gates, 227 for the IRA; for Quinton, see WNIA, *Address of the President on Current Indian Legislation, Work Needed, etc.* (Philadelphia, November 30, 1887), 7.

7. Henry M. Teller, "Debate in the Senate on Land in Severalty," in Prucha, ed., *Americanizing the American Indians*, 130–40; Prucha, *American Indian Policy in Crisis*, 246–48. Nor did allotment turn Indians into successful farmers. Instead, it led to a decline in Indian farming in the early twentieth century. See Leonard A. Carlson, *Indians, Bureaucrats, and Land: The Dawes Act and the Decline of Indian Farming* (Westport, Conn.: Greenwood Press, 1981), 4. See also Wilcomb E. Washburn, *The Assault on Indian Tribalism: The General Allotment Law (Dawes Act) of 1887* (Philadelphia: J. B. Lippincott Company, 1975); and D. S. Otis, *The Dawes Act and the Allotment of Indian Lands*, ed. and intro by Francis Paul Prucha (Norman: University of Oklahoma Press, 1973).

8. "Prof. Painter's Work at Washington and Elsewhere," *Fifth Annual Report of the Ex. Com. of the IRA for the Year Ending December 20, 1887* (Philadelphia: Office of the IRA, 1888), 14. See also Hagan, *The IRA*, 65–67.

9. CCP, *The Dawes Land in Severalty Bill and Indian Emancipation.* (Philadelphia: IRA, March 1887), *IRA Papers*, #77, reel 102. See also Genetin-Pilawa, *Crooked Paths to Allotment*, 112–33.

10. CCP, *The Dawes Land in Severalty Bill.*

11. CCP, *The Dawes Land in Severalty Bill.*

12. BIC, " Remarks of Senator Dawes," in "Journal of the Sixteenth Annual Conference," 131.

13. "Report of the Law Committee," *Fifth Annual Report of the Ex. Com. of the IRA, 1887*, quotes on 4 and 6; Valerie Sherer Mathes, "James Bradley Thayer: In Defense of Indian Legal Rights," *Massachusetts Historical Review* 21 (2020): 41–75.

14. The Worcester Association, unlike most WNIA affiliates, permitted both men and women to join. *Annual Report of the WNIA* (Philadelphia, November 17, 1885), 18 for membership.

15. James B. Thayer, "Remarks Made before the Worcester Indian Association at Worcester, Mass.," February 13, 1887, n.p., n.d. This address was most likely printed by the Massachusetts Indian Association, a branch of the WNIA.

16. HW to CCP, February 14, 1887, *IRA Papers*, reel 68; "Civilizing the Indian," *Boston Daily Advertiser*, February 14, 1887, 1; "Bright Eyes Talk: Down Easters Anxious for the Welfare of the Red Man," *New York Times*, February 14, 1887, 4.

17. HW to CCP, February 14, 1887, and CCP to HW, February 15, 1887, *IRA Papers*, reel 2. In his February 14 letter, Painter identified the source of the news account as the *Tribune*, which is presumably the *New York Tribune*.

18. Welsh informed Thayer (CCP to Thayer, February 25, 1887, *IRA Papers*, reel 68) that his plan did not seem "wise or practicable," suggesting that instead he urge the president to extend the Civil Service rules over the Indian service. See also HW to Thayer, March 14, 1887, *IRA Papers*, reel 68.

19. Report of the Law Committee, *Fifth Annual Report of the Ex. Com. of the IRA, 1887*, 7. The committee's corrections can be found in *IRA Papers*, reel 4, listed as "nd report," immediately following the December 26 letter by CCP to HW.

20. "An Act to Establish Courts for the Indians on the Various Reservations, and to Extend the Protection of the Laws of the States and Territories over All Indians, and for Other Purposes," *Proceedings of the Sixth Annual Meeting of the LMC* (LMC, 1888), 49–58. See also "The Indian Courts Bill," *Sixth Annual Report of the Ex. Com. of the IRA, 1888* (Philadelphia: Office of the IRA, 1889), 25–30; "Indian Courts Bill," A 104, *IRA Papers*, reel 102.

21. Thayer to HW, April 12, 1888, *IRA Papers*, reel 3.

22. CCP to HW, April 24 and May 1, 1888, *IRA Papers*, reel 3. On April 11, 1888, Matthew Sniffen wrote Quinton, sending her copies of the bill and asking for support to "accomplish its passage" (reel 69).

23. For timetable, see "Legislation for the Indian," *Proceedings of the Sixth Annual Meeting of the LMC*, 45; for Thayer's report, see 42–48; for comments on Dawes, see 45. Hagan writes in *The IRA* (92): "One reason that Welsh was willing to compromise his differences with Professor Thayer was that he had been seeking the support of the Boston group on a project in which he and the IRA had invested considerable time and energy—the plight of the Chiricahua Apaches held in prison at military installations in Florida and later at Mount Vernon Barracks in Alabama."

24. Hagan, *The IRA*, 92.

25. "Prof. Painter's Work at Washington," *Sixth Annual Report of the Ex. Com. of the IRA, 1888*, 19–20. In a letter to Welsh (August 1, 1888, *IRA Papers*, reel 3), Painter expresses the same opinion, wanting to give Morgan's bill "more careful study."

26. "The Introduction of Law upon the Indian Reservations, and the Proper Legal Protection of the Indian," *Second Annual Report of the Ex. Com. of the IRA, 1884*, 16–17.

27. CCP to HW, February 15, 1887, *IRA Papers*, reel 2. This was probably Lone Wolf the Younger, the adopted son of Chief Lone Wolf, who died in 1879. The elder Lone Wolf, taken captive during the Red River War, was one of the Southern Plains Indian prisoners of war educated by Capt. Richard Henry Pratt at Fort Marion in St. Augustine, Florida. This experiment led to Pratt's founding of the Carlisle Indian Industrial School.

28. For a speech by Given before the Brooklyn Indian Association, see "Indians Speak at the Meeting of the National Association," *Brooklyn Eagle*, January 24, 1889, 1. He was described as being about thirty years old, wearing eyeglasses, and speaking in "a slow and deliberate manner" that was "decidedly impressive."

29. Genetin-Pilawa, *Crooked Paths to Allotment*, 113.

30. CCP to HW, February 15, 1887, *IRA Papers*, reel 2.

31. CCP to HW, March 18, 1887, *IRA Papers*, reel 2. The meeting at Worcester was the February 13 event featuring Thayer's first public criticism of the Dawes Act.

32. In a letter to Welsh (January 22, 1887, *IRA Records*, box 226, folder 2), Painter explained he had received a petition from 350 of 720 absentee Shawnees, requesting that certificates be issued for land selected in the Indian Territory.

33. CCP to HW, February 28, 1887, *IRA Papers*, reel 2; see also CCP to HW, January 22, 1887.

34. "Rights of the Indian. What Has Been Done and What Is Needed to Be Done," *Boston Post*, April 18, 1887. Samuel Billings Capen, the keynote speaker at this meeting, was a wealthy carpet manufacturer who was engaged in other philanthropic endeavors. A member of the Boston Indian Citizenship Committee and a vice president of the Jamaica Plain WNIA branch, he was also president of the American Board of Commissioners for Foreign Missions.

35. "Prof. Painter's Work in the Southwest," *Fifth Annual Report of the Ex. Com. of the IRA, 1887*, 16–17.

36. CCP to HW, May 9, 1887, *IRA Papers*, reel 2. See CCP to HW, April 1, 1887, for Lamar's questioning of Painter about his Mohonk remarks. On April 13, 1887, Painter wrote Welsh that he hoped to get away on May 1, taking the southern route from Washington, presumably through Mississippi, Louisiana, Texas, and New Mexico, to visit the Pimas and Papagoes in Arizona.

37. "Prof. Painter's Work in the Southwest," *Fifth Annual Report of the Ex. Com. of the IRA, 1887*, 16–17; CCP, *The Proposed Removal of Indians to Oklahoma* (Philadelphia: IRA, 1887), 3–5.

38. CCP to HW, June 6, 1887, *IRA Papers*, reel 2. For the final quote, see CCP, *The Condition of Affairs*, 44. The June 6 letter to Welsh was reprinted in *The Condition of Affairs* on pages 15–20 and 34–45.

39. For schools, see "Prof. Painter's Work in the Southwest," *Fifth Annual Report of the Ex. Com. of the IRA, 1887*, 17–20, 19 for De Night; for the Comanche school, see CCP to HW, June 6, 1887, *IRA Papers*, reel 2; and for Mesa Grande, CCP, *The Condition of Affairs*, 58–59, 68.

40. A government off-reservation Indian boarding school, Chilocco Indian Agricultural School, located between Arkansas City, Kansas, and Ponca City, Oklahoma, opened in 1884. It closed in 1980.

41. CCP to HW, May 23 and June 7, 1887, *IRA Papers*, reel 2; CCP, *The Condition of Affairs*, 4–5, 7–11, quote on 4.

42. CCP, *The Condition of Affairs*, 9–10 for Ponca, 11 for Pawnee; CCP to HW, June 6 and October 31, 1887, *IRA Papers*, reel 2. In a May 9 letter to Welsh (reel 2), Painter noted that Lamar believed that Bland was "to a large extent" responsible for the difficulties at the Kiowa and Comanche Agency.

43. CCP, *The Condition of Affairs*, 34–35, 38–39, 43–45. Quotes from CCP to HW, June 6 and October 31, 1887, *IRA Papers*, reel 2.

44. CCP, *The Condition of Affairs*, 15, 20–33. Painter included Seger's account of his colony and a May 28, 1887, letter from him relative to his educational work.

45. CCP, *The Condition of Affairs*, 50; and CCP to HW, July 19, 1887, *IRA Papers*, reel 2.

46. For Ward's tenure as agent, see Mathes and Brigandi, *Reservations, Removal, and Reform*, 70–84.

47. CCP, *The Condition of Affairs*, 51–73. Painter explained that the resignation came after Ward received an insulting telegram. In a letter to Davis (June 30, 1887, *IRA Papers*, reel 2), he wrote that both friends and enemies of the Indian described Ward as "the most energetic and useful man who has held the position at this point." This

nineteen-page letter appears, with some changes, on pages 51–65 of CCP, *The Condition of Affairs*, and in an edited version in Valerie Sherer Mathes and Phil Brigandi, "Charles C. Painter, Helen Hunt Jackson and the Mission Indians of Southern California," *Journal of San Diego History* 55, 3 (Summer 2009): 89–118.

48. CCP, *The Condition of Affairs*, 72. See also "Mission Indians, Hon. J. Shirley Ward's Final Report on Them," *Los Angeles Herald*, September 14, 1887.

49. CCP to HW, July 19, 1887, *IRA Papers*, reel 2.

50. Painter may have learned about Ticknor from Jackson's description in "A Day with the Cahuillas," *New York Independent*, October 11, 1883, 1–3, and "Three Pennsylvania Women," *Christian Union*, December 28, 1882, and January 4, 1883; for an edited version of both, see Mathes and Brigandi, *A Call for Reform*, 137–48 and 149–60.

51. See Phil Brigandi and John W. Robinson, "The Killing of Juan Diego: From Murder to Mythology," *Journal of San Diego History* 40, nos. 1–2 (Winter–Spring 1994): 1–22.

52. CCP, *The Condition of Affairs*, 51–54; for quote, see CCP to Davis, June 30, 1887, *IRA Papers*, reel 2. On Ramona Lubo, see Phil Brigandi, "Debating the Existence of a 'Real' Ramona," *Valley Chronicle* (Hemet, Calif.), February 9, 2002.

53. CCP to Davis, June 30, 1887, *IRA Papers*, reel 2; CCP, *The Condition of Affairs*, 54–61, 60 for San Felipe. Oceanside Land & Water was probably the San Luis Rey Flume Company, organized in 1886, which planned to include a dam on the Warner Ranch. See William Ham Hall, *Irrigation in California (Southern)* (Sacramento: State Printing Office, 1888), 88–89.

54. CCP to Davis, June 30, 1887, *IRA Papers*, reel 2; CCP, *The Condition of Affairs*, 61–63. See also "Land in Severalty: The Mission Indians Confer about It," *Los Angeles Times*, June 30, 1887; this article placed the number of Indians in attendance at two hundred.

55. CCP, *The Condition of Affairs*, 63–65, 65 for quote; CCP to Davis, June 30, 1887, *IRA Papers*, reel 2.

56. CCP, *The Condition of Affairs*, 66; CCP to Davis, July 12 and 17, 1887, *IRA Papers*, reel 2; "Prof. Painter's Work at Washington and Elsewhere," *Fifth Annual Report of the Ex. Com. of the IRA, 1887*, 15; "Reservation News. A Raid on the Capitan Grande Indians at San Diego," *Los Angeles Herald*, July 22, 1887.

57. For the fume, see Tanis C. Thorne, *El Capitan: Adaptation and Agency on a Southern California Indian Reservation, 1850 to 1937* (Banning, Calif.: Malki-Bellena Press, 2012), 54–60.

58. CCP to Davis, July 17, 1887, *IRA Papers*, reel 2. For Preston's agreement and a November 21, 1891, letter from J. W. Sefton, company president, to Painter, see Albert K. Smiley et al., *Report of Indian Commissioners*, December 7, 1891, box 42, 75–77, in Smiley Collection, Heritage Room, A. K. Smiley Public Library, Redlands, California. For Preston's tenure as agent, see Mathes and Brigandi, *Reservations, Removal, and Reform*, 85–97.

59. CCP to HW, July 19, 1887, *IRA Papers*, reel 2.

60. CCP, *The Condition of Affairs*, 66 for quote, 68–70 for Soboba, and 92–102 for the decision; *One Case of Justice to Indians* (Philadelphia: IRA, 1888), reprinted from the *Springfield Republican*, February 23, 1888. For final quote, see "The Saboba Case," *IRA*

*Papers*, reel 3. In a letter to Welsh (March 5, 1888, *IRA Papers*, reel 3), Painter stated that after learning of the Soboba victory, he called upon the attorney general, urging him to take immediate steps to settle the threats against San Ysabel, San Felipe, and Pauma, and preparing a statement on the Mission Indian cases for him.

61. CCP to Davis, July 17, 1887, *IRA Papers*, reel 2; "Justice to Indians," *Los Angeles Times*, July 16, 1887. This "Professor James" could be Anthony H. Jannus, superintendent of schools for the Mission Indian Agency in 1887. See also "Addresses Made by Prof. Painter," *Fifth Annual Report of the Ex. Com. of the IRA, 1887*, 65. For Pasadena comment, see CCP to Davis, July 12, 1887.

62. CCP to HW, July 19, 1887, *IRA Papers*, reel 2; CCP to Davis, July 17, including the attached letter of July 19; and CCP, *The Condition of Affairs*, 74, 77.

63. CCP, *The Condition of Affairs*, 74–88 for letters and affidavits. See also the description of this event in chapter 3. In a letter to Welsh (August 15, 1887, *IRA Papers*, reel 2), Painter wrote he had "made out a most damaging case against Maclay and Widney as against their sworn statements in regard to the San Fernando ejectment."

64. CCP to Coronel, October 13, 1887, Manuscript Collection of Grant Jackson, 1828–1954, mss HM 38232, Huntington Library.

65. CCP, "The Proposed Removal of Indians to Oklahoma," quotes on 3–5, 7. Several pages of the pamphlet can be found verbatim in "Prof. Painter's Work at Washington and Elsewhere," *Fifth Annual Report of the Ex. Com. of the IRA, 1887*, 16–17.

66. CCP to HW, October 2, 1887, *IRA Papers*, reel 2.

67. "Proceedings of the Fifth Annual Meeting of the LMC," in *Nineteenth Annual Report of the BIC, for the Year 1887* (Washington, D.C.: GPO, 1888), 49.

68. CCP, "A Change of Policy Requires a Change of Method," in "Proceedings of the Fifth Annual Meeting of the LMC," quotes on 50–52.

69. CCP, "A Change of Policy Requires a Change of Method," 52, 56. See also "Friends of the Indians," *New York Times*, September 29, 1887, 4; "To Elevate the Indians: The Topics Discussed by the Friends of the Red Man," *New York Times*, September 30, 1887, 2. For more on Cleveland's proposal and the IRA's acceptance, see CCP to HW, December 5, 1887, *IRA Papers*, reel 3.

70. "Henry L. Dawes/Defense of the Dawes Act," in Prucha, ed., *Americanizing the American Indians*, 100.

71. "Devoted to the Discussion of the Dawes Bill," in "Proceedings of the Fifth Annual Meeting of the LMC," 86–87.

72. "Devoted to the Discussion of the Dawes Bill," 88–89.

73. "Third Day-Afternoon Session," in "Proceedings of the Fifth Annual Meeting of the LMC," 108.

74. "Devoted to the Discussion of the Dawes Bill," 88–89.

75. "Third Day-Morning Session," in "Proceedings of the Fifth Annual Meeting of the LMC," see 95–103 for Thayer's speech, proposals, discussion, and questions and answers; see also "The Indian Conference," *New York Tribune*, October 1, 1887, 4.

76. "Third Day-Morning Session," in "Proceedings of the Fifth Annual Meeting of the LMC," 101.

77. Abbott, a graduate of New York University, practiced law in New York and wrote the *New York Statutes and Reports* and *Abbott's Digest of New York Statutes and Reports*, as well as novels. Garrett, a Quaker and a graduate of Haverford College, worked for prison reform, improvements in administration of public charity, and as a member of the Philadelphia Committee of One Hundred, the removal of government corruption.

78. "Third Day-Evening Session," in "Proceedings of the Fifth Annual Meeting of the LMC," quotes on 111, 112, 114.

79. CCP, "Third Day-Morning Session," in "Proceedings of the Fifth Annual Meeting of the LMC," 92–93.

80. By 1887 this group's twenty-four members were becoming "more and more interested in the cause of help and justice to the Indian"; see *Annual Report of the Massachusetts Indian Association (January 1887)* (Boston: Frank Wood, 1887), 14–15. It is not known whether Martha was a member.

81. CCP to HW, October 12, 1887, *IRA Papers*, reel 2; "Addresses Made by Prof. Painter," *Fifth Annual Report of the Ex. Com. of the IRA, 1887*, 65. See also CCP to HW, October 2 and 12 and November 18, 1887, *IRA Papers*, reel 2, and December 1 and 7, 1887, reel 3. The final report with index was 114 printed pages. J. B. Harrison informed the IRA Executive Committee (April 3, 1888, *IRA Papers*, reel 3) that "it will be one of the most important publications ever issued by the Association."

82. CCP to HW, December 7, 8, 22 (for Vassar), and 31, 1887, *IRA Papers*, reel 3.

## Chapter 5. Defending an Agent, the Dakota Scouts, and a Quaker Educator

1. "Journal of the Seventeenth Annual Conference, with Representatives of Missionary Boards and Indian Rights Associations," *Nineteenth Annual Report of the BIC, 1887*, 131.

2. "Journal of the Seventeenth Annual Conference," 132.

3. "Journal of the Seventeenth Annual Conference," 133.

4. CCP to HW, January 7 and 18, 1888, *IRA Papers*, reel 3; CCP to HW, February 9, 1892, reel 8.

5. CCP to Harrison, January 24, 1888, *IRA Papers*, reel 3. Harrison, a Unitarian clergyman, public speaker, and accomplished writer, was employed beginning May 1, 1886, primarily to visit Western reservations for the IRA. See Hagan, *The IRA*, 49–50.

6. Harrison informed Painter on March 19, 1888, that his work was "attracting more attention than ever before in the public press" and that he was receiving many inquiries regarding it (*IRA Papers*, reel 69).

7. "Prof. Painter's Work at Washington," *Sixth Annual Report of the Ex. Com. of the IRA, 1888*, 5, 8–9 for Eells; CCP to HW, March 8, 1888, *IRA Papers*, reel 3.

8. CCP to Harrison, January 24, 1888, *IRA Papers*, reel 3. For Eells, see Castile, "Edwin Eells, U.S. Indian Agent," 65, 61. For Dawes, see CCP to HW, March 5, 1888, *IRA Papers*, reel 3.

9. "Prof. Painter's Work at Washington," 8–9; CCP to HW, March 5, 1888, *IRA Papers*, reel 3.

10. "Prof. Painter's Work at Washington," 8–9; CCP to HW, March 22, April 18 and 24, and August 13, 1888, *IRA Papers*, reel 3.

11. For the resolution, see [Herbert Welsh and Henry S. Pancoast], "The Sioux Bill," (Philadelphia: IRA, 1884), 4, *IRA Papers*, #A21, reel 102; "The Sioux Bill," *Sixteenth Annual Report of the BIC, 1884*, 42–43. See also IRA, *Second Annual Report of the Ex. Com. of the IRA, 1884*, 10 for the copies and 13–15 for the IRA's description of this legislation.

12. CCP to HW, March 8 for first quote, see also February 15, 1888, both in *IRA Papers*, reel 3. For last quotes, see CCP, "Washington-Agency-Review of the Year's Work," *Seventh Annual Report of the Ex. Com. of the IRA for the Year Ending December 15, 1889* (Philadelphia: Office of the IRA, 1890), 12; for background, see Prucha, *American Indian Policy in Crisis*, 169–81; Prucha, *The Great Father*, 631–40; Hagan, *The IRA*, 55–59.

13. Samuel J. Brown, "Biographic Sketch of Chief Gabriel Renville," *Collections of the Minnesota Historical Society* 10, part 2 (St. Paul, Minn.: Published by the Society, February 1905), 614–18. For his character, see 616–18; and Gary Clayton Anderson, *Gabriel Renville: from the Dakota War to the Creation of the Sisseton-Wahpeton Reservation, 1825–1892* (Pierre: South Dakota Historical Society Press, 2018).

14. Brown, the son of Susan Frenier Brown, Gabriel Renville's sister, and Major Joseph Renshaw Brown, had been captured by the U.S. Army during the 1862 uprising. Upon his release, he served as an interpreter and later as the superintendent of government scouts in Dakota Territory. Turning to teaching, he served as a lay missionary and as superintendent of the Sisseton Agency industrial school. See the Joseph R. and Samuel J. Brown and Family Papers, Minnesota Historical Society, Saint Paul, Minnesota.

15. CCP, "How We Punish Our Allies," *Lend a Hand*, October 1888, 600; later republished by the IRA (1888), *IRA Papers*, reel 102, A103.

16. Brown, "Biographic Sketch of Chief Gabriel Renville," 616.

17. CCP, "How We Punish Our Allies, *Lend a Hand*, 600–3; see also "Prof. Painter's Work at Washington," *Sixth Annual Report of the Ex. Com. of the IRA, 1888*, 12–17; "Professor Painter," *Proceedings of the Sixth Annual Meeting of the LMC*, 64–65; Hagan, *The IRA*, quote on 140. In CCP to HW, March 5, 1888, Painter wrote that he conferred with the commissioner in regard to the Sisseton Sioux and examined their treaties (*IRA Papers*, reel 3). See also CCP to Harrison, March 10, 1888; CCP to HW, March 20, 1888, *IRA Papers*, reel 3. For Painter's detailed history of this case, see CCP, "Some Dangers Which Now Threaten the Interests of the Indians," *Proceedings of the Tenth Annual Meeting of the LMC of Friends of the Indian, 1892* (LMC, 1892), 76–78. Years later (CCP to HW, June 12, 1894, *IRA Papers*, reel 11), Painter wrote that the scouts must be regarded as friendly and "the confiscation of their annuities be conserved a great injustice and wrong."

18. WNIA, "A Great Wrong to Redress," *The Indian's Friend*, January 1889, 4.

19. CCP to HW, January 31, 1891, *IRA Papers*, reel 6. See also Hagan, *The IRA*, 141; "The Passage of the Bill for the Relief of the Sisseton-Wahpeton Scouts," *Ninth Annual Report of the Ex. Com. of the IRA for the Year Ending December 15, 1891* (Philadelphia: Office of the IRA, 1892), 37–39.

20. "Prof. Painter's Work at Washington," *Sixth Annual Report of the Ex. Com. of the IRA, 1888,* 9; CCP to HW, March 5 and March 20, 1888, *IRA Papers,* reel 3; Hagan, *The IRA,* 72, and for Painter's second defense of the Menominee, see 73.

21. CCP to HW, March 20, 1881, *IRA Papers,* reel 3.

22. CCP to HW, November 15, 1888, *IRA Papers,* reel 4, and April 18 and 24, 1888, *IRA Papers,* reel 3.

23. For Garland's decision, see his letter of November 20, 1888, *Fifty-Seventh Annual Report of the CIA, 1888* (Washington, D.C.: GPO, 1888), xlv–xlvi; see also in the same location Interior Secretary William F. Villas's letter of November 23, 1888, xlv.

24. CCP to HW, November 15, 1888, and February 15, 1889, *IRA Papers,* reel 4; "Prof. Painter's Work at Washington," *Sixth Annual Report of the Ex. Com. of the IRA, 1888,* 9–11; see also "Green Bay Agency" and Thomas Jennings, Agent, August 24, 1889, *Fifty-Eighth Annual Report of the CIA to the SI, 1889* (Washington, D.C.: GPO, 1889), 88–91, 298. On December 22, 1888, Vilas wrote Welsh that he thought it wise for Congress to pass a law permitting the Indians the use of such timber; see *IRA Papers,* reel 4.

25. CCP to HW, March 5 and April 24, 1888, *IRA Papers,* reel 3.

26. Hagan, *The IRA,* 76.

27. Hagan, *The IRA,* 75; CCP, *The Proposed Removal of Indians,* 3.

28. CCP to Harrison, March 28, 1888, *IRA Papers,* reel 3.

29. CCP, "Oklahoma," *The Indian's Friend,* March 1889, 1; CCP, *The Oklahoma Bill, and Oklahoma* (Philadelphia: Office of the IRA, April, 1889), 1. In a letter to Welsh (April 4, 1888, *IRA Papers,* reel 3), Painter explained that he had spent most of the previous day "with the Oklahoma men in and out of Congress" and that the bill proposed was "nothing more than" what he had "urged with reference to the Indians concerned." On August 1, 1888 he wrote that the bill included the amendments he had suggested (CCP to HW, *IRA Papers,* reel 3).

30. "Mr. Springer's Views," *Kansas City Times,* February 18, 1888.

31. "Against Meddling with Indians. One of Atkins's Pet Schemes Exposed," *New York Tribune,* March 12, 1888.

32. CCP to Harrison, April 24, 1888, *IRA Papers,* reel 3.

33. CCP, *The Oklahoma Bill, and Oklahoma,* 4–5; CCP to HW, February 15, 1889, *IRA Papers,* reel 4. See also CCP to HW, April 1, 1889, *IRA Papers,* reel 4.

34. CCP, "Oklahoma," *The Indian's Friend,* March 1889, 1; for background, see Prucha, *American Indian Policy in Crisis,* 373–401. In January 1889, after the Creeks and Seminoles surrendered their claims to the Oklahoma District, fifty thousand homesteaders rushed in. A formal territorial government was organized in 1890, the same year the Cherokees sold the Cherokee Outlet, some 6 million acres. Three years later it was opened to homesteaders. Oklahoma Territory became a state in 1907.

35. The son of a Cherokee mother and a mixed-blood father, Smith served as principle chief of the Eastern Band of Cherokee Indians from 1880 to 1891, establishing an education system with the Quakers and gaining official state recognition for the Eastern Band. During the Civil War he had been a member of William Holland

Thomas's Confederate Legion of Cherokee and Highlanders. For his obituary, see "Chief Smith's Life," *Ashville Weekly Citizen*, August 10, 1893, 5.

36. CCP to HW, June 21, 1888, *IRA Papers*, reel 3; "Painter's Work at Washington," *Sixth Annual Report of the Ex. Com. of the IRA, 1888*, 18; *The Civil Service Record* [a monthly publication by the Civil Service Reform Associations of Boston and Cambridge], October 1888, 28–30.

37. CCP, *The Eastern Cherokees. A Report* (Philadelphia: IRA [1888]), *IRA Papers*, reel 102, quote 7. An extract was printed in the April 1889 issue of *Southern Workman and Hampton School Record*, 45.

38. CCP, *The Eastern Cherokees*, 9–10, Atkins's quote on 10.

39. CCP, *The Eastern Cherokees*, 4, 7–9, quotes on 7, 8. See also CCP to HW, September 19, 1892, *IRA Papers*, reel 9.

40. CCP, *The Eastern Cherokees*, quotes on 10–11, 13.

41. CCP, *The Eastern Cherokees*, 9, 15.

42. "Civil Service in Indian Affairs," *Philadelphia Times*, November 10, 1887; for quote see Hagan, *The IRA*, 80–81. In 1888 members of the Boston Indian Citizenship Committee also petitioned Cleveland to put the Indian service under Civil Service rules; see *IRA Records*, box 6, folder 1 (May 1888).

43. CCP to HW, August 18, 1888, *IRA Papers*, reel 3. Spray remained in his post until 1891, when the Quakers asked him to resign. In 1899 he was appointed superintendent in charge of the Eastern Cherokee Agency; see Sharlotte Neely, "The Quaker Era of Cherokee Indian Education, 1880–1892, *Appalachian Journal* 2, no. 4 (Summer 1975): 314–22. According to James Mooney, Spray was reappointed in 1898 and was still there as late as 1903; Mooney, "Myths of the Cherokee," *Nineteenth Annual Report of the Bureau of American Ethnology* (Washington, D.C.: GPO, 1902). See also *Annual Reports of the Department of the Interior, for 1903: Indian Affairs, Part I* (Washington, D.C.: GPO, 1904), 227–28.

44. In a letter to Painter (May 10, 1893, *IRA Records*, box 226, folder 4), Welsh wrote that "turning out of Spray from that school has had the most disastrous results." The present superintendent "openly acknowledges that he is only there for the money" and is "very indifferent to the welfare of the children." Following a lice infestation, parents were removing their children to Waynesville, North Carolina.

45. CCP, *The Eastern Cherokees*, 14–16.

46. CCP to HW, July 7 and 21, and September 7, 1888, *IRA Papers*, reel 3.

47. "Proceedings of the LMC," *Twentieth Annual Report of the BIC, for the Year 1888* (Washington, D.C.: GPO, 1889), 50–53 for Abbott's paper, 57 for Painter's comments.

48. "Discussion on Indian Education, Continued," *Proceedings of the Sixth Annual Meeting of the LMC*, 31–32.

49. "Legislation for the Indian," *Proceedings of the Sixth Annual Meeting of the LMC*, for Thayer's report, see 42–48; for quote, 44; for text of the committee bill (Thayer bill), 49–53; for explanation, 53–58; for Painter's comments, 63.

50. "Legislation for the Indian," *Proceedings of the Sixth Annual Meeting of the LMC*, for Painter's comments, 64–65; for Ward's resolution, 70.

51. CCP to Harrison, September 27, 1888, *IRA Papers*, reel 3.
52. "Discussion of Resolutions Concerning an Agent in Washington and Contract Schools," *Proceedings of the Sixth Annual Meeting of the LMC*, 97–98.
53. CCP to HW, October 2, 1888, *IRA Papers*, reel 3; Hagan, *The IRA*, quotes on 88, 87.
54. CCP to HW, October 2, 1888.
55. "Proceedings of the LMC," *Twentieth Annual Report of the BIC, 1888*, 97.
56. For Atkins's request, see CCP to HW, November 8, 1888, *IRA Papers*, reel 4; "Prof. Painter's Work at Washington," *Sixth Annual Report of the Ex. Com. of the IRA, 1888*, 18.
57. "Prof. Painter's Work at Washington," 19 for Thayer bill, 18 for the "tadpole" comment.
58. "Prof. Painter's Work at Washington," 19–21.
59. CCP to HW, December 25, 1888, *IRA Papers*, reel 4.

### Chapter 6. Opposing Ute Removal and Seeking a Home for the Apaches

1. "Journal of the Eighteenth Annual Conference with Representatives of Missionary Boards and Indian Rights Associations," *Twentieth Annual Report of the BIC, 1888*, 111–14, quotes on 112, 113, 114, 118, resolution on 126. For IRA opposition, see "Mr. Painter's Work," *Fourth Annual Report of the Ex. Com. of the IRA, 1886*, 14.
2. CCP to HW, January 30, 1889, *IRA Papers*, reel 4, for copies sent and quote. See also Hagan, *The IRA*, 68, 128.
3. "Journal of the Southern Ute Commission, by T. S. Childs, Secretary," *Executive Documents of the Senate of the United States* (Washington, D.C.: GPO, 1889), 2:14–19. Related documents are on 1–83.
4. CCP to HW, February 6, 1889, and for Childs, February 9, 1889; see also February 8, 1889, all in *IRA Papers*, reel 4.
5. CCP, *Civilization by Removal! The Southern Utes* (Philadelphia: IRA, 1889), 1 and 8–9 for quote. In a letter to Welsh (January 30, 1889, *IRA Papers*, reel 4), Painter wrote "I think it about the best piece of work I have done." In a second January 30 letter Painter wrote, "I have never worked so in my life." He had learned only days before that his oldest brother was at death's door and informed Welsh, "[I]t was hard to say I could not go to him, and then go before the Committee the next morning."
6. CCP, *Civilization by Removal*, quotes on 10, 11, 13–14, 15.
7. In a letter to Welsh (March 20, 1889, *IRA Papers*, reel 4), Childs expressed "surprise at the *spirit*" of the pamphlet, describing Painter's representations as incorrect, unjust, and unfair. Childs had assumed IRA publications were "carefully and conscientiously prepared," but if this one was "a fair specimen," they were a "waste of charitable funds." In a March 29 letter to Childs (*IRA Papers*, reel 4), Painter responded to him point by point.
8. Quotes are from CCP to HW, July 8, 1891, *IRA Papers*, reel 8.
9. For Oberly's tenure, see Floyd A. O'Neil, "John H. Oberly 1888–89," in Kvasnicka and Viola, eds., *The Commissioners of Indian Affairs*, 189–91. On October 25 Quinton congratulated Oberly on behalf of the WNIA Executive Board, offering her

association's cooperation in his "own earnest and just measures for the uplifting of our native Indians." She printed this letter in the October 1888 issue of *The Indian's Friend* (2).

10. Painter praised Oberly at length in a letter to Welsh on April 4, 1889 (*IRA Papers*, reel 4).

11. CCP to HW, January 28 and April 5, 1889, *IRA Papers*, reel 4. In a letter to Welsh (February 6, 1889, *IRA Papers*, reel 4), Painter recommended not pushing Oberly: "[I]t will bring him under suspicion of having given himself over to us for the sake or retaining, through us, his position." On April 11, 1889 (reel 4), Painter wrote he had received a petition from the citizens of Geneva, New York, requesting Oberly's retention, but not all reformers shared this opinion. On April 11, Strieby wrote Painter that although the former commissioner had treated him with "uniform courtesy," he had "vague and somewhat indefinite objections against him." See *IRA Papers*, box 8, folder 4.

12. Hagan, *The IRA*, 99–103; HW to CCP, January 26, 1888, and HW to ASQ, February 4, 1889, both in *IRA Papers*, reel 69; ASQ to HW, February 2 (noting she had written Harrison), February 15 (noting she had written Pennsylvania congressmen), and February 25, 1889, all in *IRA Papers*, reel 4; HW to Dawes, February 4, 1889, *IRA Papers*, box 7, folder 5; HW, "Good Indian Work," *The Indian's Friend*, February 1889, 1. For the two undated petitions directed "To the President-Elect" [Harrison], see *IRA Papers*, box 7, folder 2 (December 1, 1888–December 31, 1888).

13. "An Important Work in Good Hands," *The Indian's Friend*, May 1892, 1. This article reported that Morgan had been corresponding secretary of the Providence branch of the Rhode Island IRA at the time of his appointment. For his tenure, see Francis Paul Prucha, "Thomas Jefferson Morgan, 1889–93," in Kvasnicka and Viola, eds., *The Commissioners of Indian Affairs*, 193–203.

14. See CCP to HW, March 15, March 16, and May 18, 1889, *IRA Papers*, reel 4; Garrett to Morgan, February 17, 1890, LR #5723–1890, RG 75, SC 31, OIA, NA. Although preferring Oberly, Welsh had written Painter in late 1888 that if he "goes out," he believed that Morgan "would be an admirable successor." See HW to CCP, November 6, 1888, *IRA Papers*, reel 69.

15. ASQ to HW, December 8, December 21, and "Xmas," 1889, *IRA Papers*, reel 5; December 30, 1889, *IRA Records*, box 19, folder 6.

16. CCP to HW, March 1, 1889, *IRA Papers*, reel 4.

17. CCP to HW, July 29, 1889, *IRA Records*, box 226, folder 2.

18. CCP to HW, November 4, 1889, and CCP to Mr. Raymond, December 18, 1889, both in *IRA Papers*, reel 5.

19. CCP to HW, November 4, 1889, *IRA Papers*, reel 5.

20. "To Enlighten the Indians," *Philadelphia Inquirer*, December 18, 1889; Hagan, *The IRA*, 129–34.

21. Quoted in CCP, "Washington Agency: Review of the Year's Work," *Seventh Annual Report of the Ex. Com. of the IRA, 1889*, 18; for extensive coverage of the Ute issue, see 18–24.

22. CCP to HW, December 2, 1889, *IRA Papers*, reel 5.

23. CCP to HW, January 17, 29, and 31, 1890, *IRA Papers*, reel 5; Hagan, *The IRA*, 132–34.

24. CCP, *Removal of the Southern Utes* (Philadelphia: Office of the IRA, 1890), *IRA Papers*, reel 102, A114, quotes on 7 and 8.

25. CCP to HW, March 17, 1890, *IRA Papers*, reel 5. Painter's frustration with Dawes only intensified; see CCP to HW, February 9, 1889, and March 1, 1889, reel 4. In the February 9 letter, Painter noted that Dawes threatened to prevent the passage of another bill if the House did not permit a specific provision for the Ute Commission. Painter asked: "What are you going to do with such consummate hypocrisy?"

26. "Attempted Removal of the Southern Utes," *Tenth Annual Report of the Ex. Com. of the IRA for the Year Ending December 15, 1892* (Philadelphia: Office of the IRA, 1893), 6–8, quote on 7. See also "The Proposed Removal of the Southern Utes," *Ninth Annual Report of the Ex. Com. of the IRA, 1891*, 33–37; Hagan, *The IRA*, 129–30; and for settlement, 164.

27. ASQ to HW, February 21, 1892, *IRA Papers*, reel 8.

28. ASQ, *The Ute Question* (Philadelphia: WNIA [1890], originally in the March 20, 1890, issue of the *National Baptist*). She also wrote "A Proposed Criminal Extravagance" for the April 1890 issue of *The Indian's Friend* (2). On March 16, 1890, she described the Ute case to Welsh as "flagrant," concluding, "[I]t would be infamous to remove them" (*IRA Papers*, reel 5). See also ASQ to HW, March 18 and April 1, 1890, reel 5; ASQ to HW, January 28, 1892, reel 8. In the January 28 letter she remarked that the WNIA machinery "was pushing the [Ute] matter through the local press, letters, petitions, etc.," concluding that the previous year her association had gotten so many votes that "we felt quite sure, to spoil the bill, and I hope we can all do the same again."

29. WNIA, ASQ, "The Ute Question," *The Indian's Friend*, May 1894, 5.

30. For Welsh's involvement, see "The Apache Prisoners at Mount Vernon Barracks," *Sixth Annual Report of the Ex. Com. of the IRA, 1888*, 54–57.

31. "The Chiricahua Prisoners," *Seventh Annual Report of the Ex. Com. of the IRA, 1889*, 30; Hagan, *The IRA*, 92–96. See also HW, *The Apache Prisoners in Fort Marion, St. Augustine, Florida* (Philadelphia: Office of the IRA, 1887). In 1871 Bourke became General Crook's aide-de-camp, following him through his campaigns against the Apaches, Sioux, and Cheyennes. A student of the Indians, Bourke recorded their customs, later writing ten ethnological papers. See Joseph C. Porter, *Paper Medicine Man: John Gregory Bourke and His American West* (Norman: University of Oklahoma Press, 1986). On August 13, 1888, Bourke informed Welsh that the current situation with the Chiricahuas resulted from General Miles's "mendacity and bad faith" in falsely pretending to capture Geronimo when he had sent two scouts with a peace proposal, calling it "one of the most disgraceful incidents in American History." See *IRA Papers*, reel 3.

32. In a January 11, 1887, letter to Painter (*IRA Papers*, reel 68), Welsh initially broached the idea of looking into their condition. For his visit, see "The Apache Prisoners," *Fifth Annual Report of the Ex. Com. of the IRA, 1887*, 27–22.

33. CCP to HW, February 11, 1887. Painter made a second inquiry about Chato in a letter dated October 6, 1886 (*IRA Papers*, reel 2).

34. HW to CCP, March 17, 1887, *IRA Papers*, reel 68. Welsh provided a lengthy excerpt of Painter's response of March 18, 1887 (*IRA Papers*, reel 2), in his *The Apache Prisoners in Fort Marion* (Philadelphia: Office of the IRA, 1887); see 45 for Welsh's quote.

35. CCP to HW, March 18, 1887, *IRA Papers*, reel 2. In a March 24 letter to Welsh (*IRA Papers*, reel 2), Painter provided additional information on the Apaches.

36. CCP to HW, March 28, 1887, *IRA Papers*, reel 2.

37. CCP to HW, April 1, 1887, *IRA Papers*, reel 2. "It seems to me that unless the [War] Department can show that the locality is unhealthy, there can be no escape from an awkward position unless the offer to locate these Indians is accepted," Painter wrote Welsh on July 21, 1888 (*IRA Papers*, reel 3).

38. Hagan, *The IRA*, 92–95; CCP to HW, May 10, 1888, and February 11, 1889, *IRA Papers*, reel 3 and 4, respectively. On June 29, 1888, General Crook informed Welsh that he "knew no one more fitted than you people [the IRA] who have the Indians [*sic*] interest at heart" (*IRA Papers*, reel 3). He wanted a permanent home for them so they could start "on the road to a future life that will elevate them out of their present condition."

39. On August 27, 1888, Welsh had informed Painter he was pleased with the farm as a possible permanent home (*IRA Papers*, reel 69).

40. CCP to HW, May 27 and June 7 and 17, 1889, and Bourke to HW, May 27 and 28, 1889, all in *IRA Papers*, reel 4.

41. "From the Report of Capt. Bourke," *Seventh Annual Report of the Ex. Com. of the IRA, 1889*, 32–33. For the conference at Mount Vernon Barracks, see "Geronimo's Band," *Baltimore Sun*, July 22, 1889.

42. "From the Report of Capt. Bourke," 34–36.

43. "From the Report of Capt. Bourke," 36–38; "The Chiricahua Prisoners," *Seventh Annual Report of the Ex. Com. of the IRA, 1889*, 39. See also Proctor to HW, July 3, 1889, *IRA Papers*, reel 4. In a letter to Welsh (October 10, 1889, *IRA Papers*, box 9, folder 3), the secretary wrote he did not think North Carolinians seriously objected. Congress had authorized him to purchase no more than ten thousand acres from the Cherokees for a Chiricahua home. See undated statement sent by Bourke to HW, in *IRA Papers*, box 7, folder 2 (December 1, 1888–December 31, 1888).

   Two years later, invited by the Massachusetts auxiliary that sponsored two teachers at Mount Vernon, Quinton visited the Apache prisoners there, describing their pleasant village, their vegetable garden, and a visit to the school. Although she hoped this civilization plan for the captive women and children would succeed, she concluded "[I]t *is* an experiment and an expensive one." See ASQ, "A Visit to the Apache Prisoners, *The Indian's Friend*, May 1891, 1.

44. CCP to HW, July 29, 1889, *IRA Records*, box 226, folder 2; CCP to HW, September 9, 1889, *IRA Papers*, reel 4.

45. CCP to HW, March 11 and 13, 1890, *IRA Papers*, reel 5; "Work in Washington—Report of C. C. Painter," *Eighth Annual Report of the Ex. Com. of the IRA, 1890* (Philadelphia: Office of the IRA, 1891), 13–14. On January 17, 1890, Painter wrote that he did not "know what tribes will say about taking Apaches to Indian Territory," but "we will have to work for the best that we can get" (*IRA Papers*, reel 5).

46. "The Indian and His Property," in "Proceedings of the LMC," *Twenty-First Annual Report of the BIC, for the Year 1889* (Washington, D.C.: GPO, 1890), 104–6, 110, reprinted as "Charles C. Painter/The Indian and His Property," in Prucha, ed., *Americanizing the American Indians*, 114–21; see also "The Indian Conference," *New York Times*, October 4, 1889, and *Essex County Herald* (Guildhall, Vermont), October 11, 1889.

47. "Work in Washington—Report of C. C. Painter," *Eighth Annual Report of the Ex. Com. of the IRA, 1890*," 16–17.

48. CCP to HW, January 23 and February 12, 1890, *IRA Papers*, reel 5.

49. CCP to HW, March 6, 1890, *IRA Papers*, reel 5.

50. CCP to Perkins, April [day missing; probably April 18], 1890, *IRA Papers*, reel 6. See CCP to HW, April 18 and 19, 1890, *IRA Papers*, reel 6. See also CCP, *A Plea for Enlarged School Work* (Philadelphia: Office of the IRA, 1890), 1.

51. CCP, *A Plea for Enlarged School Work*, 2–3 for statistics, 4–5 for quote.

52. In a letter to Welsh (June 28, 1890, *IRA Papers*, reel 6), Painter noted that Morgan felt "some degree of anxiety about the Educational Appropriation Clauses." See also "Report of C. C. Painter, Agent of the Association," *Eighth Annual Report of the Ex. Com. of the IRA, 1890*, 12; for educational monies and schools, see "Indian Legislation," *The Indian's Friend*, September 1890, 1.

53. On August 23, 1890, Painter informed Welsh that Morgan had written him the previous day, "expressing earnest hope that I may be present at the investigation of the Murphy claim" (*IRA Papers*, reel 6).

54. CCP to HW, September 19, 1890, reel 6. According to *The Indian's Friend* (May 1897, 6), Belt was an attorney from Maryland and had been in the Indian service for thirty years. Five letter books of his correspondence from 1885–1898 can be found in the Western History Collections at the University of Oklahoma Libraries.

   On February 23, 1889, Agent John Blair wrote Oberly that James Murphy was not an Indian, although his Menominee grandmother was on the Sac and Fox roll. Blair was unable to learn how she had been placed there. See *Executive Documents of the Senate of the U.S. for the First Session of the Fifty-First Congress*, vol. 9 [Ex. Doc. No. 82] (Washington, D.C.: GPO, 1890), 4; this source includes eighty pages of letters, affidavits, and testimonies relative to this issue.

55. CCP to HW, January 1, 1891, *IRA Papers*, reel 6.

56. CCP to HW, September 19, 1890, and January 1, 1891, *IRA Papers*, reel 6. See also "Report of C. C. Painter, Agent of the Association," *Eighth Annual Report of the Ex. Com. of the IRA, 1890*, 31–32.

57. CCP to HW, August 20, 1890, *IRA Papers*, reel 6.

58. CCP to HW, October 8 and 20, 1890, *IRA Papers*, reel 6.

59. "Report of C. C. Painter, Agent of the Association," *Eighth Annual Report of the Ex. Com. of the IRA, 1890*, 31–32; CCP to HW, January 1, 1891, *IRA Papers*, reel 6.

60. "Washington Agency: Report of C. C. Painter," *Twelfth Annual Report of the Ex. Com. of the IRA for the Year Ending December 15, 1894* (Philadelphia: Office of the IRA, 1895), 27–30, quote on 30.

61. "Report of C. C. Painter, Agent of the Association," *Eighth Annual Report of the Ex. Com. of the IRA, 1890*, 32–38, quote on 38.

62. "Report of C. C. Painter, Agent of the Association," 39–47, quote on 39. In a letter to Belt dated November 17, 1890, Morgan described his visit to government schools at Soboba and Potrero and his interview with the superintendent of the Mission Indian schools (LR #35960–1890, RG 75, SC 31, OIA, NA). Mission Indian Agent Rust, who believed in the importance of an off-reservation manual training school along the lines of Carlisle, selected a site in Perris, California. The school was opened in October 1892 and replaced in 1902 by Sherman Institute (today's Sherman Indian High School). See Mathes and Brigandi, *Reservations, Removal, and Reform*, 104–6.

63. "Report of C. C. Painter, Agent of the Association," *Eighth Annual Report of the Ex. Com. of the IRA, 1890*, 47–52, school description on 49.

64. CCP to HW, November 6, 1890, *IRA Papers*, reel 6.

65. For his description, see "Chilocco," in "Report of C. C. Painter, Agent of the Association," 45–47.

66. CCP to HW, November 28, 1890, *IRA Papers*, reel 6. For a description of his 1890 experience with the Ghost Dancers among the Cheyennes and Arapahos, see CCP, "The Indians' New Messiah. Interview with Sitting Bull," *Cheyennes and Arapahoes Revisited and a Statement of Their Agreement and Contract with Attorneys* (IRA, March 1893), 10–15.

67. CCP to HW, December 2 and 13, 1890, *IRA Papers*, reel 6; For final quote, see CCP, "The Indians' New Messiah. Interview with Sitting Bull," *Cheyennes and Arapahoes Revisited*, 11. In a December 12 letter to Welsh, Painter repeated his opinion: "To my mind the danger of an outbreak lies with the whites rather than with the Indians" (*IRA Papers*, reel 6).

68. Elaine Goodale Eastman, "The Ghost Dance War and Wounded Knee Massacre of 1890–91," *Nebraska History* 26 (January 1945): 26–42; Elaine Goodale Eastman, *Sister to the Sioux: The Memoirs of Elaine Goodale Eastman, 1885–91*, ed. Kay Graber (Lincoln: University of Nebraska Press, 1978), 145–46. While treating the victims of Wounded Knee, Goodale met her future husband, Santee Sioux physician Charles Eastman. For a contemporary history of the dance, see James Mooney, *The Ghost Dance Religion and the Sioux Outbreak of 1890*, ed. Anthony F. C. Wallace (Chicago: University of Chicago Press, 1965).

69. "The Sioux Outbreak: Its Causes and the Reforms in Indian Management to Which It Should Lead," *Eighth Annual Report of the Ex. Com. of the IRA, 1890*, 4–8.

70. WNIA, "The Indian 'War'," *The Indian's Friend*, February 1891, 2.

### Chapter 7. The California Mission Indian Commission

1. CCP to Noble, June 4, 1891, LR #20927–1891 [box 25], and CCP to Morgan, August 10, 1891, LR #30088–1891, both in RG 75, SC 31, OIA, NA.

2. Painter, while continually condemning the reservation system, was nonetheless responsible for the creation of these new reservations. This he could easily justify

because the Mission Indians were already village dwellers engaged in agriculture, and the preservation of their lands gave them a better chance to continue their way of life while integrating into the dominant culture, as Painter envisioned for all Indians.

3. "Journal of the Twentieth Annual Conference, with Representatives of Missionary Boards and Indian-Rights Associations," *Twenty-Second Annual Report of the BIC, for the Year 1890* (Washington, D.C.: GPO, 1891), quotes on 186, 175. In "The Old Grannies Meet" (*Topeka State Journal*, January 9, 1891), Painter described reservations as "an infernal system." See also "Sentimentalists: Oppose the Transfer of the Indian Bureau," *Reno Gazette-Journal*, January 9, 1891.

4. CCP to HW, n.d., *IRA Papers*, reel 6; original in *IRA Records*, box 17, folder 1 (n.d.; based on the content, this was likely written around January 20, 1891).

5. CCP to HW, January 13, 1891, *IRA Papers*, reel 6. See also CCP to HW, February 13, 1891, *IRA Papers*, reel 7; "The Extension of the Civil Service Reform Rules to the Indian Service," *Ninth Annual Report of the Ex. Com. of the IRA, 1891*, 4–9. On April 13, 1891, Harrison extended Civil Service rules to Indian service physicians and school superintendents, assistants, teachers, and matrons. This was amended on March 30, 1896, to include additional personnel below the level of agent. Agents remained under the spoils system until Theodore Roosevelt became president.

6. CCP to HW, January 20, 1891, *IRA Papers*, reel 6.

7. U.S. Department of the Interior, OIA, "Indian Legislation Passed during the Second Session of the Fifty-First Congress," *Sixtieth Annual Report of the CIA to the SI, 1891*(Washington, D.C.: GPO, 1891), 612–14 and 47–48.

8. CCP to HW, March 11 and December 12, 1890, *IRA Papers*, reel 5.

9. CCP to HW, January 20, 1891; CCP to HW, n.d. (somewhere between January 20 and 24, 1891), *IRA Papers*, reel 6. Aside from Painter's letters there is no extant documentation to suggest how Painter came to be appointed to the commission. What is clear is that he was certainly the hardest working member, remaining in California for a full eleven months while the other two members returned home much earlier.

10. For Smiley and Eliphalet Whittlesey's 1884 visit, see "Visit to Agencies in New Mexico, Arizona, and California," *Sixteenth Annual Report of the BIC, 1884*, 14–22; "Mr. A. K. Smiley," *Proceedings of the Ninth Annual Meeting of the LMC, 1891* (LMC, 1891), 24–25. See also Mathes and Brigandi, *Reservations, Removal, and Reform*, 112–117, including criticism of the commission's work by agents Francisco Estudillo and Lucius A. Wright.

11. Moore attended the University of Michigan Law School in 1868 and was admitted to the bar the following year. He was elected a circuit court commissioner for Lapeer County in 1870, a prosecuting attorney in 1872, and the mayor of Lapeer in 1874, and he was a one-term state senator. In 1888 he was elected a circuit judge of the Sixth Judicial Circuit, a position he held until 1896, when he became an associate justice of the Supreme Court of Michigan. See "Moore, Hon. Judge Joseph B.," *Men of Progress: Embracing Biographical Sketches of Representative Michigan Men* (Detroit: Evening News Association, 1900), 119; "Hon. Joseph B. Moore," *Portrait and Biographical Record of Genesse, Lapeer and Tuscola Counties, Michigan* (Chicago: Chapman Bros., 1892),

192–93; "Hon. Joseph B. Moore," *Cyclopedia of Michigan: Historical and Biographical* (New York: Western Publishing and Engraving, 1900), 104–5.

12. "The Mission Indians. Members of the Commission Chosen by Secretary Noble," *San Francisco Chronicle*, January 24, 1891; see also "Mission Indians Commission," *San Francisco Call*, January 24, 1891; "Mission Indian Commissioners," *Los Angeles Times*, January 24, 1891; "Mission Indian Commission," *San Francisco Call*, February 19, 1891, 1. For Painter's perspective, see Valerie Sherer Mathes, "The California Mission Indian Commission of 1891: The Legacy of Helen Hunt Jackson," *California History* 73, no. 4 (Winter 1993–94): 339–59, notes on 390–95; for Smiley's perspective, see Larry E. Burgess, "Commission to the Mission Indians: 1891," *San Bernardino County Museum Association Quarterly* 35, no. 1 (Spring 1988): 2–47.

13. CCP to HW, January 30, 1891, *IRA Papers*, reel 6. In a letter to Welsh (February 16, 1891, *IRA Papers*, reel 7), Painter again brought up the issue of salary.

14. CCP to HW, January 24 and 28, 1891; CCP to Pancoast, January 24, 1891, *IRA Papers*, reel 6.

15. CCP to HW, January 28, 1891; see also January 30 and 31, 1891—all in *IRA Papers*, reel 6.

16. CCP to HW, January 28, 1891. A week earlier, on January 20, Painter informed Welsh he had been "urging this Sisseton matter all I can"; see also CCP to HW, January 31, 1891, *IRA Papers*, reel 6.

17. Henry Guy Carleton, "Government Perfidy. That Has Been a Powerful Cause of This Indian Trouble," *Chicago Daily Tribune*, January 23, 1891.

18. "The Passage of the Bill for the Relief of the Sisseton-Wahpeton Scouts," *Ninth Annual Report of the Ex. Com. of the IRA, 1891*, 37–39.

19. This last task would be especially complicated. To expand its line through San Gorgonio Pass across the desert to Yuma, Southern Pacific had been granted a government subsidy in land for ten miles on either side of the tracks. "To prevent a complete monopoly, the land was divided into alternating sections of 640 acres each, with odd-numbered sections going to the railroad and even-numbered remaining public land.... The result was a bewildering checkerboard of ownership, made even worse by a lack of accurate surveys in the field. The confusion would plague most of the reservations in what is now Riverside County for decades" (Mathes and Brigandi, *Reservations, Removal, and Reform*, 27).

20. For typed instructions to the commission, see Noble to Morgan, January 24, 1891, and Morgan to Smiley, Morse [Moore], and CCP, January 31, 1891, both in LR #3101–1891, RG 75, SC 31, OIA, NA. For a typeset copy, see Acting Secretary, George Chandler to Morgan, February 9, 1891, and Morgan to Smiley, Morse [Moore], and CCP, January 31, 1899, both in LR #5319–1891, RG 75, SC 31, OIA, NA. For complaint about funding, see CCP to Morgan, February 12, 1891, LR #5817–1891, RG 75, SC 31, OIA, NA.

21. For late start, see CCP to Morgan, February 28, 1891, LR #9084–1891, and Smiley, CCP, and Moore to Noble, April 1, 1891, LR #12973–1891, both in RG 75, SC 31, OIA, NA. For Painter dinner, see "3/5," and for San Manuel, see "3/9" through "3/11," in Albert K. Smiley, *Account of a Trip through Southern California, Spring of 1891*, A. K.

Smiley Public Library, Redlands, California; also CCP to HW, April 3, 1891, *IRA Papers*, reel 7.

22. Belt to Noble, December 19, 1891, LR #9299–1891 [#44477–1891], RG 75, SC 31, OIA, NA; this letter is an abbreviated version of the final report in Albert K. Smiley et al. *Report of Indian Commissioners*, A. K. Smiley Public Library. For an explanation of "odd-numbered," see note 19 above.

23. Smiley, CCP, and Moore to Noble, March 16, 1891, LR #11277–1891, and Smiley, CCP, and Moore to Noble, April 1, 1891, LR #12973–1891, both in RG 75, SC 31, OIA, NA. For an explanation of "odd-numbered," see note 19.

24. Belt to Noble, December 19, 1891, LR #9299–1891 [#44477–1891], RG 75, SC 31, OIA, NA.

25. Smiley, CCP, and Moore to Noble, March 16, 1891, and Belt to Smiley, Morse [Moore], and CCP, April 1, 1891, both in LR #11277–1891, RG 75, SC 31, OIA, NA.

26. Smiley, CCP, and Moore to Noble, April 1, 1891, LR #12973–1891, RG 75, SC 31, OIA, NA.

27. For the division of work, see CCP to Morgan, April 3, 1891, LR #12984–1891, and Smiley and Moore to Noble, April 14, 1891, LR #14877–1891; see also CCP to Noble, April 14, 1891, LR #14878–1891—all in RG 75, SC 31, OIA, NA. For Smiley's trip, see *Account of a Trip through Southern California*, A. K. Smiley Public Library.

28. CCP to Noble, April 14, 1891, LR #14878–1891, and CCP to Noble, May 5, 1891, LR #17210–1891 [box 25], both in RG 75, SC 31, OIA, NA.

29. Smiley to Noble, April 1, 1891, LR #13939–1891, RG 75, SC 31, OIA, NA. For leaves, see Noble to Moore, April 9, 1891, LR #13695–1891 [box 25], and Noble to CCP, April 11, 1891, LR #13694–1891 [box 25], both in RG 75, SC 31, OIA, NA. In a June letter to Morgan (June 4, 1891, LR #20194–1891, RG 75, SC 31, OIA, NA), Moore wrote he would try and arrange his affairs and return in the fall.

30. "Letter Appointing Frank D. Lewis as Clerk to the Mission In. Commission," George Chandler, Acting Interior Secretary, May 20, 1891, LR #18465–1891, RG 75, SC 31, OIA, NA. In March Rust had recommended that Lewis be instructed to accompany the commission with expenses provided; see Rust to Morgan, March 27, 1891, LR #12233–1891, RG 75, SC 31, OIA, NA.

31. CCP to HW, April 20 and April 3, 1891, *IRA Papers*, reel 7.

32. CCP to Noble, May 5, 1891, LR #17210–1891 [box 25], and CCP to Morgan, May 11, 1891, LR #18195–1891 [box 25], both in RG 75, SC 31, OIA, NA. See also "Report of Mr. C. C. Painter, Washington Agent of the Association," *Ninth Annual Report of the Ex. Com. of the IRA, 1891*, 15. Morongo and the Coachella Valley proved to be the most complicated cases with reference to railroad lands.

33. CCP to HW, May 13 and June 8, 1891, *IRA Papers*, reel 7.

34. "The Southern Utes," *Colorado Sun*, January 25, 1892; see reprint in *IRA Papers*, A 142, reel 102.

35. CCP to Noble, June 4, 1891, LR #20927–1891 [box 25], RG 75, SC 31, OIA, NA; CCP to HW, June 8, 1891, *IRA Papers*, reel 7.

36. CCP to Noble, June 4, 1891, LR #20927–1891 [box 25].

37. CCP to Morgan, July 2, 1891, LR #24215–1891 [box 25], and for last two quotes and Rust, see CCP to Morgan, July 7, 1891, LR #25081–1891 [box 25], both in RG 75, SC 31, OIA, NA. On May 13 Lewis recommended to Morgan that an allotting agent be sent to these four villages, as the Indians were ready and circumstances were favorable; see LR #18263–1891, RG 75, SC 31, OIA, NA.

38. Shields to Noble, July 22, 1891, enclosed with Chandler to Morgan, October 23, 1891, LR #38241–1891 [4039; box 25], RG 75, SC 31, OIA, NA. For Rincon allotment, see "Report of Mission Tule River Agency, Francisco Estudillo to Commissioner Daniel M. Browning, August 31, 1893," *Sixty-Second Annual Report of the CIA to the SI, 1893* (Washington, D.C.: GPO, 1893), 128.

39. CCP to Noble, July 6, 1891, LR #24778–1891, RG 75, SC 31, OIA, NA.

40. CCP to Noble, July 6, 1891, LR #24778–1891; CCP to HW, July 1, 1891, *IRA Papers*, reel 8.

41. CCP to Morgan, August 10, 1891, LR #30088–1891, RG 75, SC 31, OIA, NA.

42. CCP to HW, October 6, 1891, *IRA Papers*, reel 8; Smiley, *Account of a Trip through Southern California,* A. K. Smiley Public Library. For Moore and Painter in San Francisco, see "Mission Indians. Two Government Commissioners in This State," *San Francisco Chronicle,* October 29, 1891.

43. WNIA, "Association News and Notes," *The Indian's Friend,* September 1891, 3.

44. CCP to HW, November 12, 1891, *IRA Papers*, reel 8; CCP to Morgan, November 20, 1891, LR #42168–1891, RG 75, SC 31, OIA, NA. See also Belt to Noble, December 19, 1891, LR #9299–1891 [44477], RG 75, SC 31, OIA, NA. Hensley and A. P. Knowles were early occupants at Capitán Grande, with Hensley claiming to have purchased land as early as June 1881 from an Indian. In the fall of 1887 both were evicted by military troops. For more, see Thorne, *El Capitan,* 49–58, 61, 78, 179–180.

45. CCP to Morgan, December 4, 1891, LR #44055–1891, RG 75, SC 31, OIA, NA.

46. Albert K. Smiley et al., "Smiley Commission Report: Mission Indians," *Report of Indian Commissioners,* December 7, 1891, Smiley Collection, A. K. Smiley Library, for quotes, see 2, 68–69, and for Lewis, see 71, 72.

47. Lewis to Morgan, December 7, 1891, LR #44547–1891, RG 75, SC 31, OIA, NA. Smiley, "Smiley Commission Report": for Barker's offer, see Exhibit L, 94–98, for the Southern Pacific Railroad, see Exhibit G, 86–90, and for President Harrison's approval, see 99–100. For reservation numbers and acreage, see Belt to Noble, December 19, 1891, LR #9299–1891 [44477]. See also Mathes and Brigandi, *Reservations, Removal, and Reform,* 114.

48. For a list of all of the reservations, see Burgess, "Commission to the Mission Indians," 18–32; see also 33–35 for summary and acreage returned, quote on 34. See also "Report of Mr. C. C. Painter, Washington Agent of the Association," *Ninth Annual Report of the Ex. Com. of the IRA, 1891,* 11–23, especially 17–18, which lists the original executive order reservations and new ones.

49. CCP to HW, December 15, 1891, *IRA Papers*, reel 8.

50. CCP to Morgan, December 15 or 16 [illegible], 1891, LR #44765–1891, RG 75, SC 31, OIA, NA. The letter was written on either December 15 or 16 because Smiley's telegram

was received on the fifteenth and this letter was received in the Indian Office on December 17.

51. CCP to HW, December 28, 1891, *IRA Papers*, reel 8.

52. CCP to Belt, December 28, 1891, LR #46029–1891, RG 75, SC 31, OIA, NA.

53. "Message of the President of the United States," H. Ex. Doc. 96, 52d Cong. 1st Sess., 1892: 15 for Harrison's December 29 letter, 15 for Noble's December 30 letter, 5–11 for Shield's December 19 letter, 2–5 for Morgan's January 13 letter to Noble, 1–2 for Noble's January 23 letter to Harrison, and 1 for Harrison's response. For an extract of the commission's report on Morongo, see 11–13. See also "The Mission Lands. The Indian Commission's Report Before Congress," *San Francisco Call*, January 27, 1892.

54. CCP to HW, March 23, 1892, *IRA Papers*, reel 9; CCP to Noble, April 7, 1892, LR #12740–1892, RG 75, SC 31, OIA, NA; for settled cases, see Lewis to CCP, April 14, 1892, LR #15767–1892, RG 75, SC 31, OIA, NA.

55. CCP to HW, December 12, 1892, *IRA Papers*, reel 9.

### Chapter 8. Defending Indian Education and Stockbridge Enrollment

1. "Journal of the Twenty-First Annual Conference of the United States BIC with Representatives of Missionary Boards and Indian Rights' Association," *Twenty-Third Annual Report of the BIC, for the Year 1891* (Washington, D.C.: GPO, 1892), 140–41. In a letter to Welsh (January 9, 1892, *IRA Papers*, reel 8), Painter noted that the Thayer bill had come up for discussion privately among members of the BIC. "I think it is pretty generally agreed that the *Bill* is impracticable, but the conviction stronger than ever that *something* must be done." Months later, in December 1892 before the annual WNIA convention, Commissioner Morgan explained that he had studied the Thayer bill, listened at Mohonk to its provisions, and read the American Bar Association's resolutions, concluding that even without new legislation, "there could be sufficient protection of Indians in their present transitional state by the correction and extension of the present police courts among them." See WNIA, "The Annual Convention," *The Indian's Friend*, January 1893, 2.

2. CCP, "Report of Washington Agent," *Tenth Annual Report of the Ex. Com. of the IRA, 1892*, 9 for quote, 12–13 for Utes, 9–11 for education.

3. CCP to HW, January 1 and 13, 1892, see also March 7 and February 19, 1892, all in *IRA Papers*, reel 8. Quinton supported Welsh's position, writing on January 2, 1892: "We must man every gun. Give me any new points"—a reference to a future article for *The Indian's Friend* (*IRA Papers*, reel 8).

4. HW, "Letter from Mr. Herbert Welsh. A Crisis in the Cause of Indian Education," *Southern Workman*, February 1892, 32. In a letter to Welsh (February 16, 1892, *IRA Papers*, reel 8), Painter wrote that although the bill made no monetary change for Hampton or Lincoln, there was a reduction for buildings, not schools; "No special harm done." For Painter's comments on Welsh's open letter, see CCP to HW, February 23, 1892. On February 15, 1892, after Welsh asked Quinton to visit the capital and meet with Indian Office officials, she wrote that she was using "every nerve &

muscle," working "in many ways, & on many lines" on behalf of the appropriation bill, as well as the Ute case (*IRA Papers*, reel 8).

5. CCP, *Extravagance, Waste and Failure of Indian Education* (Philadelphia: IRA, March 1, 1892), 5–6, 22. In a speech at "Indian Citizenship Day," on February 8, 1892, Painter compared the cost of Indian education to that of a military engagement. See "Economy from Standpoint of the War Department," *The Hampton Normal and Agricultural Institute and Its Work for the Education of the Indian*, n.d. (1892 or 1893).

6. CCP to HW, March 2, 1892, *IRA Papers*, reel 8.

7. "Indian Rights: Herbert Welsh Replies to Senator Wolcott," *New York Times*, March 31, 1892; "Not Run by Pittsburgers. An Office of the Indian Rights Association Writes a Stinging Letter to Senator Wolcott—Why the Ute Removal from Colorado Is Opposed," *Pittsburgh Dispatch*, March 31, 1892; CCP to HW, March 10, 1892, *IRA Papers*, reel 8, and March 30, and April 1, 1892, reel 9.

8. CCP to HW, April 11, *IRA Papers*, reel 9; "Attempted Removal of the Southern Utes," *Tenth Annual Report of the Ex. Com. of the IRA, 1892*, 7. For vote, see *Southwestern Christian Advocate*, May 12, 1892, 3.

9. CCP to HW, April 19, April 21, and August 4, 1892, *IRA Papers*, reel 9. In a May 18, 1892, letter to Welsh (*IRA Papers*, reel 9), Painter wrote that Dawes was working with Wolcott to modify the Ute bill to possibly consolidate the Colorado Utes with the Navajos. This never became a reality.

10. CCP to HW, April 16, 1892, *IRA Papers*, reel 9.

11. CCP to HW, April 26, 1892, *IRA Papers*, reel 9; "Oneida Indians in Council," *Green Bay Weekly Gazette*, April 27, 1892, see also short news item in the May 4, 1892, issue.

12. CCP to HW, May 9, and May 31, 1892, *IRA Papers*, reel 9.

13. Assigned with his troops to protect the southern border of Kansas, Lee had taken over as agent in late July 1885. In a letter to the commissioner of Indian Affairs, Lee reported that this troop presence had brought a "quieting influence," and he was now working closely with John H. Seger, who was encouraging the Indians to take up farming and stock-raising; see Lee to CIA, August 31, 1886, *Annual Report of the CIA to the SI, 1886* (Washington, D.C.: GPO, 1886), 114–24.

14. CCP to HW, May 11, June 17 and 29, and July 1 and 16, 1892, *IRA Papers*, reel 9. In a letter to Welsh (September 19, 1892, *IRA Papers*, reel 9), Painter noted that Lee had agreed to accompany him.

15. CCP, *Cheyennes and Arapahoes Revisited*, 43–44 for meeting, 45–46 for Noble's explanations.

16. CCP, "Some Dangers Which Now Threaten the Interests of the Indians," *Proceedings of the Tenth Annual Meeting of the LMC of Friends of the Indian*, 78; Lee to CCP, July 18, 1892, *IRA Papers*, reel 9. See also "Captain Lee's Findings and Charges," in CCP, *Cheyennes and Arapahoes Revisited*, 52.

17. CCP to HW, August 10, 1892, *IRA Papers*, reel 9.

18. During the fifth conference session, Moore gave an address on the government's policy toward the Mission Indians. In "Our Policy toward the Mission Indians" (*Proceedings of the Tenth Annual Meeting of the LMC, 1892* [LMC: 1892], 113–17), he

found much to praise: governmental teachers who did admirable work and several Indian men who possessed an "executive ability of a high order," building comfortable homes, planting vineyards and orchards and living lives "which would in any man be worthy of commendation" (115). There was not an able-bodied man who did "not possess the necessary intelligence . . . to enable him to earn all the necessaries of life for himself and those dependent upon him" (116).

19. CCP, "Some Dangers Which Now Threaten the Interests of the Indians," quotes on 72, 73.

20. A March 3, 1891, law had required that the Interior Department's investigation of depredation claims cease and be transferred to the Court of Claims. See "Indian Depredation Claims," *Sixty-Second Annual Report of the CIA to the SI, 1893* (Washington, D.C.: GPO, 1893), 71.

21. In late March Painter attended the Court of Claims to hear its opinion on the "constitutionality of the law referring depredation claims to that Court." The decision to sustain the law caused him to fear there would be "an unbounded vista of assault" on tribal funds. See CCP to HW, March 29, 1892, and January 30, 1893, *IRA Papers*, reel 9. In May 1892, accompanied by Whittlesey, Painter appeared before the court to testify on behalf of the Sisseton-Wahpeton scouts. His "How We Punish Our Allies" was included as evidence; see CCP to HW, May 25 and June 29, 1892, *IRA Papers*, reel 9.

22. CCP to HW, February 23, 1892, *IRA Papers*, reel 9.

23. CCP, "Some Dangers Which Now Threaten the Interests of the Indians," 75–76; "Washington Agency: Report of C. C. Painter," *Tenth Annual Report of the Ex. Com. of the IRA, 1892*, 17–18, quote on 18.

24. "Mohonk Indian Conference of 1892," *IRA Papers*, reel 9. The flyer's signatories were Garrett, Moses Pierce, Davis, Elliott F. Shepard, and Edward L. Pierce, the latter replacing Austin Abbott.

25. CCP to HW, October 26, 1892, *IRA Papers*, reel 9.

26. CCP to HW, November 5, 1892, *IRA Papers*, reel 9; CCP, *Cheyennes and Arapahoes Revisited*, quote on 8, see also 21.

27. CCP, *Cheyennes and Arapahoes Revisited*, 3 for quotes, 22 for Kiowa school, 5–7 for government impact on mission schools; see also CCP to HW, November 25, 1892, *IRA Papers*, reel 9.

28. CCP, *Cheyennes and Arapahoes Revisited*, 15 for quotes, 24 and 25 for Morgan; Hagan, *The IRA*, 112 for quote on Noble, see also 113. For Morgan comment, see CCP to HW, February 1, 1893, *IRA Papers*, reel 10.

29. CCP to HW, November 25, 1892, *IRA Papers*, reel 9; "Cheyenne and Arapahoe Indians: Serious Trouble Is Threatened Unless They Are Supplied with Food," *Brooklyn Daily Eagle*, November 18, 1892; "About to Put on War Paint," *Dallas Morning News*, November 11, 1892.

30. CCP, *Cheyennes and Arapahoes Revisited*, 36 and 41 for quotes, 53–57 for the first contract, 58–62 for the second, 38–52 for explanation of both. In a February 7, 1893, letter to Welsh, Painter stated that he had a copy of the first one, "the important one;" but the second was in Indian Office records. On February 10 he noted that after

considerable trouble he finally obtained a copy of the second contract (both letters in *IRA Papers*, reel 10).

31. CCP to HW, December 14, 1892, and February 20 and 27, 1893, *IRA Papers*, reels 9 and 10. In a letter to Welsh dated January 19, 1893, Painter wrote he had finished the report and was unable to make it any shorter and still "possess you full of all the facts" (*IRA Papers*, reel 9). See also CCP to HW, January 20, 1893, *IRA Papers*, reel 9; Hagen, *The IRA*, 142; and CCP, "Report of Washington Agent" ["Contract with Cheyennes and Arapahoes Approved"], *Tenth Annual Report of the Ex. Com. of the IRA, 1892*, 20–22.

32. "Report of Matters Looked after since May, 1892," *IRA Papers*, box 19, folder 6 (n.d., probably late in 1892).

33. CCP to HW, November 5, 1892, *IRA Papers*, reel 9; Hagan, *The IRA*, 147; CCP to HW, March 21, 1893, *IRA Papers*, reel 10. Cleveland's second term coincided with the Panic of 1893, triggered by the failure of the Philadelphia and Reading Railroad, and the subsequent panic on Wall Street, which plunged the country into a depression that lasted until 1897.

34. CCP to Cleveland, April 26, 1893, *IRA Papers*, reel 10. For Cleveland's policy, see Hagan, *The IRA*, 157–58, 160.

35. "Journal of the Twenty-Second Annual Conference of the United States BIC with the Representatives of Missionary Boards and Indian Rights Associations," *Twenty-Fourth Annual Report of the BIC, for the Year 1892* (Washington, D.C.: GPO, 1893), 115–16. For final quote, see CCP to HW, February 6, 1893, *IRA*, reel 10.

36. "Journal of the Twenty-Second Annual Conference of the United States BIC," 122, 141–42.

37. CCP to HW, January 14, 1893, *IRA Papers*, reel 9. For Bartholomew, see CCP to HW, April 26, 1893, and for last quote, see CCP to HW, January 9, 1893—both in *IRA Papers*, reel 10.

38. CCP to HW, February 8, 1893, *IRA Papers*, reel 10. See also CCP to HW, February 13, 1893; and HW, "To Members of the Indian Rights Association, and to All Who Are Interested in a Prompt and Wise Solution of the Indian Problem"—both in *IRA Papers*, reel 10. On January 24, 1893, Painter had written that monies paid to religious contract schools would be reduced (*IRA Papers*, reel 9).

39. CCP to HW, February 10, 1893, *IRA Papers*, reel 10.

40. Painter had referred to Morgan's extravagant expenditures, especially school buildings "placed where it will be impossible to utilize them successfully, and this to satisfy the demands of Congressmen." See CCP to HW, January 29, 1892, *IRA Papers*, reel 8; February 1, 1893, *IRA Papers*, reel 10.

41. CCP to HW, February 23 and 28 and March 17, 1893, *IRA Papers*, reel 10.

42. CCP to HW, February 17, 1893, *IRA Papers*, reel 10; "Jas. C. Bridgman, Agent, to the Indian Commissioner, September 18, 1875," *Annual Report of the CIA to the SI, 1875* (Washington, D.C.: GPO, 1875), 369; "Chase to the Indian Commissioner, September 1, 1874," *Annual Report of the CIA to the SI, 1874* (Washington, D.C.: GPO, 1874), 186; see also the report of Henry R. Wells on p. 18. For background, see "Work in Washington—Report of C. C. Painter," *Eighth Annual Report of the Ex. Com. of the IRA, 1890*, 11–12; Hagan, *The IRA*, 137–38.

43. "Mr. Painter's Work," *Fourth Annual Report of the Ex. Com. of the IRA, 1886*, 15.

44. In a letter to Welsh (February 9, 1892, *IRA Papers*, reel 8), Painter had described Stockbridge as Sawyer's timber business partner, who only voted for measures that interested him personally, soliciting votes of other senators "as a personal favor in such measures." See also CCP to HW, April 26, 1892, *IRA Papers*, reel 9.

45. CCP to HW, March 1, 1889, *IRA Papers*, reel 4; for quote, CCP to HW, February 17 and 20, 1893, *IRA Papers*, reel 10.

46. CCP to HW, February 25, 1893, *IRA Papers*, reel 10.

47. CCP to HW, March 2, 1893, *IRA Papers*, reel 10.

48. CCP to HW, March 1, 1893, *IRA Papers*, reel 10; "Washington Agency: Report of C. C. Painter," *Eleventh Annual Report of the Ex. Com. of the IRA for the Year Ending December 15, 1893* (Philadelphia: Office of the IRA, 1894), 29. In a March 6, 1893, letter to Welsh, Painter had not yet learned whether the Stockbridge bill had been signed (*IRA Papers*, reel 10).

49. CCP to HW, August 30 and September 1, 1893, *IRA Papers*, reel 10. For more on Browning's tenure, see William T. Hagan, "Daniel M. Browning, 1893–97," in Kvasnicka and Viola, eds., *The Commissioners of Indian Affairs*, 205–9.

50. CCP to HW, September 23, 1893, *IRA Papers*, reel 10. For the logging report, see CCP, "Washington Agency," *Eleventh Annual Report of the Ex. Com. of the IRA, 1893*, 48–50; CCP to HW, November 4, 1893, *IRA Papers*, reel 10.

51. CCP, "Washington Agency," *Eleventh Annual Report of the Ex. Com. of the IRA, 1893*, 29–30; for enrollment, see 41. For approval, see CCP to HW, June 20, 1894, *IRA Papers*, reel 11.

52. In a letter to Welsh (December 26, 1893, *IRA Papers*, reel 10), Painter noted that time had come for "some kind of protection" for the Christian minority.

53. CCP, "Washington Agency," *Eleventh Annual Report of the Ex. Com. of the IRA, 1893*, 43–48; for submission, see "Stockbridge and Munsee Enrollment," *Annual Report of the CIA, 1894* (Washington; GPO, 1895), 89.

54. CCP to HW, October 1 and 9, 1893, and November 4, 16, 25, and 27, 1893, *IRA Papers*, reel 10. In an October 28 letter, Painter wrote that Martha had sat up for a few moments. For the last three weeks he had been anxious about her health and his work. On November 16 he wrote that she had dismissed her nurse and was improving, but he would feel easier when his work was done.

55. CCP to HW, December 1, 6, and 13, 1893, *IRA Papers*, reel 10.

56. CCP to HW, December 25, 1893, *IRA Papers*, reel 10.

### Chapter 9. The Apache Prisoners and the Florida Seminoles

1. CCP to HW, March 17, 21, and 24 for Martha's illness and weather, March 28 for departing, and April 18, 1893, for return, *IRA Papers*, reel 10.

2. Miss J. L. Axtell, "The Story of the Florida Seminoles," November 1889, 3; "Association News and Notes," September 1890, 1; ASQ, "A Visit to the Seminoles," April 1891, 1, all in *The Indian's Friend*; CCP to HW, June 5, 1893, *IRA Papers*, reel 10.

3. "The Seminole Mission," *The Indian's Friend*, December 1891, 2; Clara R. Brecht, "In the Wilderness," *The Indian's Friend*, June 1893, 1, 3. See also CCP to HW, June 5, 1893, *IRA Papers*, reel 10.

4. "Washington Agency: Report of C. C. Painter," *Eleventh Annual Report of the Ex. Com. of the IRA, 1893*, 30–36, quotes on 34, 35.

5. CCP to HW, May 8, 1893, *IRA Papers*, reel 10.

6. CCP to HW, June 5, 1893, *IRA Papers*, reel 10. The WNIA sold eighty acres to the government, upon which Dr. Brecht "put up buildings and did preparatory work"; see "Mrs Quinton," in "Proceedings of the BIA," *Twenty-Sixth Annual Report of the BIC, for the Year 1894* (Washington: GPO, 1895), 113 for sale.

7. CCP to HW, March 17, 1893, *IRA Papers*, reel 10. Wotherspoon had served in the navy from 1870 to 1873, fought in the Indian wars from 1874 to 1881, and since 1890 had been training a company of Apache prisoners at Mount Vernon. For his presentation, see "Capt. Wotherspoon," *Proceedings of the Eleventh Annual Meeting of the LMC, 1893* (LMC, 1893), 12–16.

8. CCP to HW, June 5, 1893, *IRA Papers*, reel 10. In a February 12, 1892, letter to Welsh (*IRA Papers*, reel 8), Painter noted his recent visit to General Oliver O. Howard, who like Bourke and others asserted there was nothing for the Indians in Alabama. See also "Washington Agency: Report of C. C. Painter," *Eleventh Annual Report of the Ex. Com. of the IRA, 1893*, 36–39.

   In late April 1891, Quinton visited the Shepard sisters; see ASQ, "A Visit to the Apache Prisoners," *The Indian's Friend*, May 1891, 1. See also Rose Stremlau, "WNIA Missions in the South," in Mathes, ed., *The Women's National Indian Association*, 111–13, 115, 117–18; Valerie Sherer Mathes, "The Banner Association: Twenty-Five Years in Massachusetts," in *The Women's National Indian Association*, 159–60.

9. CCP to HW, April 18, 1893, *IRA Papers*, reel 10.

10. CCP to HW, January 4, 1892, *IRA Papers*, reel 8; CCP to HW, December 28, 1892, *IRA Papers*, reel 9. See also Hagan, *IRA*, 153–55. In CCP to HW, March 17, 1893, Painter noted that Quinton, assuming he would be appointed, had already requested that the superintendent of her Seminole school be reappointed (*IRA Papers*, reel 10).

11. HW to Garrett, January 11, 1893, *IRA Papers*, reel 72.

12. CCP to HW, April 20 and May 13, 1893, *IRA Papers*, reel 10. For more on Browning and Smith, see Hagan, *The IRA*, 155–56.

13. CCP to HW, May 13, 1893, *IRA Papers*, reel 10.

14. CCP to HW, June 5, 1893, *IRA Papers*, reel 10. In his June 12 letter, Painter followed up with additional information on some of the issues he had previously mentioned.

15. CCP to HW, August 7, 1893, *IRA Papers*, reel 10. Other addresses were in Richmond, Massachusetts, and Cattaraugus and Irving, New York. For all of Painter's addresses, see his December 25, 1893, letter to Welsh (*IRA Papers*, reel 10).

16. CCP to HW, October 17 and 25, 1893, *IRA Papers*, reel 10. A November 8 letter to Welsh revealed improvement that allowed him to leave Martha under a nurse's care. Painter wrote, in a rare personal note, "I continue to receive good news in regard to Mrs. Painter's convalescence. The nurse wrote me a few days since that Mrs. Painter

had received a box of beautiful flowers which you were kind enough to send her. If she had been able, I know she would have written you a letter of thanks. Please accept my, as well as her, grateful acknowledgement." (*IRA Papers*, reel 10).

17. "Journal of the Twenty-Third Annual Conference of the U.S. BIC, with Representatives of Missionary Boards and Indian Rights Associations," *Twenty-Fifth Annual Report of the BIC, for the Year 1893* (Washington, D.C.: GPO, 1894), 108.

18. "Journal of the Twenty-Third Annual Conference," 123–24; CCP to HW, December 26, 1893, *IRA Papers*, reel 10.

19. CCP to HW, January 9, 1894, *IRA Papers*, reel 11.

20. *Twenty-Sixth Annual Report of the BIC, 1894* (Washington, D.C.: GPO, 1895), 3; CCP to HW, February 2, 1894, *IRA Papers*, reel 11.

21. For the Ute Bill, see CCP to HW, January 4, April 17, and June 11, 1894, *IRA Papers*, reel 11. In the latter he wrote that two prominent proponents for Ute removal had told him that he "had whipped them out completely."

22. "Washington Agency: Report of C. C. Painter," *Twelfth Annual Report of the Ex. Com. of the IRA, 1894*, quote on 33.

23. "Washington Agency: Report of C. C. Painter," 20–64 for his entire report.

24. In his letter to President Cleveland, dated by hand as April 26, 1893, Painter included facts on seven other issues as well, including the removal of the Umatilla Indians' agent at their request, removal of the Nez Perce agent and the Southern Ute agent, and dispossession of the Puyallup Indians (*IRA Papers*, reel 10).

25. CCP to HW, September 1, 1893, *IRA Papers*, reel 10. For Estudillo's appointment, see *Journal of the Executive Proceedings of the Senate of the United States of America*, vol. 28 (Washington; GPO, 1909), 461. For a history of his tenure, see Mathes and Brigandi, *Reservations, Removal, and Reform*, 133–59.

26. *The Indian's Friend*, November 1892, 2. In a September 19, 1892, letter to Welsh (*IRA Papers*, reel 9), Painter wrote that he "greatly" feared that "what had been so hopefully begun out there will be suffered to peter out in utter failure" because of Foote's appointment. "It is an infernal shame and outrage."

Land at Rincon was difficult to subdivide; therefore, "to do justice to the Indians," Foote had informed Morgan that she needed permission to divide it into irregular lots. Acting Interior Secretary Cyrus Bussez gave his permission to ensure the Indians received "arable lands with the best water privileges." See Bussez to Morgan, November 5, 1892, LR #40040–1892, RG 75, SC 31, OIA, NA. In "Association News and Notes" (*The Indian's Friend*, February, 1893, 1), Foote had described her allotment of two thousand acres, beginning in Rincon, giving twenty acres to heads of households and ten acres to those under twenty-one. While at Rincon she lived in an adobe house with no need for locks.

27. In late August of that year, Painter requested that Dorn be paid; see CCP to Noble, August 23, 1892, LR #30985–1892, RG 75, SC 31, OIA, NA. It is not known if he was.

28. All quotes in this paragraph are from CCP to Cleveland, no typed date but "[1893 Apr 26]" appears in top right, *IRA Papers*, reel 10.

29. CCP to HW, January 22, 1894, *IRA Papers*, reel 11.

30. White had tried earlier to have Dorn removed, ordering the agent to dismiss him, but Dorn refused to leave and complained to the Interior Department. See CCP to HW, November 4, 1893, *IRA Papers*, reel 10. See also "Copyists Suffer. Land Office Patronages," *San Francisco Call*, March 1894. Painter wrote Welsh that he could not "but feel anxious in regard to the allotments" in California" (CCP to HW, January 9, 1894, *IRA Papers*, reel 11).

31. CCP to HW, January 26, 1894, *IRA Papers*, reel 11.

32. CCP to HW, February 2 and 23, 1894; see also CCP to HW, January 26, 1894, all in *IRA Papers*, reel 11.

33. CCP to HW, February 2, 1894, and Howry to CCP, January 31, 1894, *IRA Papers*, reel 11. Quinton also addressed the issue, claiming that some damage claims against the Indians were twenty-five years old and the total of claims was nearly double that of all Indian trust funds. See ASQ, "A Large Hope," *The Indian's Friend*, January 1894, 4.

34. Quinton had asked Painter in December to write an article for the WNIA newsletter. See CCP to HW, December 25, 1893, *IRA Papers*, reel 10.

35. CCP to HW, March 13, 1894, *IRA Papers*, reel 11; CCP to ASQ, January 1894, "Indian Depredation Claims, *The Indian's Friend*, February 1894, 8. See also "Washington Agency: Report of C. C. Painter," *Twelfth Annual Report of the Ex. Com. of the IRA, 1894*, 26–27.

36. CCP to HW, February 15 and 19 (for Browning's opposition), February 23, and April 17, 1894, *IRA Papers*, reel 11.

37. CCP to HW, February 23 and 27, 1894, *IRA Papers*, reel 11.

38. CCP to HW, April 9 and 17, 1894, *IRA Papers*, reel 11.

39. "Washington Agency: Report of C. C. Painter," *Twelfth Annual Report of the Ex. Com. of the IRA, 1894*, 57–58, quote on 57. See ASQ, "A Visit to the Apache Prisoners," *The Indian's Friend*, May 1891, 1.

40. CCP to HW, April 17, 19, and 30, 1894; for detailed description and quote on BIC members, see CCP to HW, May 16, 1894—all in *IRA Papers*, reel 11.

41. "Washington Agency: Report of C. C. Painter," *Twelfth Annual Report of the Ex. Com. of the IRA, 1894*, 20; CCP to HW, April 9 and May 2 and 16, 1894, *IRA Papers*, reel 11.

42. CCP to HW, May 16 and July 12 and 20, 1894, *IRA Papers*, reel 11; "Washington Agency: Report of C. C. Painter," *Twelfth Annual Report of the Ex. Com. of the IRA, 1894*, 20–23, quote on 22. On August 8, he wrote that "Holmanism" prevailed, and the BIC's appropriation had been reduced by one thousand dollars.

43. *Twelfth Annual Report of the Ex. Com. of the IRA, 1894*, 10 for explanation of the bill, 12 for last quote.

44. CCP to HW, April 9, May 7 and 22, and June 1 (for New York), 1894, *IRA Papers*, reel 11.

45. CCP to HW, July 20 and August 8, 1894, *IRA Papers*, reel 11. For the conference, see "Report of C. C. Painter," in "Report of the BIC," *Executive Documents of the House of Representatives for the Third Session of the Fifty-third Congress, 1894–95* (Washington, D.C.: GPO, 1895), 146–51, condensed; much of this report appeared in the IRA's twelfth annual report. See also CCP to HW, June 27, 1894, *IRA Papers*, reel 11, relative to accompanying Hailmann to the summer institutes.

46. "Washington Agency: Report of C. C. Painter," *Twelfth Annual Report of the Ex. Com. of the IRA, 1894,* 24–26.

47. CCP to HW, October 5, 1894, *IRA Papers,* reel 11.

48. CCP to HW, October 5, 1894. For WNIA homebuilding, see Lori Jacobson, "'Environed by Civilization': WNIA Home-Building and Loan Department," in Mathes, ed., *The Women's National Indian Association,* 65–83.

49. CCP, "The Leasing of Indians' Lands," *Proceedings of the Twelfth Annual Meeting of the LMC, 1894,* quotes on 86 and 88.

50. Painter concluded that Hill, acting as a private citizen, had persuaded the Indians to go to Oklahoma with him. For his labors, Congress awarded Hill five thousand dollars out of the Indians' money; see "Washington Agency: Report of C. C. Painter," *Twelfth Annual Report of the Ex. Com. of the IRA, 1894,* 45, see also 44–46.

51. "Washington Agency: Report of C. C. Painter," *Twelfth Annual Report of the Ex. Com. of the IRA, 1894,* 39–41.

52. "Washington Agency: Report of C. C. Painter," 42–43, quote on 42.

53. "Washington Agency: Report of C. C. Painter," quotes on 43–44; see also "Kickapoo Mission, in Report of Sac and Fox Agency," *Sixty-Second Annual Report of the CIA to the SI,* 262, 264.

54. "Washington Agency: Report of C. C. Painter," 48–51, quote on 53. On 49–52 Painter details cases of sales and leases. See also CCP to HW, November 24, 1894, *IRA Papers,* reel 11. In a letter to Welsh (September 19, 1892, *IRA Papers,* reel 9), Painter noted that both the Pottawatomies and Shawnees were disturbed about the manner in which their allotments were made.

55. "Washington Agency: Report of C. C. Painter," 53–57, quotes on 53 and 56–57. For schools visited, see CCP to HW, November 20, 1894, *IRA Papers,* reel 12.

56. "Washington Agency: Report of C. C. Painter," quotes on 58–59; CCP to HW, November 24, 1894, *IRA Papers,* reel 11; for Baldwin's first report and date of arrival, see "Baldwin to Browning, August 29, 1895," *Annual Report of the SI, 1895* (Washington, D.C.: GPO, 1896), 250–53.

57. "Washington Agency: Report of C. C. Painter," quotes on 44; for more on the Cherokee Commission, see Prucha, *The Great Father,* 2:746–47.

58. "All for the Indians," *Philadelphia Inquirer,* December 7, 1894.

59. CCP to HW, December 18 and 19, 1894, *IRA Papers,* reel 12.

60. CCP to HW, January 7, 1895, *IRA Papers,* reel 12.

61. Seaman to HW, January 13, 1895, Whittlesey to HW, January 14, 1895, Leupp to HW, January 14, 1895, and Garrett to HW, January 15, 1895—all in *IRA Papers,* box 25, folder 4; ASQ to HW, January 24, 1895, and ASQ to Roosevelt, January 23, 1895, *IRA Papers,* box 25, folder 5.

## Conclusion

1. *Twelfth Annual Report of the Ex. Com. of the IRA, 1894,* 64–65; "The Late Rev. Charles C. Painter," *Springfield Republican,* January 20, 1895, 3.

2. "Our Washington Agent," *Thirteenth Annual Report of the Ex. Com. of the IRA for the Year Ending December 14, 1895* (Philadelphia: Office of the IRA, 1896), 9.

3. "Report of the BIC," *Twenty-Sixth Annual Report of the BIA, 1894* (Washington, D.C.: GPO, 1895), 4.

4. "Journal of the Twenty-Fourth Annual Conference of the United States BIC with Representatives of Missionary Boards and Indian Rights Associations," *Twenty-Sixth Annual Report of the BIC, 1894*, 38 for first quote, 72 for Abbott and Eaton.

5. "Journal of the Twenty-Fourth Annual Conference of the United States BIC with Representatives of Missionary Boards and Indian Rights Associations," 72–73.

6. "Stafford Springs, Ct.," *Springfield (Mass) Republican*, January 27, 1895. A copy was sent to Martha, who despite all her ailments, lived to be 101 years old, dying on December 19, 1940. She was buried in Great Barrington.

7. "Tribute to Mr. Painter," *Berkshire Courier*, January 31, 1895, for the first quote; "Charles C. Painter," *Berkshire Courier*, January 17, 1895, for the second. An example of Painter's support of young people is found in his care for W. E. B. DuBois, a Great Barrington High School classmate of his son, Charles. Although DuBois wanted to attend Harvard, Painter and members of four Congregational parishes funded a scholarship for him to Fisk. DuBois did attend Harvard later, becoming the first African American to receive a doctorate. See Bernard A. Drew, *Dr. DuBois Rebuilds His Dream House* (Great Barrington: Attic Revivals Press, 2006), 70–71; Bernard A. Drew, "Charles C. C. Painter, Advocate," *Berkshire Eagle* (November 3, 2003).

8. "A Great Loss," *The Indian's Friend*, February 1895, 4; *Southern Workman*, February 1895, 19.

9. *Proceedings of the Thirteenth Annual Meeting of the LMC, 1895* (LMC, 1896), 39.

▼ ▼ ▼

# BIBLIOGRAPHY

## Manuscript Collections and Government Documents

American Missionary Association. Archives. Amistad Research Center, Tulane University, New Orleans, Louisiana.

Armstrong, Samuel C. Papers. Hampton University Archives, Hampton, Virginia.

Board of Indian Commissioners (BIC). *Annual Report.* Washington, D.C.: Government Printing Office (GPO), 1882–95.

Brown, Joseph R. and Samuel J. Family Papers. Minnesota Historical Society, St. Paul, Minnesota.

Bureau of Indian Affairs, Record Group 75. National Archives, Washington, D.C.

Commissioner of Indian Affairs (CIA). *Annual Report of the CIA to the Secretary of the Interior (SI).* Washington, D.C.: GPO, 1874–75, 1882–86, 1888–89, 1891, 1893,1895.

Coronel, Anthony F. Collection. Seaver Center for Western History Research, Los Angeles County Museum of Natural History, Los Angeles, California.

Dawes, Henry Laurens. Papers. Library of Congress, Washington, D.C.

Indian Rights Association. Papers, 1864–1973. Series I-A, Incoming Correspondence, 1864–1968. Microfilm Edition. Historical Society of Pennsylvania, Philadelphia, Pennsylvania.

———. Records (Collection 1523). Historical Society of Pennsylvania, Philadelphia, Pennsylvania.

Indian Rights Association, Cambridge Branch. Secretary's Records. Cambridge Public Library, Cambridge, Massachusetts.

Jackson, Grant. Manuscript Collection. Henry E. Huntington Library, San Marino, California.

Jackson, Helen Hunt. Collection. Clifton Waller Barrett Library, Alderman Library, University of Virginia, Charlottesville, Virginia.

———. Papers. Tutt Library, Colorado College, Colorado Springs, Colorado.

Jackson, Helen Hunt. Manuscripts. Henry H. Huntington Library, San Marino, California; *Proceedings on Occasion of the Presentation of the Petition of the Women's National Indian Association, by Hon. H. L. Dawes, February 21, 1882.* Washington, D.C.: GPO, 1882.

Rust, Horatio Nelson. Papers. The Henry E. Huntington Library, San Marino, California.

Smiley, Albert K. Collection. A. K. Smiley Public Library, Redlands, California.

Weinland, William Henry. Papers. The Henry E. Huntington Library, San Marino, California.


### Contemporary Sources

American Missionary Association. *The American Missionary*, numerous years.

———. *Annual Report*. New York: AMA, 1877, 1879–83.

———. *History of the American Missionary Association with Illustrative Facts and Anecdotes*. New York: AMA, 1891.

*The Bi-Centennial Celebration of the Founding of the First Baptist Church of the City of Philadelphia*. Philadelphia: American Baptist Publication Society, 1899.

*Catalogue of the Officers and Students of Williams College for the Academic Year 1854–55.* Williamstown, Mass. 1854.

*Catalogue of the Officers and Students and Register of Societies in Williams College, for the Academic Year 1857–58*. Williamstown, Mass.: The Sophomore Class, 1857.

Child, Hamilton. *Part First: Gazetteer of Berkshire County, Mass., 1725–1885*. Syracuse, N.Y.: Printed at the Journal Office, January 1885.

———. *Part Second: Business Directory of Berkshire Count, Mass., 1884–85*. Syracuse, N.Y.: Printed at the Journal Office, 1885.

*The Congregational Year-Book, 1896*. Boston: Congregational Sunday.

*The Delta Upsilon Decennial Catalogue*. Published by the Fraternity, 1902.

*The Delta Upsilon Quinquennial Catalogue*. N.p.: Delta Upsilon Fraternity, 1884.

*First Congregational Church: Great Barrington, Mass. Parish Bulletin, 1895*. Great Barrington: Edward V. Foote, Book and Job Printer, 1895.

Hartsorne, Henry. "Memoir of James E. Rhoades." *Proceedings of the American Philosophical Society* 34, no. 149 (December 1895): 354–57.

Hartzell, Rev. J. C. *Christian Educators in Council: Sixty Addresses by American Educators with Historical Notes upon the National Education Assembly Held at Ocean Grove, N.J., August 9–12, 1883*. New York: Phillips & Hunt, 1884.

*Historical Catalogue of the Theological Institute of Connecticut*. Hartford: Press of the Case, Lockwood & Brainard Company, 1881.

*The Indian Question: Report of the Committee Appointed by Hon. John D. Long*. Boston: Frank Wood, Book and Job Printer, 1880.

Indian Rights Association. *Annual Report of the Executive Committee*. Philadelphia: Office of the IRA, 1884–1896.

———. *The Case of the Mission Indians in Southern California, and the Action of the Indian Rights Association in Supporting the Defence of Their Legal Rights*. Philadelphia: Office of the IRA, 1886.

———. *One Case of Justice to Indians*. Philadelphia: Office of the IRA, 1888.

Lake Mohonk Conference (LMC). *Proceedings of the Annual Meeting*. 1886, 1888, 1891–94.

———. *Second Annual Address to the Public of the Lake Mohonk Conference*. Philadelphia: Printed by the Order of the Executive Committee of the Indian Rights Association, 1884.

*Lend a Hand: A Record of Progress and Journal of Organized Charity*, ed. Edward E. Hale. (Boston: Lend a Hand Company), numerous issues.

Massachusetts Indian Association. *Annual Report of the Massachusetts Indian Association*. Boston: Frank Wood Printer, 1887.

Pancoast, Henry S. *Impressions of the Sioux Tribe in 1882, with Some First Principles in the Indian Question*. Philadelphia: Franklin Printing House, 1883.

Painter, C. C. *Cheyennes and Arapahoes Revisited and a Statement of Their Agreement and Contract with Attorneys*. Philadelphia: Office of the IRA, 1893.

———. *Civilization by Removal! The Southern Utes*. Philadelphia: Office of the IRA, 1889.

———. *The Condition of Affairs in Indian Territory and California*. Philadelphia: Office of the IRA, 1888.

———. *The Dawes Land in Severalty Bill and Indian Emancipation*. Philadelphia: Office of the IRA, 1887.

———. *The Eastern Cherokees. A Report*. Philadelphia: IRA, 1888.

———. *Extravagance, Waste and Failure of Indian Education*. Philadelphia, Office of the IRA, March 1, 1892.

———. *The Indian Rights Association, Its Aims Methods and Work*. Philadelphia: Office of the IRA, 1890.

———. *The Oklahoma Bill, and Oklahoma*. Philadelphia: Office of the IRA, April 1889.

———. *A Plea for Enlarged School Work*. Philadelphia: Office of the IRA, 1890.

———.*The Proposed Removal of Indians to Oklahoma*. Philadelphia: IRA, 1887.

———. *Removal of the Southern Utes*. Philadelphia: Office of the IRA, 1890.

———. *A Visit to the Mission Indians of Southern California and Other Western Tribes*. Philadelphia: Office of the IRA, 1886.

Quinton, Amelia Stone. *The Lake Mohonk Indian Conference*. Leaflets of the Women's National Indian Association, 1885.

———. *Suggestions to Friends of the Women's National Indian Association*. Philadelphia, 1884.

———. *The Ute Question*. Philadelphia: WNIA, 1890.

*The Southern Workman and Hampton School Record*, numerous issues. Hampton Institute, Hampton, Virginia.

Taylor, Charles J. *History of Great Barrington (Berkshire County) Massachusetts*. Great Barrington: Clark W. Bryan & Co., Publishers, 1882.

Tibbles, Thomas Henry. *Buckskin & Blanket Days*. Lincoln: University of Nebraska Press, 1957.

———. *The Ponca Chiefs: An Account of the Trial of Standing Bear*. Lincoln: University of Nebraska Press, 1972.

———. *The Ponca Chiefs: An Indian's Attempt to Appeal from the Tomahawk to the Courts*. Boston: J. S. Lockwood, 1887.

Welsh, Herbert. *The Apache Prisoners in Fort Marion, St. Augustine, Florida*. Philadelphia: Office of the IRA, 1887.

——. *Four Weeks among Some of the Sioux Tribes of Dakota and Nebraska, Together with a Brief Consideration of the Indian Problem*. Germantown, Philadelphia: Horace F. McCann, Steam-Power Printer, 1882.

——. *Report of a Visit to the Great Sioux Reserve, Dakota, Made during the Months of May and June, 1882, in behalf of the IRA, by Order of the Executive Committee*. Office of the IRA, 1883.

*The Williams Obituary Record*. Williamstown: Society of Alumni, 1895.

*The Women's Baptist Home Mission Society 1877 to 1882*. Chicago: R. R. Donnelley & Sons Printers, 1883.

Women's National Indian Association (WNIA). *Address of the President on Current Indian Legislation, Work Needed, etc*. Philadelphia: November 30, 1887.

——. *Annual Report*. Philadelphia: November 17, 1885.

——. *Fourth Annual Report of the Women's National Indian Association*. Philadelphia: November 1884.

——. *The Indian's Friend*. Various issues, 1888–97.

## Secondary Sources

Anderson, Gary Clayton. *Gabriel Renville: From the Dakota War to the Creation of the Sisseton-Wahpeton Reservation, 1825–1892*. Pierre: South Dakota Historical Society Press, 2018.

Apostol, Jane. "Horatio Nelson Rust: Abolitionist, Archaeologist, Indian Agent." *California History* 58, no. 4 (Winter 1979–80): 304–15.

Bates, J. C. *History of the Bench and Bar of California*. San Francisco: Bench and Bar Publishing Company, 1912.

Beard, Augustus Field. *A Crusade of Brotherhood: A History of the American Missionary Association*. Boston: The Pilgrim Press, 1909.

Brigandi, Phil, and John W. Robinson. "The Killing of Juan Diego: From Murder to Mythology." *Journal of San Diego History* 40, nos. 1–2 (Winter–Spring 1884): 1–22.

Brown, Samuel J. "Biographic Sketch of Chief Gabriel Renville." *Collections of the Minnesota Historical Society* 10, part 2 (St. Paul: Published by the Society, February 1905): 614–18.

Burgess, Larry E. "Commission to the Mission Indians: 1891." *San Bernardino County Museum Association Quarterly* 35, no. 1 (Spring 1988): 1–46.

——. "The Lake Mohonk Conferences on the Indian, 1883–1916." PhD diss., Claremont University, 1972.

Burton, Jeffrey. *Indian Territory and the United States, 1866–1906: Courts, Government, and the Movement for Oklahoma Statehood*. Norman: University of Oklahoma Press, 1995.

Castile, George P. "Edwin Eells, U.S. Indian Agent, 1871–1895." *Pacific Northwest Quarterly* 72, no. 2 (April 1981): 61–68.

Carlson, Leonard A. *Indians, Bureaucrats, and Land: The Dawes Act and the Decline of Indian Farming*. Westport, Conn.: Greenwood Press, 1981.

Daniels, Morris S. *The Story of Ocean Grove: Related in the Year of Its Golden Jubilee*. New York: The Methodist Book Concern, 1919.

Drew, Bernard. *Dr. DuBois Rebuilds His Dream House.* Great Barrington, Mass.: Attic Revivals Press, 2006.

———. *Great Barrington Great Town Great History.* (Great Barrington, Mass.: Great Barrington Historical Society, 1999.

Eastman, Elaine Goodale. *Sister to the Sioux: The Memoirs of Elaine Goodale Eastman, 1885–91.* Edited by Kay Graber. Lincoln: University of Nebraska Press, 1978.

———. "The Ghost Dance War and Wounded Knee Massacre of 1890–91." *Nebraska History* 26 (January 1945): 26–42.

Ellis, Elmer, *Henry Moore Teller: Defender of the West.* Caldwell, Idaho: Caxton Printers, 1941.

Fear-Segal, Jacquiline, "The Man on the Bandstand at Carlisle Indian Industrial School." In *Boarding School Blues: Revisiting American Indian Educational Experience*, edited and with an introduction by Clifford E. Trafzer, Jean A. Keller, and Lorene Sisquoc, 99–122. Lincoln: University of Nebraska, 2006.

Fear-Segal, Jacquiline, and Susan D. Rose, eds. *Carlisle Indian Industrial School: Indigenous Histories, Memories, and Reclamations.* Lincoln: University of Nebraska Press, 2016.

*Felix S. Cohen's Handbook of Federal Indian Law.* Albuquerque: University of New Mexico Press, 1971.

Foster, Sarah Whitmer, and John T. Foster Jr. "Historical Notes and Documents: Harriett Ward Foote Hawley: Civil War Journalist." *Florida Historical Quarterly* 83, no. 4 (Spring 2005): 448–67.

Gates, Merrill Edwards, ed. "Eliphalet Whittlesey." In *Men of Mark in America: Ideals of American Life Told in Biographies of Eminent Living Americans*, vol. 2. Washington, D.C.: Men of Mark Publishing Company, 1906.

Genetin-Pilawa, C. Joseph. *Crooked Paths to Allotment: The Fight Over Federal Indian Policy after the Civil War.* Chapel Hill: University of North Carolina Press, 2012.

Green, Michael D. "Porter Pleasant." In *Encyclopedia of North American Indians.* Edited by Frederick E. Hoxie, 502–4. Boston: Houghton Mifflin Company, 1996.

Hagan, William T. *The Indian Rights Association: The Herbert Welsh Years, 1882–1904.* Tucson: University of Arizona Press, 1985.

Hall, William Ham. *Irrigation in California (Southern).* Sacramento: State Printing Office, 1888.

Hebert, Edgar W. "The Last of the Padres." *San Diego Historical Society Quarterly* 10, no. 2 (April 1964): 15–22.

Holmes, Elmer Wallace. *History of Riverside County.* Los Angeles: Historic Record Company, 1912.

Jackson, Helen Hunt. *A Century of Dishonor: A Sketch of the United States Government's Dealings with Some of the Indian Tribes.* Norman: University of Oklahoma Press, 1995.

Mark, Joan. *A Stranger in Her Native Land: Alice Fletcher and the American Indians.* Lincoln: University of Nebraska Press, 1988.

Mathes, Valerie Sherer. "Boston, the Boston Indian Citizenship Committee, and the Poncas." *Massachusetts Historical Review* 14 (2012): 119–48.

———. "The California Mission Indian Commission of 1891: The Legacy of Helen Hunt Jackson." *California History* 73, no. 4 (Winter 1993–94): 339–58, notes 390–95.

———. *Divinely Guided: The California Work of the Women's National Indian Association.* Lubbock: Texas Tech University Press, 2012.

———. "Helen Hunt Jackson, Amelia Stone Quinton, and the Mission Indians of California." *Southern California Quarterly* 96, no. 2 (Summer 2014): 172–205.

———. *Helen Hunt Jackson and Her Indian Reform Legacy.* Austin: University of Texas Press, 1990.

———, ed. *The Indian Reform Letters of Helen Hunt Jackson, 1879–1885.* Norman: University of Oklahoma Press, 1998.

———. "James Bradley Thayer: In Defense of Indian Legal Rights." *Massachusetts Historical Review* 21 (2020): 41–75.

———. "Mary Lucinda Bonney and Amelia Stone Quinton, Founders of the Women's National Indian Association." *American Baptist Quarterly* 28, no. 4 (Winter 2009): 421–40.

———, ed. *The Women's National Indian Association: A History.* Albuquerque: University of New Mexico Press, 2015.

Mathes, Valerie Sherer, and Phil Brigandi. *A Call for Reform: The Southern California Indian Rights of Helen Hunt Jackson.* Norman: University of Oklahoma Press, 2015.

———. "Charles C. Painter, Helen Hunt Jackson and the Mission Indians of Southern California." *Journal of San Diego History* 55, no. 3 (Summer 2009): 89–118.

———. *Reservations, Removal, and Reform: The Mission Indian Agents of Southern California 1878–1903.* Norman: University of Oklahoma Press, 2018.

Mathes, Valerie Sherer, and Richard Lowitt. *The Standing Bear Controversy: Prelude to Indian Reform.* Urbana: University of Illinois Press, 2003.

McNeil, Teresa Baksh. "St. Anthony's Indian School in San Diego, 1886–1907," *Journal of San Diego History* 34, no. 3 (Summer 1988): 186–200.

Meyer, Annie Nathan, ed. *Woman's Work in America.* New York: Henry Holt and Company, 1891.

Miller, Larisa K. "The Secret Treaties with California's Indians." *Prologue* (Fall–Winter, 2013): 38–45.

Mooney, James. *The Ghost Dance Religion and the Sioux Outbreak of 1890.* Edited by Anthony F. C. Wallace. Chicago: University of Chicago Press, 1965.

———. *Myths of the Cherokee.* Washington, D.C.: Government Printing Office, 1902.

O'Neil, Floyd. A. "Hiram Price 1881–85." In *The Commissioners of Indian Affairs, 1824–1977.* Edited by Robert M. Kvasnicka and Herman J. Viola. Lincoln: University of Nebraska Press, 1979: 173–79.

Otis, D. S. *The Dawes Act and the Allotment of Indian Lands.* Edited by Francis Paul Prucha. Norman: University of Oklahoma Press, 1973.

Plane, Ana Marie, and Gregory Button. "The Massachusetts Indian Enfranchisement Act: Ethnic Contest in Historical Context, 1849–1869." *Ethnohistory* 40, no. 4 (Autumn 1993): 587–618.

Porter, Joseph C. *Paper Medicine Man: John Gregory Bourke and His American West.* Norman: University of Oklahoma Press, 1986.

Prucha, Francis Paul. *American Indian Policy in Crisis: Christian Reformers and the Indian, 1865–1900.* Norman: University of Oklahoma Press, 1976.

———, ed. *Americanizing the American Indians: Writings by the "Friends of the Indian," 1880–1900.* Cambridge, Mass.: Harvard University Press, 1973.

———. *Documents of United States Indian Policy.* (Lincoln: University of Nebraska Press, 1990.

———. "A 'Friend of the Indian' in Malwaukee: Mrs. O. J. Hiles and the Wisconsin Indian Association." *Historical Messenger of the Milwaukee County Historical Society* (Autumn 1973): 78–95.

———. *The Great Father: The United States Government and the American Indians.* 2 vols. Lincoln: University of Nebraska Press, 1894.

Thorne, Tanis C. *El Capitan: Adaptation and Agency on a Southern California Indian Reservation, 1850 to 1937.* Banning, Calif.: Malki-Ballena Press, 2012.

Wanken, Helen M. "Woman's Sphere and Indian Reform: The Women's National Indian Association, 1879–1901." PhD diss., Marquette University, 1981.

Washburn, Wilcomb E. *The Assault on Indian Tribalism: The General Allotment Law (Dawes Act) of 1887.* Philadelphia: J. B. Lippincott Company, 1975.

## Newspapers

*Berkshire Courier*

*Boston Daily Advertiser*

*Boston Post*

*Brooklyn Daily Eagle*

*Cambridge Tribune*

*Cherokee Advocate*

*Chicago Tribune*

*Dallas Morning News*

*Fort Scott Weekly Monitor*

*Kansas City Times*

*Lancaster Daily Intelligencer*

*Los Angeles Times*

*New York Times*

*New York Tribune*

*Newton Graphic*

*Philadelphia Inquirer*

*Pittsburgh Dispatch*

*Reno Gazette-Journal*

*River Press*

*San Francisco Call*

*San Francisco Chronicle*

*Springfield Sunday Republican*

*Times-Picayune*

*Topeka State Journal*

*Valley Chronicle*

▼ ▼ ▼

# INDEX

*References to illustrations appear in italic type.*

PRINCE ALBERT PUBLIC LIBRARY
**31234900095033**
Charles C. Painter : the life of an Indi

CPSIA information can be obtained
at www.ICGtesting.com
Printed in the USA
LVHW091703291020
670189LV00003B/59

9 780806 166322